SUSTAINABLE GOLF COURSES

SUSTAINABLE GOLF COURSES

A Guide to Environmental Stewardship

RONALD G. DODSON

Audubon International

FOREWORD BY ARNOLD PALMER

WILEY

John Wiley & Sons, Inc.

Library of Congress Cataloging-in-Publication Data:
Dodson, Ronald G.
   Sustainable golf courses : a guide to environmental stewardship / by Ronald G. Dodson.
      p. cm.
   Includes index.
   ISBN 0-471-46547-X (cloth)
1. Golf courses—Design and construction—Environmental aspects—United States.
2. Golf courses—Management—Environmental aspects—United States.   I. Title.
   GV975.3.D63 2005
   796.332'068—dc22

                                        2004025916

Printed in the United States of America
10 9 8 7 6 5 4 3

I would like to dedicate this book to the staff of Audubon International and the United States Golf Association. Without the continuing support of the USGA, there would be no golf and environment programs, golf and environment research, and no Audubon Cooperative Sanctuary Program. Were it not for the dedicated staff of Audubon International, who work hard every day to provide education and information, much of which forms the basis of this book, I would not be in the position to make this information available to an even broader audience. History will show that the work and dedication of the people who make up the USGA and Audubon International were and are critical to the future of the game.

CONTENTS

FOREWORD

Golf is my business, my pastime, and my passion. I believe that the game of golf can be any or more of those things for people of all ages and abilities. It is a game of history played in settings as varied as there are landscapes.

From its beginning in Scotland, golf has been connected to nature by playing and enjoying the game in natural surroundings. I have always enjoyed the natural environment in and around the courses I have played and designed.

Golf instills honesty and builds character by encouraging the golfer to know and apply the rules of golf to monitor his or her own game. In the same manner, the golf industry has taken responsibility to ensure the environment is preserved and protected within the golf course corridor. Palmer Course Design Co. and the members of the American Society of Golf Course Architects have studied environmental issues as they pertain to golf course design for decades, and along with our partners in the industry, the USGA, Golf Course Superintendents Association, and the PGA, we take pride in providing environmentally sustainable golf courses for future generations to enjoy.

With sound management practices, a golf course can make economic sense while protecting, and in many cases, restoring the environment. New golf courses create new job opportunities and an increased tax base to our communities. When irrigated with reclaimed water or built on degraded sites such as landfills or brownfields, the golf course benefits a community in far-reaching ways while conserving our natural resources.

Audubon International has created a great program and reference material that defines the principles we all should follow. This book is an important guide for all who love and play the game. The integrity of the game is exemplified by golf industry professionals who share in the responsibility to protect our ecosystems while preserving one of golf's most appealing aspects . . . the natural environment.

Arnold Palmer

Arnold Palmer and Ron Dodson, Bay Hill Golf International Tournament, April 1998.

ACKNOWLEDGMENTS

If I were to list all of the individuals and organizations that deserve recognition for their support in regard to this text, the list might be longer than the book itself. Consequently, it is not possible to list every individual name. But to those of you who have been there when I had a question or a problem (and you know who you are), thank you very much. Thanks for putting up with my questions, but more than that, thank you for being my friends.

That said, I would like to acknowledge certain individuals who have gone above and beyond, not only in regard to this text, but in regard to their personal involvement in promoting environmental stewardship and golf course management. Thanks first to the financial support from The Bonita Bay Group, Bonita Springs, Florida, and Arthur Hills/Steve Forest Golf Design Company for their generous financial support for this publication and their commitment to creating more sustainable golf courses. Although there were many golf course superintendents and others associated with golf course management that should be acknowledged, I'd like to personally thank Tim Hiers (The Old Collier Golf Club); Joel Howard, PhD, Al Dougherty, Ed Griffith, Terrey Dolan, David Fry, and Karen Childress (WCI Communities); and George Kelley (Stevinson Ranch).

I would also like to specifically acknowledge the following Audubon International staff and associates for their contributions. In particular, Nancy Richardson, Director of the Audubon Signature Program, for her continued dedication and commitment to the Audubon Signature Program and its members; Jean MacKay, Audubon International Education Director; and Joellen Zeh, Manager of the Audubon Cooperative Sanctuary Programs, for their continued education and outreach to our members; and for significant portions of best management practices and other technical information and guidance, Miles "Bud" Smart, PhD (Environmental Planning, Director), Larry Woolbright, PhD, (Research, Director), Kraig Marquis, and Charles Peacock, PhD. I would also like to acknowledge Mary Jack, my able assistant, who has read and reread this text, rearranged sentences and entire sections of the book to make it flow better, and helped me look through the Audubon International photograph library for so long I'm certain that she dreams about golf courses! You would not be reading this were it not for Mary.

The United States Golf Association has been critical to the success of our efforts to maintain the traditions of the game of golf while bringing an environmental ethic to golf and golfers. I would, however, like to specifically recognize several individuals for their continued support. First of all, Michael P. Kenna, PhD, Research Director, should be recognized for his continued dedication to organize, manage, and shepherd the USGA Turfgrass and Environmental Research Program. The USGA does not get the kind of public recognition it deserves for all that has been accomplished through this program, and Mike deserves special mention for his efforts. Along with Mike, both Kimberly Erusha, PhD, Education Director, and Jeff Nus, PhD, Manager, Research Program, deserve special recognition for taking often complicated agronomic, genetic, and wildlife management topics and transforming them into words that ordinary people can understand. But most especially, I would like to acknowledge James T. Snow, National Director of the USGA Green Section. Jim was the original supporter of the creation of the Audubon Cooperative Sanctuary Program for Golf Courses. For more than 15 years, he has been supporter, advocate, watchdog, and protector of the program for which we owe him a debt of appreciation. Thanks, Jim, for all your support!

Finally, I want to thank my family—Theresa, Kelly, Eric, and Travis Dodson—for sticking with me through many long years of travel, meetings, telephone calls, and what I'm sure were many boring evenings of listening to me talk about the latest new idea I had dreamed up concerning golf and the environment. (But wait until you hear the one I thought of yesterday!)

SUSTAINABLE GOLF COURSES

INTRODUCTION

The aim of this book is to serve as a reference for all those who are involved in planning, developing, and constructing new golf courses, as well as for those who are involved in the management of golf courses once they are built. It is not intended to be a comprehensive, all-encompassing text that covers in detail every aspect of building new, or managing old, golf courses. It is, however, useful information that can be applied on a case-by-case basis with the ultimate goal of helping meet the economic, ecological, and social issues facing the game of golf and the entire golf course industry.

I have been told that what I want for golf is beyond the means of the golf course industry. I hope those who believe that are wrong. What I want for golf is for it to be the best it can be. That said, golf is many things to many people. To some it is simply a game. To others it is a way of life or a profession. To others it is land development that uses large quantities of natural resources and causes adverse impacts to the quality of the environment. And, truth be told, it is all of that and more.

As a sport, golf is a game that is played at all ages. The playing field is in nature, and the system of creating "handicaps" or "indexes" actually gives golfers of varying levels of talent the chance to "level the playing field" during a friendly contest. It is simply a sport that is enjoyed by all sorts of people from all walks of life.

Golf is not essential to our lives. From an ecological perspective, golf courses do not contribute to the essential elements of human survival—food, cover, water, and space. Unlike agriculture, golf courses do not produce food that we all need to eat. Nor does it provide shelter. Even though many people live around golf courses, residential properties that sometimes surround golf courses are frequently exclusive, sprawling developments that only wealthy people can afford.

1

FIGURE I-1. INDIAN RIVER CLUB, VERO BEACH, FL. *Modern-day golf can blend the beauty of nature and the beauty of golf into a compatible and sustainable system that works for the benefit of developers, golfers, wildlife, the environment, and an entire community.*

While there are plenty of water "features" around many golf courses, a course does not provide water, and, in fact, many people believe that golf is one of the largest users and abusers of both water quality and quantity. And even though there is plenty of space in and around golf courses, it is frequently only available to those who can afford to use it.

Those of us who have been involved with golf courses for many years, however, know that this provides only one side of the golf course story. Golf courses provide jobs, contribute to the tax base, and play a role in communities and economics the same as any type of development. On a global basis, make no mistake, golf is *big* business. Additionally, golf courses can provide habitat for wildlife, including threatened and endangered species, and they provide open space and allow for plenty of "green" space in otherwise urban areas. Golf courses can also be built and managed to treat wastewater and act as part of the storm water management systems for entire communities.

My view of golf is that golf courses should be sited, designed, constructed, and managed in a manner that allows them to become an important part of any community's "green infrastructure." And, what, you might be asking, is green infrastructure? Every community needs open space and clean water. Every community must provide places for wildlife to live and to raise the next generation of whatever species is supposed to be found in a particular region. Most often we think of these types of places as wildlife refuges, nature reserves, or parks. But the fact is that there simply is not enough money to purchase every piece of property that could become a nature reserve. And, even more importantly, there is a dwindling supply of money to manage the properties even if there were enough dollars to buy them in the first place. This is where golf can play a critical role. Golf courses, *if properly sited, appropriately designed, and effectively managed,* may provide many of the same attributes of a nature reserve, but come with the money necessary to manage not only the places on which the game is played but the natural areas that are included in the golf course budget.

To a great extent, golf needs to return to its roots. That doesn't mean that we shouldn't use new technologies when available, but it does mean that we should remember that the true game of golf was played in nature. The modern age of golf course development has brought the "machine age" to nature, with developers depending on the extensive use of heavy equipment and a sense of human domination. Rather than designing golf courses as part of the natural landscape, developers have changed the natural course of watersheds and cut up wildlife habitat into smaller and smaller pieces. This has often been done in the name of aesthetics, but more often, with overinflated budgets that pay for a significant or well-known "brand name" to help ensure its success and cache.

I say all of this not because I'm so "pro-golf," as some of my environmental peers have claimed. I say this because I am "pro-sustainable development." I steadfastly believe that it is not a matter of "we" versus "they." It is not a matter of whether we need development—development is not an inherently bad thing. We just need the right kind of development, in the correct locations, built and managed in effective ways that minimize any negative impact on the environment while optimizing potential benefits. Building golf courses is an economic engine that can drive opportunities for future generations. We need open spaces to walk and listen to the sounds of nature. We need to relax and rejuvenate. At the same time, we need to be vigilant to ensure the safety of land, water, and air. We cannot wish ourselves to this sustainable future; we will have to make some difficult decisions. To achieve the lofty goals associated with sustainability, it will take all of us—every person,

FIGURE I-2. ST. ANDREWS, SCOTLAND. *The heritage of golf is rooted in nature, and the playing of the game is rooted in personal adoption of both the rules of the game and the rules of nature. Source: Ron Dodson.*

every company, every governmental agency, every educational institution at all levels—working together to form a collection of programs, policies, and practices that will be effective and benefit everyone. Anything less will certainly lead to unsustainable destinations, unsustainable lifestyles, and a widening gap between the "haves" and "have nots."

I believe that golf can be a catalyst for change. Golf can bridge the gap between what is thought of traditionally as "development" and what is thought of traditionally as "sanctuary." I believe that golf can be the leader of a new conservation movement within the free enterprise system and a true agent of change in the way we live, work, and recreate.

CHAPTER 1

SUSTAINABLE GOLF AND THE ENVIRONMENT

Sustainable Golf Courses—An Oxymoron?

It is thought by some that the word "sustainable" and the words "golf course" shouldn't even be in the same sentence. Some believe that golf courses by their very nature are not sustainable. To a degree that is a correct statement—depending on both your personal definition of sustainability and whether you include human beings in the overall concept of sustainability. In general, the elements most often associated with sustainability include ecology, economy, and society. In other words, to an extent, there must be a balance between these three "legs of the stool," or the stool will fall over. Some, on the other hand, focus mostly, if not entirely, on the ecological leg and then zero in on concerns over water quality and loss of rare species and pristine habitat. Others focus on the economic bottom line and say, "If we can't make this project work from an economic point of view, then there will be no project!" This tends to be the basis for the old argument of "the environment versus the economy." Or, "Take your pick. Birds or jobs!" These arguments and various versions of them are reflective of unsustainable attitudes. We can do better than this. We need birds and we need jobs and we need an economy that is built on the use *and* protection of our environment and natural resources and the social fabric that makes places special. Anything less, in the long term, is unsustainable both in terms of our economy and our environment and to all living things, including people.

The History of Golf

The history of the game of golf is a bit shrouded in mystery, but most golf aficiona-
dos believe that the modern-day game traces its roots back to Scotland and the
oldest links-style courses. "Links land" is that somewhat barren land that is found
between the more productive agricultural lands and the sea. It is land that is
sparsely vegetated and wind-blown, and to many, it is not good for much of anything. This links land is where the birth of golf is considered to have taken place.
Many of the original golf layouts started with the first hole being found at the city's
edge, with succeeding holes going out into the links land, and then returning on
nearly the same piece of land back toward the city. In many cases, greens were
large enough to accommodate two separate holes. For example, one might find
hole #3 on the front side of the green and #12 on the backside of the same green.
Not only did this save on building and maintenance costs, but it also gave golfers a
chance to talk to others who were playing along the way. Both the equipment used
and the terrain in which the game of golf was played were absolutely nothing like
today. In the beginning, golf was certainly a game that was played in nature, and it
was truly nature of the wildest sort. Wind, rain, rocks, and bare brown spots
between sparsely and somewhat poorly managed turf were all elements of the
game when it started. The origin of golf is a long way from the manicured condi-

FIGURE 1-1. ST. ANDREWS, SCOTLAND. *The history of the community around the links at St.
Andrews is an important part of the golf course. This is a golf course managed with the belief
that less is more. Source: Ron Dodson.*

tions that we find today on many golf courses and certainly a long way from the steel-headed, titanium-shafted clubs that we find in use in the modern game. It is this transition from a game that was truly played in nature to a game that is played in an artificial form of nature that is the taproot of some of the environmental and economic concerns that are facing the game today. (See Figure 1-1.)

The game of golf has seen periods of slow to no growth, then to significant growth, to explosive growth. Some link the growth of the game to televised golf tournaments, and to the popularity of professional golfers like Arnold Palmer in the early 1960s, and to the explosive growth to the U.S. economic conditions of the mid-1980s and 1990s, coupled with Tiger Woods' arrival on the professional golf stage (see Figure 1-2). This growth and public fascination with the touring professional and the courses on which they play their game also has changed the way that golf courses are designed and managed. While change can be good, if uncontrolled, these changes can drastically alter the ultimate outcome. In reality, the modern game of golf bears little resemblance to the original game of golf. Other than trying to get a ball (which today is certainly not the same kind of ball as originally used) into a hole in the ground (of course, today's "hole" is metal sleeved, perfectly placed, and painted white) in the fewest number of strokes, the two games can hardly be compared. In addition, the game that today's touring professional and the game that the rest of us mortal, everyday golfers play can hardly be compared. That is where the problems associated with the sustainability of the game of golf rests.

By and large, we, the public, are demanding that courses be designed and managed as though we could all play like Tiger Woods. We want fast greens and "perfect" turfgrass (no matter where we might actually hit the golf ball), and we want club manufacturers to create equipment that will guarantee that we can hit as

FIGURE 1-2. 2002 UNITED STATES OPEN. *Black Course, Bethpage State Park, Long Island, NY. Tiger Woods at the 2002 U.S. Open.*

straight and far as any touring professional can. And, because we are all busy making all the money that we need so that we can afford to join the private golf club or pay the high green fees necessary to fund the artificial maintenance necessary to keep our trumped-up golf courses playable, we want to be able to get on the course and finish our round in less than four hours. I argue that this approach is not even golf at all. It is some form of speeded-up business-dealing opportunity masquerading as golf. It is this masquerade that in the end could be the demise of the game itself.

There are presently more than 17,000 golf courses in the United States, and between the mid-1980s and late 1990s, one new golf course per day was opened in the country. Although the golfing public and golf investors were enthusiastic about this growth, many governmental agencies, environmental organizations, and the public have expressed concern about the environmental impact of golf course development and management. As a result, agencies have increased their regulatory oversight of golf course development, legal actions have been taken against many, and restrictions on course management have been put into place. While some support these actions, others have indicated that this merely increases the cost of doing business for golf courses and is increasingly burdensome to the public and regulators alike.

The game of golf—already thought by many to be expensive and exclusive—may increasingly preclude the general public from enjoying the natural and recreational benefits of the game. In addition, it appears in the early 2000s that what was once considered the golf course boom has now slowed to a crawl or completely stopped in many places. While increased regulatory and citizen pressure can be connected to this slowdown to a degree, much of it can be directly connected to unsustainable economic strategies that many have taken in regard to the game of golf. These strategies include, but are not limited to (1) building courses in places that will not support the necessary rounds of golf and a reasonable green fee to allow the course to be solvent; (2) building courses in a manner in which the associated maintenance costs to keep the courses playable put undue economic stress on the maintenance budgets and course staff; (3) attempting to build courses in the wrong locations from an environmental point of view and therefore causing the expenditure of millions of dollars in attempts to gain governmental permits, which in the end may or may not be granted; and (4) managing existing courses in ways that cause environmental problems such as adverse water quality and public or employee health concerns that can cause both economic and social problems. All of these lead to economically, ecologically, and socially unsustainable golf courses. That means that proposed courses have a more difficult time getting permits and, consequently, getting built.

It also means that existing courses have an increasingly difficult time finding acceptable products with which to manage their courses, find themselves facing financial emergencies, and often face closing down or being purchased by others.

The ramifications are frequently that golf course personnel lose their jobs, course designers can't find work, irrigation companies don't get contracts, and the list of bad news goes on and on.

The Case for Sustainability

"The word 'sustainable' implies perpetuity, constant rebirth and renewal, and an inexhaustible system. 'Development' connotes change, growth, expansion, production, movement. Development, to be sustainable, must somehow incorporate renewal that ensures the continuity of matter, resources, populations, and cultures. Sustainability, to incorporate development, must allow change and adaptation to new conditions. Today, the two ideas together speak of balancing economic and social forces against the environmental imperatives of resource conservation and renewal for the world of tomorrow" (Porter, ULI, *The Practice of Sustainable Development*).

For those associated with the golf course industry, that means that you should strive for economically viable, ecologically healthy, and socially acceptable golf courses. The primary focus of this book is to offer information that will help those associated with managing existing golf courses, as well as those involved in planning, designing, and permitting new golf courses, the necessary tools to reach those goals. If any one of the three concerns—economically viable, ecologically healthy, or socially acceptable—is rooted in unsustainable positions, the long-term and short-term results for a golf course and those associated with the golf course industry will not be pleasant. You not only have a responsibility to the economic viability of golf, but you have an ecological and social responsibility too.

For those associated with governmental agencies and environmental organizations, that means that you should also support the concepts associated with sustainability and you should reconsider the standard one-size-fits-all approach to regulation. Those courses that voluntarily adopt and document implementation of more sustainable practices should be encouraged and rewarded, not punished. While it is true that golf courses, or anything else for that matter, should not be built on some sites, you need to rethink your positions concerning the manner in which you determine which sites are acceptable to develop and which are not, because all sites are not alike. Finally, you need to rethink the financial implications of the decisions that you make, because those implications are merely being passed on to the public. You have an ecological responsibility to the concepts of sustainability, but you also have economic and social responsibilities.

For those individuals who have personal reasons for opposing new golf course development or who put undue pressure on golf course superintendents to manage courses in ways that have adverse impacts on the sustainability of a course, you need to rethink your actions. While it is a person's right to expresses his or her position in regard to any topic, if that personal position leads to adverse impacts on the economic, ecological, or social fabric of a golf course, a neighborhood, or a community, that personal position lacks credibility and should be questioned strongly. While a person has a right to express his or her position, the person also has ecological, economic, and social responsibilities that go beyond personal interests.

There Is No "One Size Fits All"

To a great extent, those associated with golf need to understand and believe that there really is no one set of rules that can be applied to the design and management of all golf courses. The goals associated with the game of golf should be to provide optimum playing conditions, based on scientifically sound management strategies that are based upon the specific site that is being managed. There is a method to accomplishing this, whether you are managing a golf course that has been in

FIGURE 1-3. COUNTRY CLUB OF FLORIDA, VILLAGE OF GOLF, FL. *Wetlands are recharge areas for groundwater aquifers, play a role in storm water runoff, and provide home for many species of wildlife. Properly managed, they can also play important roles in regard to visual beauty of a golf course.*

existence for years or you are planning the development of a new course. (See Figure 1-3.)

Step one in the process is to take a look at the "region" in which the golf course is located. By *region*, I mean both terrestrial (land) and aquatic (water) regions. It should be clear that if a course is located in a desert region, as opposed to a southern wetland setting, different management strategies will be required for each to keep the courses playable. It should also be clear then that different design strategies will be necessary, or at least should be necessary, to make various courses more manageable based on the specific site being designed to become a golf course. In addition to the land "types" (desert versus wetland), surrounding land uses are of equal importance (see Figure 1-4). The location of a course in a rural, suburban, or urban setting can greatly affect the manner in which the course should be designed, or needs to be managed, from both an economic and environmental point of view. Finally, the position of the golf course in the overall watershed is an important consideration. A watershed is described as an area of land on which all the water that falls onto it drains to a common point. Watersheds come in all sorts of shapes and sizes. It is important for the golf course designer and manager to know exactly what watershed their property is located within and exactly where

FIGURE 1-4. TPC AT THE CANYONS, LAS VEGAS, NV. *Even in a desert setting there are watersheds. When rains do come to the desert, improper watershed planning can be disastrous, as most rainwater will not seep into the ground but run off in a torrent of water. The uses of watershed planning and appropriate plant selection are keys to ecologically sensitive golf course design and management.*

within that watershed the property fits. In other words, is the course at the top or bottom of the watershed? This is important because course management can impact the overall watershed and those associated with golf should want that impact to be a positive one, not a negative one.

Sound Economics Based on Ecological Facts

We must all come to grips with the fact that our ultimate economic fate is based on the state of the ecological processes around us. Note that I didn't say "environmental" conditions. Environmental conditions are results, or reflections, of what has happened to the ecological systems around us. For example, poor water quality is an environmental condition. But that result is an action that was taken to the aquatic ecological system in which the water that we are monitoring is located. That is why there are many ways to adversely impact the quality of water. Water quality can be impacted directly or indirectly. So, the goal of being an "environmentally friendly" golf course, while laudable, is really only a "defensive" position that says, "OK, I'm not as bad as you think I am." But for the golf course industry to say "We want and we work for clean water from an ecological systems point of view" is a much bolder statement that goes beyond self-interest. And the fact is that we all need clean water! In addition, our economic health is based on a system, and that economic system is directly connected to an ecological system. This is a fact, and until we act like we believe that this is a fact, our path toward a more sustainable culture is doomed. Being sustainable is not a "thing." Being sustainable is not a "place." Being sustainable is a way, it is a method, it is a process. Being environmentally friendly is good, but it could be an "ornament on a dead tree." We should work toward a healthy system that will ensure that the "tree" remains alive and well, and not just celebrate the ornaments that we hang on it.

For those managing existing golf courses, your challenges could be great because of decisions that have been made long before you arrived on the scene (see Figure 1-5). But you can do something positive, and that is why Audubon International created the Audubon Cooperative Sanctuary Program for Golf Courses. There are those who think the golf course Cooperative Sanctuary Program was created just to help golf look good—or at the very least, to help golf not look as bad as some believe golf to be. Nothing could be further from the truth. The program was created to serve as an educational and motivational vehicle to encourage people to merge environmental stewardship into their businesses and personal lives. It is a baby step toward the adoption and use of the principles of sustainability. It forms a common frame of reference for all those who choose to take action. It is a framework to follow, and it is a forum from which public recognition can be given to those that take action. But those actions taken at many existing golf courses are

FIGURE 1-5. BONITA BAY MARSH COURSE, BONITA SPRINGS, FL. *Golf course superintendents have tremendous responsibilities that range from turf management to wildlife management, coupled with administrative responsibilities that range from employee supervision to the management of people who are often the very people that the golf course superintendent works for! Source: Maryle Barbe.*

governed by the decisions that have been made prior to today. For example, if decisions were made in the design of the course that preclude the use of modern-day management practices, that would be a limiting factor to the present golf course management efforts. If the course has an old, out-of-date irrigation system, it will be very difficult to conserve the amounts of water that one may wish, unless the entire irrigation system is replaced. But if the course is presently being managed as a "wall-to-wall" turfgrass system, that most certainly can be changed. Of course, the golfers will have to go along with the change, but it can be done, and in the process, great strides can be made in the areas of water conservation, energy conservation, and wildlife and habitat enhancement. This will result in positive action for both the economic and ecological attributes of a golf course. But to be effective, these actions must be supported by the golfers who utilize the facility.

CHAPTER 2

ESTABLISHING AN ENVIRONMENTAL PHILOSOPHY

Building a Sustainable Foundation

In order for golf courses to become more sustainable, those individuals connected to the development, design, construction, and management of golf courses need to think beyond the game of golf, and they certainly need to think beyond the confines of one golf course. They must believe that golf can and must be woven into the fabric of a community in a sustainable manner if the game of golf is to be viable economically, ecologically, and socially. What follows is a set of *Principles for Sustainability* that was created by Audubon International.

Audubon International believes that a properly sited, designed, and managed golf course can be a fine example of sustainable development. If not properly sited, designed, and managed, it can also represent the worst that humans have to offer and will eventually cave in on itself because of its *un*-sustainability. In order for the golf course industry to move toward a more sustainable future, everyone associated with golf must adopt a set of principles to be used in guiding decisions in regard to the siting, design, and management of golf courses. Trying to just "skim by" or just doing what it is minimally required by regulation is not a sustainable path. In order to become more sustainable, those associated with golf must embrace a set of guiding principles and stick to them in a leadership and focused manner. These principles must be bigger than the game of golf. They must focus on the underpinnings of environmental and economic life. This is the way for golf to become not just "environmentally friendly," but a real agent for change in the way the entire country develops and manages land, and that should really be the ultimate goal of the golf course industry.

Principles for Sustainable Resource Management[1]

FIGURE 2-1. *Audubon International logo.*

AN ENVIRONMENTAL VISION

Audubon International envisions a world where people from all walks of life act in ways that demonstrate their understanding and responsibility as stewards of our environment. We envision global and local landscapes that conserve and sustain biodiversity. And we believe that all people should be educated and motivated to participate pro-actively in environmental decisions that confront our society and choose sustainable actions individually and collectively.

BUILDING A FOUNDATION FOR SUSTAINABILITY

Sustainable development and sustainable resource management means using natural resources in ways beneficial to human beings, now and into the future, and at the same time not depleting those resources nor adversely impacting biological diversity. Biological diversity is a key to the ultimate health and survival of the environment. How we protect and enhance that diversity depends in part on the protection and conservation of natural resources like water, plant, life, and energy resources.

People from all walks of life must learn to act in ways that demonstrate their commitment and responsibility as stewards of our environment. We all must work toward global and local landscapes that sustain intricate ecosystem relationships and include a diversity of plants, wildlife, and people.

Audubon International believes that all people must be educated and motivated to participate proactively in resource management decisions that confront our society and choose sustainable actions on an individual and collective level.

Sustainable development and sustainable resource management includes the following concepts. These concepts should be articulated and embraced by landowners

[1]An Audubon International Guidance Document ©1998 Audubon International. All rights reserved. Published with Permission.

FIGURE 2-2. HENDERSON, NV. *Initial site planning from a watershed perspective is a key to the long-term success of any project.*

and developers at the inception of any land use change (development), adopted by everyone who is associated with the project, and finally, passed along to those who will live, work, or play in the community after it is built (see Figure 2-2).

> ➤ Sustainable resource management ensures that the effects of our actions do not diminish, and may even enhance, the quality of life as it relates to our environment for our future generations.

> ➤ Sustainable resource management includes focusing on human behavior that encourages resource conservation and resource management activities that maintain natural resources and the continued functioning of the ecosystem.

> ➤ Sustainable resource management focuses on physical production practices that encourage the use of resources in such a way that allows us to utilize those resources indefinitely.

> ➤ Sustainable resource management requires both short and long term decision-making that ensures that watershed, plants, wildlife, people, and our economic and social systems are protected and enhanced for future generations.

In an effort to promote more sustainable patterns of land use and sustainable resource management, Audubon International created a set of principles. These principles represent the basic tenants that we believe are crucial in leading us to a more sustainable future. Keep in mind that total sustainability will not happen overnight.

FIGURE 2-3 QUAIL RUN GOLF COURSE, LAPINE, CO. *As habitat in many areas is converted to other uses, wildlife is being displaced. Golf courses can provide necessary habitat in areas developed primarily for human use.*

Audubon International's principles, however, form a philosophical foundation by which a community, or any part of it, may work toward a sustainable future (see Figure 2-3). To that end, Audubon International believes that the local and global community should:

➤ Encourage resource management practices that have the greatest positive impact on wildlife species, water, and the ecosystems that sustain life.

➤ Strive to use resources that are most easily renewed.

➤ Strive to reduce or eliminate the use of resources that are difficult or impossible to renew.

➤ Encourage activities that result in identifying new resources and technologies and enhance our present resource base in ways that will maximize positive impacts to the overall quality of life and the environment.

➤ Encourage human activities and practices that conserve water and continually enhance water quality on a local and global basis.

➤ Encourage human activities, practices, and land uses that support ecosystems that maintain and enhance biodiversity.

➤ Consider the geographic and ecological context in which our actions take place, and at the same time strive to manage resources within the natural limitations and opportunities defined by ecosystems and geographic boundaries.

TURNING PRINCIPLES INTO ACTION

The following are examples of resource management activities that demonstrate how the principles for sustainable resource management should apply to present and future resource management decisions. Audubon International's *Principles for Sustainable Resource Management* are designed to serve the community as it evolves and serves as an educational and philosophical foundation as well as a living guide for all those who work, live, or recreate in the community. Consequently, these principles should be displayed throughout the community as a joint commitment between those who build the community and those who live in it (see Figure 2-4).

Site Specific Assessment

Before land-use changes take place, it is crucial to understand the "properties" of the site subject to proposed changes. A comprehensive site survey should do the following:

1. Identify the geographic and topographic features of the area.
2. Identify the area's unique resources to protect and conserve them.
3. Make it possible to choose power sources in accordance with the area's physical attributes.

FIGURE 2-4. PELICAN PRESERVE, FORT MYERS, FL. *Audubon International planning team, Larry Woolbright and Kraig Marquis, survey the land and plans a WCI Communities project. Identification of significant ecological elements early in the planning stages on the site to be developed is critical. Areas are not only those identified by government but also include areas that may be restored to functioning habitat.*

4. Identify and conserve areas of archeological, natural, historical, and cultural significance.

5. Identify land use in the vicinity and seek compatibility regarding proposed changes and use.

6. Specify the area of change and establish parameters for future changes beyond this area.

Habitat Sensitivity

Sustainable resource management entails factoring in the wildlife habitat of an area or region (see Figure 2-5). Managing land in a habitat-sensitive way includes the following:

1. Not disturbing local wildlife populations by degrading sources of food, shelter, or water.

2. Protecting ecologically sensitive areas from all degrading impacts.

3. Not posing threats to species directly or indirectly through increased air and water pollution.

4. Avoiding the increase of ambient noise levels in the area during and following changes in land use.

FIGURE 2-5. OLD MARSH GOLF CLUB, PALM BEACH GARDENS, FL. *Protecting habitat for nesting, resting, feeding, and hiding from predators are key to providing homes for wildlife during all phases of their life cycles. Source: Alice Semki.*

5. Assuring migratory species access to habitual routes, food sources, and breeding grounds.

6. Maintaining corridors and greenspace that will allow for the movement of plants and animals.

Native and Naturalized Plants and Natural Landscaping

Sustainable resource management should provide the use of material and resources native to an area (see Figure 2-6). Using native or naturalized plants reduces the need for special watering and ground preparation, while natural landscaping can help hold valuable topsoil. For this reason, native and naturalized plants and natural landscaping should

1. Be used exclusively, except for social-purpose areas such as agricultural lands, recreational use areas, and work areas.

2. Be designed and implemented to reduce natural vegetation loss.

3. Encourage biodiversity.

4. Not require the need for pesticides, herbicides, and fertilizers; minimize their use on special-purpose areas mentioned in requirement no. 1 above;

FIGURE 2-6. SONNENALP GOLF CLUB, EDWARDS, CO. *Not only does natural landscaping save water, but even small areas can provide important wildlife benefits for species such as butterflies, hummingbirds, and native pollinators.*

FIGURE 2-7. QUAIL RIDGE COUNTRY CLUB, BOYNTON BEACH, FL. *Using a computerized irrigation system that will detail the amount of water that needs to be applied to turf is the most effective way to conserve water resources while managing turfgrass on golf courses.*

and promote the use of management practices and materials that, through their source and production process, are a component of the Earth's natural cycles.

5. Use efficient irrigation methods and practices.
6. Maximize the use of integrated resource management.

Water Conservation

Water is vital to all life, yet it is one of our most misused, mismanaged, and misunderstood resources. We make deserts bloom year round and have expanded populations in areas that are running out of water. A water conservation program should

1. Utilize a rainwater collection or gray-water system for watering grounds, flushing toilets, and so on.
2. Minimize water usage by monitoring water usage and installing low-flow devices (see Figure 2-7).
3. Evaluate sustainable yields for the lowest flow periods of the supply and be designed to accommodate those periods.
4. Recapture and reutilize water resources.
5. Integrate native and naturalized plants that are biologically appropriate for the geographic region.

Waste Management

The first goal of waste management should be to not generate waste. We must rethink how we purchase and consume goods. If waste is generated, the following should apply:

FIGURE 2-8. TOP OF THE ROCK GOLF
COURSE, RIDGEDALE, MO. *Waste
management is an important part of
course management. The goals should
be to reduce, reuse, and recycle as much
as possible. This includes a focus on
getting golfers to practice waste
management on the golf course too.*

1. Solid and hazardous wastes must be reduced, recycled, or reused whenever
   possible (see Figure 2-8). Continuously monitor and assess how much solid
   and hazardous waste is generated.
2. Nonrecyclable wastes must be disposed of in an environmentally sensitive
   manner. Periodically review waste reduction strategies and recycling methods used.
3. Compost all organic wastes.
4. Explore low-capital, low-maintenance alternatives for wastewater treatment
   systems.

Energy Conservation and Renewable Energy Sources

Nothing short of weaning ourselves from oil and coal will be sustainable. Until that
time, an infrastructure change should

1. Explore the utilization of
   a. Photovoltaics
   b. Solar power (see Figure 2-9)
   c. Wind power

FIGURE 2-9. *Solar power panels provide an opportunity to use a renewable energy resource and reduce dependence on oil and coal.*

  d. Geothermal power
  e. Wave and tide generated power
  f. Hydroelectric power
  g. Clean-burning fuels
2. Minimize consumption of nonrenewable resources while more energy-efficient sources are being developed.
3. Include energy-efficient technologies in manufacturing, building design, and transportation.

FIGURE 2-10. GRANITE BAY GOLF CLUB, GRANITE BAY, CA. *Wildlife need to be able to move from area to area without being put in danger by predators or exposed to death by vehicles. A wildlife corridor is an area that allows safe passage from one habitat area to another area.*

Greenspace and Corridors

Urban parks, forested zones, native grassland areas, and stream corridors reaching into urban areas are necessary elements of sustainability (see Figure 2-10). In this regard, we should

1. Provide access to appropriate greenspaces for educational and recreational experiences.
2. Maintain corridors that connect areas and allow for wildlife movement within the property boundary and adjacent areas.
3. Identify and preserve greenspaces and corridors of high wildlife habitat and water quality value within a city or community.

Agriculture

Reaching sustainability will include sustainable agricultural practices. Therefore, we should

1. Protect prime agricultural production areas.
2. Promote regional food self-sufficiency (see Figure 2-11).

FIGURE 2-11. TURNING STONE CASINO, SHENANDOAH GOLF COURSE, VERNONA, NY. *Protecting prime agricultural production areas and promoting regional food self-sufficiency are critical aspects of land planning and impact regional sustainability.*

3. Improve the efficiency of low-input farming methods.

4. Improve irrigation and drainage systems.

5. Integrate livestock management with food crop and vegetative management to improve soil fertility.

6. Encourage the use of integrated pest management (IPM) practices at all farms and agriculture facilities.

7. Explore the use of greenhouse farming.

8. Increase the use of aquaculture.

Community Design

Beyond the specific design of a structure, there is the issue of how it is all put together in a community (see Figure 2-12). Where does the food come from? Where do the people work and play? How are the sustainable patterns of behavior extended into the larger community? Community developments and changes should

1. Protect the area's sustainable resources.

2. Encourage low-impact transportation like walking, bicycling, and so on.

3. Work with the contours of the land to avoid excessive mechanical land and soil movement, such as blasting and filling.

FIGURE 2-12. *Aside from providing homes for wildlife, many golf courses are either surrounded by homes or located in the middle of a city. The pattern of human movement and the patterns of wildlife movement need to be compatibly planned with a golf course design.*

4. Include recycling/composting centers and encourage exchange/reuse stations.

5. Include support stations for forms of transportation that rely on alternative sources of energy.

6. Include a multipurpose community/environmental education center.

7. Include clustering of residences when possible.

8. Minimize the use of impermeable surfaces for drives and parking lots.

9. Continually look for opportunities to "reclaim" previously degraded environments.

10. Cluster structures and maximize open space.

Transportation

To move toward sustainability, we should

1. Encourage the expanded use of public transportation.

2. Encourage and utilize low-impact transportation by providing sidewalks, walking trails, and bicycle paths.

FIGURE 2-13. WILLIAMSTON, NC. *Automobiles and our dependence on them for nearly every aspect of our lives is at the taproot of many of our environmental concerns. A sustainable society will be less dependent on this form of transportation for personal transportation and for the transportation of goods and services.*

3. Ensure the availability of energy-efficient public transportation to new areas of development and city centers.
4. Reduce cross-country transportation of goods by diversifying local resources.
5. Encourage infrastructure changes that support the use of more energy efficient technologies in vehicles (such as electric-battery-charging stations). (See Figure 2-13.)

Building Design

The design of individual buildings is essential to developing sustainable patterns of behavior. Everything from lighting to composting food scraps must be considered (see Figure 2-14). In this regard, the building designs should

1. Incorporate energy efficient design approaches for
   a. Heating/cooling
   b. Ventilation
   c. Building material

FIGURE 2-14. WCI EVERGRENE MODEL HOME, PALM BEACH GARDENS, FL. *The "green" model home referred to as "Geni-G" (Generation Green) was judged by the Florida Green Building Coalition as the most energy-efficient home ever built in Florida at the grand opening in 2004. The various features displayed in this model are available to homeowners who are purchasing new homes in the WCI Evergrene Community, and who are interested in incorporating them into their own homes.*

    d. Appliances

    e. Lighting

    f. Cooking

    g. Water use

    h. Space

2. Include efficient waste handling and recycling programs.

3. Apply landscaping practices that minimize maintenance, such as employing native or naturalized plants.

4. Use building materials that will not become hazardous waste or impossible to dispose of in an ecologically beneficial manner at the end of their useful life.

CHAPTER 3

ECOLOGICAL PRINCIPLES

Introduction

Sustainable resource management means that we will utilize resources, but we will do so in ways that will not diminish opportunities for people in the future to meet their own needs. Why is this important to golf? If golf courses, and those associated with the golf course industry, are seen as those who use, waste, and possibly damage natural resources, it will become increasingly difficult to build new courses or manage existing courses without public outcry. This is not a sustainable path to follow from an economic point of view. In addition, actually wasting and damaging natural resources is not a sustainable path from an ecological or social point of view either. Once again, that means that those associated with golf need to think beyond the game itself and to remember that the game is to be played in nature—not on it!

Principles form the fabric of belief of an individual or an organization. Sustainable resource management constitutes actions that can deliver on those principles or beliefs. In other words, a principle might be "I believe that all living things, including human beings, need clean water." A sustainable resource management statement may be "I will develop and manage our golf course from a watershed perspective, and I will not adversely impact the quality of water in the watershed." (See Figure 3-1.)

Following is a list of the prime areas of concern for those who build new or manage existing golf courses. Each item is based upon the best that science has to tell us at the present time. While it is true that those associated with the management of existing courses will face some limitations because of previously made decisions, or because of previously completed surrounding land development, the

FIGURE 3-1. TOP OF THE ROCK, RIDGEDALE, MO. *The sights and sounds of nature are not only a part of the game but to a great degree make the game a more enjoyable experience. It is an experience that should be relished and not ignored.*

facts are clear and still useful. Continuous improvement should be the goal. That means continuous improvement on ecological (environmental), economic (budgets), and social (community, employers, and employees) aspects should be used to judge our overall successes. Sustainable resource management and the components for environmental protection and enhancement when a golf course is being designed, constructed, and managed is central to the long-term sustainability of all golf courses. The basic ecological goals should be to maintain and enhance water resources, habitat value and quantity, and biodiversity. By understanding and becoming familiar with these concepts, one has the foundation for achieving environmental protection.

Environmental Planning Principles and Guidelines

Environmental planning is an imprecise science, and an ecological understanding of complex ecosystems is not well developed. What works in one type of habitat or ecosystem might not work in another. The current astonishing rate of species extinction and changes in global climate make even what we do know uncertain in the future. Therefore, the impact of any management plan must be evaluated after it is in place, and we must be ready to revise and adjust it. This kind of adaptive management is a key to successful conservation planning, and it is the reason why incremental planning should be undertaken.

To implement an adaptive management program, basic ecological concepts need to be understood. By understanding and becoming familiar with these concepts, one has the foundation for achieving environmental protection. For example, one of the basic concepts is that multiple connections between patches is better for wildlife than a single connection, and infinitely better than none at all. By knowing this, the design of a new golf course, or the management of an existing golf course, can incorporate the maximum number of connections for the site. It follows, then, that if during construction the connections are not altered, and that during operations, the connections are maintained as wildlife connections, an increase in biological diversity is not only possible, but money will be saved through the restoration process too.

Sustainable resource management principles are divided into three areas: spatial principles and guidelines, biological community principles and guidelines, and water quality principles and guidelines.

SPATIAL PRINCIPLES AND GUIDELINES

The following spatial principles should serve as a guide not only for planning a specific site but for integrating the biological attributes of the site into the general ecological region in which it is situated. As many of these principles as possible should be incorporated in the design of new course development, or redevelopment, or incorporated as management actions on existing golf courses.

> ➤ *Large areas of habitat sustain more species than small areas.* Preserve as many large habitat areas as possible in single tracts for each ecosystem, or increase the size of existing patches of habitat to the minimum size needed to sustain viable wildlife populations.

> ➤ *Many small patches of habitat in an area will help sustain regional diversity.* Where there is no opportunity to preserve, increase, or create large patches of habitat, increase the number of small habitat patches (see Figure 3-2).

FIGURE 3-2. BONITA BAY EAST, BONITA BAY, FL. *While small patches of habitat will serve well for some species, fragmenting habitat areas with roads can limit their value. Some species will not cross a road, or may meet their demise while attempting to cross.*

> *The shape of a habitat patch can sometimes be nearly as important as the size.* Modify or design the shape of habitat patches to create more interior habitat. If space is limited, a circular area will maximize interior habitat.

> *Fragmented habitats and ecosystems reduces diversity.* Avoid fragmenting large patches of natural vegetation. Even a narrow access road through a forest can be a barrier to movement of small organisms, eliminate interior habitat, and introduce unwanted species.

> *Isolated patches of habitat sustain fewer species than closely associated patches. Minimize the isolation of patches.* Corridors and an increased number of patches can prevent isolation.

> *Species diversity in patches of habitat connected by corridors is greater than that of disconnected patches.* Maintain or develop many corridors of similar vegetation to connect isolated patches of the same or similar community types. Opportunities exist along roadways, rivers and streams, urban ravines, fencerows, hedgerows, and railroad rights-of-way, to name a few. Wider corridors provide more wildlife benefits and protect water quality better than narrower ones. Breaks in the corridor should be avoided.

> *Water bodies should be connected to the surrounding natural community by continuous corridors of natural vegetation for maximum wildlife value.* This allows wildlife to migrate to and from the water. Corridors should be as wide as possible for the specific location.

> *A mixture of habitat types sustains more species and is more likely to support rare species than a single habitat type (monostand).* On large parcels, mixtures of habitat types should be restored as the diversity of the landscape allows.

> *Transition areas (ecotones) between habitat types are natural and support a variety of species from both specific habitat areas and species that may only be found in the ecotone.* Ecotones should be allowed to naturally develop between adjacent habitat areas. Increasing the mix (interspersion) of habitat

types on a given parcel can increase the amount of area in ecotones, but this should not be done at the expense of reducing interior habitat.

➤ *Sustainable resource management requires native and naturalized plants.* This practice accomplishes a variety of positive goals, including (a) providing animals with the same food and cover plants they evolved with; (b) minimizing the need to supply extra water, fertilizer, cultivation, and other care; and (c) reducing or eliminating the need for pesticides because plants are coevolved with local pests. Introduce as many native species as possible into a restoration area. This maximizes both plant and, subsequently, animal biodiversity.

BIOLOGICAL COMMUNITY PRINCIPLES AND GUIDELINES

A biological community is a collection of habitat types that are in proximity to one another and connected to each other. The biological community principles should serve as a guide not only for planning a specific site but also for helping integrate biological communities into the larger ecological region. Try to incorporate as many of these principles in the golf course as possible. (See Figure 3.3.)

➤ *Restoration of native plant communities helps to sustain diverse wildlife populations.* The more fully restored biological community has higher diversity. This means introducing as many components of the biological community as possible.

➤ *An increase in the structural diversity of vegetation increases species diversity.* The vegetational structure of a biological community can be enhanced by restoring tree, shrub, and herbaceous layers that are reduced or lacking. Retain an understory shrub layer around all trees. Biological systems are composed of layers of vegetation, typically including big trees, small trees, shrubs, and herbaceous plants. Wildlife are largely dependent on structural habitat, so species diversity of almost all groups can be increased by adding vertical layers of vegetation to the plant community.

➤ *A high diversity of plant species ensures a year-round food supply for the greatest diversity of wildlife.* Introduce as many species known to be part of the biological community as possible. Also retain dead, standing, and fallen trees, as they provide important nesting sites for many cavity-nesting species and a source of food for other species.

➤ *Species survival depends on maintaining minimum population levels.* Different species will have different minimum population requirements. The minimum population in a particular parcel will depend upon many factors.

FIGURE 3-3. POTTAWATOMIE GOLF COURSE, ST. CHARLES, IL.
Restoring habitat with native plants will help many native wildlife species. Even small restoration projects can add beauty to the game, reduce water consumption, and help wildlife conservation efforts.

> *Low-intensity land management sustains more species and costs less than high-intensity management.* Reducing management intensity can often reduce the maintenance costs and environmental impacts associated with landscape management. Converting areas to native vegetation adapted to site conditions can reduce management intensity. Forest, grassland, and wetland communities are low-intensity landscapes.

WATER QUALITY PRINCIPLES AND GUIDELINES

These water quality principles should serve as a guide for planning at a specific site, and because of the scale of water processes, they will help maintain water quality of the watershed. The aim should be to conserve water and to keep water

FIGURE 3-4. TETON PINES COUNTRY CLUB & RESORT, JACKSON, WY. *Golf course drainage is critically important, and the goal for all golf courses should be to document that water leaving the course is cleaner than water entering the course. Best management practices should be implemented to make that happen.*

clean. The water quality principles should be incorporated into the design and management of all golf courses. However, the specific measures taken at each golf course should be determined on a case-by-case basis. (See Figure 3-4.)

> *Water quality protection begins with a regional watershed perspective.* The watershed and water that it drains to are inseparably linked, and the linkage is important to maintaining good water quality. Watershed management must focus on maximizing natural biogeochemical cycling and minimizing chemical and soil losses from the watershed.

> *All drainage from golf courses should not be discharged directly to water without adequate filtration.* Drainage should first be filtered through native plant materials, or otherwise be cleaned through appropriate best management practices.

> *The water quality of all water bodies (e.g., ponds, lakes, streams, etc.) should be protected by having a vegetative buffer around them.* The width of the buffer should be determined on a case-by-case basis. Establishing management zones around water bodies will protect water quality. Highly managed turf to the edge of a water body should be avoided. When practical, diffusors in lakes can reduce fish kills due to lack of oxygen.

➤ *Poor-quality irrigation water can negatively impact turfgrass.* Irrigation water should be taken from the upper one-third of the water column of all irrigation holding ponds.

➤ *Management strategies for water bodies should be developed and should include a program for scouting water bodies for potential problems* (e.g., high concentrations of algae that may result in a "bloom," or unwanted submersed aquatic weeds like Eurasian milfoil (*Myriophyllum spicatum*). Invasive species should be removed.

➤ *A high diversity of aquatic plant species ensures a year-round food supply for the greatest diversity of aquatic life.* If a water body is restored, introduce as many species known to be part of the biological community as possible. Restoration of native plant communities helps to sustain diverse aquatic wildlife populations. The more fully restored aquatic biological community has higher diversity of wildlife and reflects on overall water quality (see Figure 3-5).

➤ *An increase in the structural diversity of vegetation increases species diversity.* Emergent, floating leaves and submersed plants naturally occur in water bodies. Restoring these layers that are reduced or lacking can enhance the vegetational structure of a community. Native plants should make up the vegetation.

FIGURE 3-5. KALAMAZOO COUNTRY CLUB, KALAMAZOO, MI. *Including aquatic vegetation in and around all golf course water bodies not only provides important wildlife habitat but also serves as part of the water-quality treatment system for the golf course.*

> *An increase in various habitats in deeper waters, as well as in the littoral areas, favors an increase in biodiversity of the water body.* Habitats may be created from such diverse items as old tires, used Christmas trees, and other material that will add three-dimensional structure to the water body.

> *A water quality monitoring program should be instituted for surface water, groundwater, and sediments.* Background quality should be established, and criteria for management responses should be identified. Specific laboratory detection levels/methods should be identified.

> *If available, appropriately treated reclaimed water should be used for irrigation of golf courses.*

> *A prescription, computerized irrigation system with a weather station that controls the irrigation program should be designed for the application of water in the amount necessary to maintain healthy turf.* Irrigation head locations should be placed so that only areas where golf is typically played are watered. Part-circle and full-circle heads should be used as appropriate to minimize drift to native areas. (See Figure 3-6.)

> *Water-saving devices that promote minimal use of water are better than devices that waste water.* Water-saving devices such as low-volume toilets and low-flow faucets should be used throughout the golf course and community. Vacuum flush toilets and infrared faucet cutoffs are also valuable considerations.

FIGURE 3-6. QUAIL RIDGE COUNTRY CLUB, BOYNTON BEACH, FL. *Designing an irrigation system for "prescription" use of water is essential to allow water to be used only where it is needed, when it is needed, and in the amount that it is needed.*

➤ *Storm water management that includes large concrete basins and conduits or other "hard" surfaces is less desirable than using a larger number of smaller-sized basins or wetlands to store water.* Conduits should be made of natural materials, and these riparian corridors generally can provide good water management and habitat value.

CHAPTER 4

CHOOSING SITES FOR NEW GOLF COURSES

Introduction

New golf course development projects are the projects that are most often the center of controversy and concern. Everyone has an opinion about a new development, and the media tends to focus on the concerns being expressed by local citizens and local organizations. Many times, all the negative things that are said about a proposed golf course are wrapped in an "environmental flag." Concerns are expressed about pesticide use, water contamination, loss of habitat for rare species of wildlife, and loss of the "rural character" of the area in which the proposed development is to take place. These concerns are sometimes based on little fact and lots of emotion. I am greatly concerned that this "environmental flag-waving" approach will be damaging to both the environmental movement and to the general public.

Many places in the United States have made it so expensive to build anything that it is only those with the necessary financial and legal resources who can stay in the permitting process long enough to bring a proposal to fruition. In the end, that means that the developments are so expensive that only the wealthy can afford them. What does that mean to the rest of us "regular folk"? Where are we going to live, work, and play? While we need to protect the quality of the environment, we must also ensure that this is for all types of people, at all economic levels. We also need to protect some areas from any development, including golf courses. These areas are significant in regard to the overall ecologically functioning of systems that we all depend upon to live. But there are also many areas that are acceptable to develop. Nevertheless, even those areas should be developed in a sustainable manner. There is a process to determine the appropriateness of a site for golf course development. When a developer commits to siting, designing, and managing a development sustainably, the developer should adopt the *Principles for Sustainable Resource Management* as a guide to the development and management of the property. The adoption of these principles should be verified by planning, design, construction, and management review and assessment, and should serve as part of the basis for judging the ultimate success of the development.

Watershed Context

Site selection and evaluation of potential golf course locations within a watershed should be the first step in the golf course development or management process. A properly sited, designed, and managed golf course can coexist with nature and other land uses within the watershed. If the site is not appropriate for the activities associated with developing and maintaining a golf course, there are likely to be problems. The golf course location should be evaluated relative to the watershed. The watershed and waters that it drains to are inseparably linked, and the watershed must be managed effectively to maintain water quality.

There are two primary reasons that land-use changes must be understood in terms of the watershed. The first is that large-scale processes that directly influence water quality are readily determined with this level of inspection. This includes, for example, drainage patterns, riparian corridors, and other land uses in the watershed. Second, potential pollutant pathways to the water may not be within a given political or legal boundary, and thus to establish these pathways, the entire watershed must be evaluated. If a golf course is located miles away from a significant water feature, but over a connecting cave system, for example, the golf course has the potential to adversely impact that water feature. Not only should the specific site characteristics be taken into account, but the interaction of this development with the site-specific watershed, and the greater watershed, needs to be considered.

Site Analysis

To avoid siting a golf course at an inappropriate location, a thorough analysis of the site should be done to evaluate its suitability (see Figure 4-1). Best management practices (BMPs) will not be able to resolve environmental problems if the golf course is located in an unsuitable location. Three key indicators of the suitability of a site include geology, soils, and topography.

FIGURE 4-1. RAPTOR BAY GOLF CLUB, BONITA SPRINGS, FL. *Every golf course project is located in areas with significant opportunities for community-wide positive results. The only way to maximize those opportunities is to spend considerable time studying the site and the region in which that specific site is located.*

While these are the keys to site suitability, additional indicators include existing significant site elements (e.g., wetlands, buffers, and natural areas). These site elements are important because (1) they may affect the availability of developable land, or may affect the land necessary for a golf course; (2) they may impact the interconnected, natural drainage systems for water management; and (3) they may serve to filter water. An added benefit to preserving natural areas, buffers, and significant site elements is that they provide habitat for wildlife, along with connections between habitat patches, and they provide possible opportunities for passive recreation and education.

The key factors to a site's suitability, geology, soils and topography, and ecologically significant site (and surrounding) elements are evaluated with the following steps. These same steps are also used to produce an effective environmental design for the project and are used in the construction and management phases of development too. The steps begin at a relatively general level with siting and become progressively more specific through each development phase. The steps are as follows:

1. *Identify the biological, chemical, and physical resources of the property.* Knowing the characteristics of the site facilitates informed decisions about the site. Identify environmental and ecological areas on the property that require protection. Identification allows protection of the sensitive areas or species.

2. *Examine the golf course and its surroundings relative to its position in the watershed.* Land and land-use changes must be understood in terms of the landscape.

3. *Identify construction and management practices that will afford protection for all aquatic resources or pathways to the water.* Management practices that should be included in a comprehensive program are (1) construction management; (2) conservation management zones; (3) drainage; (4) best management practices; and (5) integrated pest management, including selection of pesticides and fertilizer and restrictions on the use of certain materials based not only on regulation but also on the ecology of the site and areas around the site.

4. *Implement an environmental monitoring program.*

The first three steps above should be conducted during site selection to make sure that (1) the watershed has the appropriate key characteristics, (2) that there is enough land to design a golf course and provide adequate protection for water resources, and (3) that environmentally friendly construction and management practices will work on the property and be an appropriate part of the design. Before a site is selected for a golf course, it is critical to work through this process to ensure that all phases and various practices of golf development are protective of all regional and site specific significant elements. (See Figure 4-2.)

FIGURE 4-2. ROBERT TRENT JONES GOLF CLUB, GAINESVILLE, VA. *It is important to determine the status of a site before construction begins, during construction, and after the golf course is built. The goal should be to prove increased wildlife diversity and improved water quality.*

Site Inventory

To determine the appropriateness of a site, a site inventory should be conducted. The site inventory provides a means of gathering information about the site and its surroundings and putting it into a form that can be used as a basis for assessing site suitability and as the basis for the course design. Information that should be gathered and evaluated includes the following:

> - Physical setting
> - Topography
> - Soils
> - Hydrogeology (presence of karst conditions, depth to aquifer, direction of groundwater flow)
> - Surface water on-site (including presence of sinkholes or springs)
> - Climate
> - Existing land uses
> - Vegetation
> - Sensitive areas
> - Regulatory requirements (e.g., buffers or setbacks)

Each site will have a unique set of characteristics that should be evaluated, with additional information added to the list as necessary for a given site.

In order to make the gathered information useful, it is a common practice to prepare a series of maps, beginning with a base map and adding layers of information to the base map. Geographical Information Systems (GIS) are powerful and widespread tools for developing the maps necessary to evaluate the site. GIS can produce a relatively simple layered map, or it can be used to model the natural system. (See Figure 4-3.)

FIGURE 4-3. *The use of Geographic Information Systems (GIS) is a technology that allows for the gathering of various "layers" of information and then to visually depict those layers on a map. This can greatly add to the ability to make informed decisions concerning land management.*

Depending on the amount of information available, additional site-specific investigations may need to be conducted. The focus of the investigations is on assessing key indicators of the suitability of a site including geologic connections, soil structure, and the location of key water elements (subsurface and surface) and surface water connections with the subsurface and surface water. The presence and extent of sinkholes, cave entrances, or fissure systems connecting to subsurface water can make the site unsuitable.

Assessments may include geological evaluations to determine soil structure, location of aquifers, and geologic connections to the subsurface water. Surface evaluations (e.g., pathways of surface water movement) may augment the subsurface investigations so that all potential pollution pathways that may link the golf course site to the water should be identified. This is an important step and is often complex, time-consuming, and, therefore, may be costly to determine. Once the potential pathways are identified, site-specific data should be used to identify ways to close those pathways through design and use of BMPs. If those pollution pathways are too numerous, or not able to be reduced through implementation of BMPs, another location should be considered.

In addition to determining the site's suitability relative to the key indicators, significant site elements should also be identified. They are important because of the land area they occupy and because they are components of the natural drainage systems for water management and serve to filter water. Significant site elements may include wooded areas, or other native or restored areas, water resources and associated buffers, corridors or filter strips, and wildlife habitat patches, especially for species of special interest.

Properly siting golf course projects is *the key* to developing ecologically, economically, and socially sustainable golf projects. Proposing projects that will impact ecologically significant natural resources just doesn't make sense or cents! That is not to say that golf courses can't be near or around some wonderful natural areas, or even enhance natural areas if they are properly designed. Golf is a game played in nature, but not on it. On the other hand, there are those who promote the belief that all golf courses should be built on seriously degraded or brownfield sites. I disagree with this as a general approach because I believe that, when compared to other types of developments, properly sited, designed, and managed golf courses can work very well as "buffers" to other less "environmentally friendly" types of land use and development. Therefore, why would we want to relegate golf courses to degraded land parcels? Aren't brownfield sites more appropriate for less environmentally friendly development? It is not that I oppose golf course development on brownfield sites, but let's not promote that all golf courses be built on them. Finally, there are sites that are not appropriate for golf course development at all. And if the site is not appropriate for a golf course for ecological reasons, then it is not appropriate for any kind of development at all!

All sites are different from one another. Most sites that are proposed for golf course development are not "pristine" habitat. Many sites have been impacted by some past human activity, such as agricultural farming. However, this doesn't mean that an impacted site has no value. The value or potential value from an ecological point of view has to be determined (see Figure 4-4). Determining the significance of a site can and should be accomplished through a standard process that can be applied to all sites, in all types of regions and ecological settings. This information will help set the stage for both an ecologically and economically successful project.

Jim Moore, director of the United States Golf Association's Construction Education Program, has stated that

> Site selection has the greatest single impact on the eventual cost of building a new golf course since heavy earth-moving tasks are the most labor and equipment intensive. These tasks include general clearing, stockpiling and purchase of topsoil, excavation of the subgrade, rock removal, rough shaping, and fine grading. Although there are a few notable exceptions, the majority of sites selected for the construction of new golf courses are less than ideal in terms of contouring. As a result, it is now common to move tremendous amounts of soil in the form of cuts and fills. At one time, moving more than 200,000 cubic yards of earth was considered unusual if not excessive. Today, it is not uncommon to move over 1,000,000 cubic yards to build and shape the new course. As a result the cost of the heavy earth-moving tasks alone can easily exceed $1,000,000. Obviously, hole routing that results in large cuts and fills add greatly to the cost of construction, as do design features such as excessive bunkers, hollows and mounds (*Building and Maintaining the Truly Affordable Golf Course—USGA Green Section Record*).

FIGURE 4-4. SANCTUARY GOLF COURSE AT WESTWORLD, SCOTTSDALE, AZ. *Construction is not dainty. Although earth must be moved and shaped, the goal should be to minimize both and to protect sensitive resources while construction is going on.*

Audubon International, with input from Dr. Larry Woolbright, Director of Research, and others associated with Audubon International's Environmental Planning Department, and other organizations and agencies have designed a site classification system that is being used as a guide for projects enrolled in the Audubon International Gold Signature Program. It should be remembered that this classification system is aimed at wildlife and habitat evaluation and is only a portion of what should be considered when evaluating a potential site for a golf course. Obviously, if the site is judged to be wonderful for a golf course from an ecological point of view, but there is no market for golf, then the project probably won't work from an economic point of view.

Site Classification System

In order to achieve Audubon International certification as a Gold Signature Project, each property must have a biologically functioning system of wildlife habitat. The amount and design of the habitat system is based on a multistep site evaluation process undertaken by Audubon International, and a recommended ecological design is produced for the member based on this process. Exact acreage and minimum habitat requirements for certification may vary from site to site based on the site evaluation. The final requirements maximize the wildlife value of the site while taking into account the potential economic return on development investments. (See Figure 4-5.)

It is important to evaluate the current condition of the ecosystems on each property, as well as in the surrounding landscape, before determining expectations

FIGURE 4-5. THE OLD COLLIER GOLF CLUB, NAPLES, FL. *Larry Woolbright, Bud Smart, and Tim Hiers survey the look of The Old Collier Golf Club, the first golf course in the United States to use Seashore Paspalum turfgrass for all golf playing surfaces. Uniquely, paspalum can be irrigated with saltwater.*

for the project. The habitat requirement is less for a property with little existing natural community on it than for one that is in pristine condition. The habitat requirement will also be greater for a property that is adjacent to significant natural areas than for one that is surrounded by other developments.

It is important to note that each property is unique. Some properties, such as those containing endangered species or rare communities, may have specific habitat requirements in excess of these guidelines. Some properties, such as urban infill sites, may have open space or green space requirements substituted for habitat requirements.

Audubon International uses the site classification system to complete a site classification for each property attempting to become certified in the Gold Signature Program. The Audubon International Site Classification Form, along with a complex mathematical evaluation, is used to establish the minimum requirements in connection to each individual site to obtain certification. Although this may sound a bit complex, it is the only manner presently being used to deliver on the belief that there is no one-size-fits-all approach to determining what the requirements should be on each individual site. In other words, the typical government permit approach is to develop a standard set of requirements and uniformly apply them to every proposed development. In reality, this doesn't work in a sustainable way. It may be uniform, but the one-size-fits-all approach does not give enough flexibility to the realities of what is found in the real world on each individual site.

As an initial step in the analysis of the ecological significance of a parcel of property, Audubon International assigns it to one of five classes that are modified from the system developed by O'Connell & Noss for the Society for Conservation Biology. These site classes include consideration of the size of the parcel, the presence of any significant species or communities, and the degree to which natural communities on the site have been degraded. In addition, adjacent properties are categorized according to similar criteria. Both the site class and landscape category have management implications for Audubon International's recommendations on appropriate land uses.

Definitions

Following are a number of definitions that are useful in understanding Audubon International's site classification system.

Natural Heritage Inventory, or NHI, is a system created by The Nature Conservancy (TNC) in partnership with other organizations and governmental agencies. It is a system that ranks species of plants and animals and habitat communities based on their rareness. Species with a rating of G are considered globally significant, with a sliding scale of from 1 to 5 and with a rating of G1 being the most rare on a global basis. Elements considered state or regionally significant are rated S, with a sliding scale of 1 to 5 and with S1 being most rare on a state or regional basis.

Endangered Species Act, or ESA is a federal law that focuses on the protection of endangered and threatened species and on "candidate" (C) species that may become listed as endangered or threatened under the ESA after further study.

International Union for the Conservation of Nature, or IUCN is an international body with endangered and threatened species lists that guide decision making in areas where the ESA is not utilized.

Convention on International Trade in Endangered Species, or CITES, is another international body that focuses on protection of extremely rare species that are being adversely impacted by poaching and international trade.

Wildlife habitat is a native ecosystem that is included in the project specifically to support local wildlife species. It may include limited opportunities for passive recreation, but its main function is for wildlife, not people. Wildlife habitat typically includes core preserve areas and the corridors that connect them.

A *core habitat preserve* is a patch of intact native vegetation suitable to the ecological region and historically accurate for the site. Core habitats should be existing communities that are protected from impact during development. Only in cases of prior habitat damage may restored habitat be substituted for naturally occurring habitat. The nature of the property may dictate a single large core habitat preserve (site classes 1, 2, and 3). The location of the preserves may be constrained by off-site natural elements (landscape categories A, B, C, and D).

A *wildlife corridor* is a linear habitat that connects two core preserves. It must be composed of intact vegetation of the same type as the habitats it connects. A corridor must be wide enough to ensure that the middle of it is not subject to external impacts. The exact width of this requirement varies with habitat types but may be no less than 25 feet in any habitat. For a typical temperate forest corridor, Audubon International recommends a width of 100 feet, but even 10 feet is preferable to nothing.

A *wildlife underpass* is a device to allow wildlife to cross obstructions such as roads. Roads are not allowed in core habitat patches, but sometimes corridors must cross roads. In this situation, we recommend that the road be equipped with an acceptable critter-crossing. The best way to accomplish this is to elevate the road on a bridge that allows the corridor to pass below it. The bridge must be high enough to allow passage of the wildlife typical of the property. Frequently, corridors are associated with streams or other running water. In this case the bridge must be wide enough to allow for terrestrial passage on either side of the normal flow of water. However, open-topped box culverts may be approved as critter-crossings in certain locations on certain projects.

Other open spaces include picnic areas, playing fields, visual buffers, drainage basins, and many other places where there are no roads or buildings. They may have a variety of functions but are not primarily designed as habitat for wildlife. They are included in this evaluation in recognition of the fact that they may offer marginal uses to wildlife, as well as improving the quality of the project for human use.

SITE CLASSES

The following site classes refer only to the parcel under study, not to the surrounding landscape.

Class 1

Sites Supporting (in any way) Globally Significant Elements, including

> NHI G1 through G3 species and communities

> ESA endangered, threatened, C1 and C2 species

> Outstanding examples of community types

> IUCN endangered and threatened species

> CITES Appendix I and Appendix II species

> Other elements considered by Audubon International to be of global significance (see Figure 4-6)

FIGURE 4-6. *Certain species are listed as endangered, threatened, or rare. These species must be identified and specific measures taken to ensure their protection. The wood stork is a rare species that is often seen feeding and resting on well-managed golf course properties.*

MANAGEMENT OBJECTIVE: reservation and recovery of significant elements, including expectation of population increase and range expansion.

MANAGEMENT IMPLICATIONS: Management in support of imperiled significant elements is necessary. Preservation of the resource base used by significant elements is important, and substantial buffering is required. Protection is required for sites critical to any stage of the life cycle of an endangered element, and for any site with a high probability of future occupation by the species. The proportion of the parcel that can be used for other functions is limited by these factors. In the absence of special considerations, habitat should be one large, unfragmented preserve.

Class 2

Sites Supporting (in any way) State/Regionally Significant Elements, Including

➤ State endangered, threatened, and candidate species

➤ NHI S1–S3 species and communities

➤ Outstanding examples of communities of regional significance

➤ Other elements considered by Audubon International to be of regional significance (see Figure 4-7)

FIGURE 4-7. TETON PINES COUNTRY CLUB & RESORT, JACKSON, WY. *All species of wildlife have different space requirements to survive. Some need large areas, while others spend their entire lives in a very small area.*

MANAGEMENT OBJECTIVE: Preservation of significant elements, including no decline or degradation. May or may not include expectation of population increase and range expansion.

MANAGEMENT IMPLICATIONS: Similar to Class 1. Management in support of imperiled significant elements is necessary. Preservation of the resource base used by significant elements is important, and substantial buffering is required. Protection is required for sites critical to any stage of the life cycle of an endangered element. Protection may also be required for some areas with a high probability of future occupation by the species, depending on landscape category. The proportion of the parcel that can be used for other functions is limited by these factors. Habitat should be one large, unfragmented preserve.

Class 3

Large Sites (generally exceeding 1,000 acres) Supporting Natural Occurring Species Assemblages, Including NHI G4-G5 or S4-S5 Species and Communities

MANAGEMENT OBJECTIVE: Maintain native species composition and ecological processes.

MANAGEMENT IMPLICATIONS: Preservation of self-sufficient examples of native communities and species is necessary. A single large preserve area is usually required to ensure critical mass of native ecosystem. The arrangement of preserve areas must include all resources required for continued functioning of critical processes and must not fragment continuous natural ecosystems in the surrounding landscape. Location of the main preserve should be chosen to ensure a strong connection to off-site resources. The proportion of the parcel available for development will be restricted.

Class 4

Small Sites (generally less than 1,000 acres) Supporting Natural Occurring Species Assemblages, Including NHI G4–G5 or S4–S5 Species and Communities

MANAGEMENT OBJECTIVE: Maintain native species and prevent further degradation of natural communities.

MANAGEMENT IMPLICATIONS: Preservation of best remaining examples of natural assemblages. This is likely to be multiple core preserves. Creation or preservation of on-site network of corridors connecting habitat fragments. Connection, as possible depending on landscape category, to off-site matrix of similar natural assemblage.

Class 5

Degraded Parcels with Few Native Species and Little Natural Community

MANAGEMENT OBJECTIVE: No further degradation; restoration if feasible.

MANAGEMENT IMPLICATIONS: Preservation of any remnant natural elements. Restoration of patches of appropriate native community. Emphasis on providing food and cover for generalists, and on educational opportunities.

LANDSCAPE CATEGORIES

These categories refer to the immediately adjacent properties, in their aggregate, as they contribute to the regional landscape and provide a natural context for the property under study.

Category A

Surrounding Landscape Supports Globally Significant Elements, Including

> ➤ NHI G1 through G3 species and communities
> ➤ ESA endangered, threatened, C1 and C2 species
> ➤ Outstanding examples of community types
> ➤ IUCN endangered and threatened species
> ➤ CITES Appendix I and Appendix II species
> ➤ Other elements considered by Audubon International to be of global significance

MANAGEMENT IMPLICATIONS: Subject property is evaluated primarily in light of its potential to support future expansion of significant or imperiled elements, and secondarily for its ability to serve as a buffer against future degradation of significant elements on adjacent properties. A single large core preserve area should augment off-site habitat and buffer it from impact of development. Restricted use of portions of the parcel is expected.

Category B

Surrounding Landscape Supports State/Regionally Significant Elements, Including

> ➤ State endangered, threatened, and candidate species
> ➤ NHI S1-S3 species and communities
> ➤ Outstanding examples of communities of regional significance
> ➤ Other elements considered by Audubon International to be of regional significance (see Figure 4-8)

FIGURE 4-8. PLANTATION COURSE, KAPALUA, HI. *Many golf courses are located in areas of tremendous ecological significance. While this provides breathtaking beauty for the golfers using those courses, it is of paramount importance that those golf courses also take their management responsibilities beyond the course and focus on protecting regional resources.*

MANAGEMENT IMPLICATIONS: Similar to Category A. Subject property is evaluated primarily in light of its potential to support future expansion of significant or imperiled elements, and secondarily for its ability to serve as a buffer against future degradation of significant elements on adjacent properties. Single large core preserve is located so as to augment off-site habitat and buffer it from impact from development. Restricted use of portions of the parcel is expected.

Category C

Surrounding Landscape Includes Significant Natural Area (generally 5,000 acres or more, and/or fronting subject parcel on multiple sides) Supporting Native Species Assemblages, Including NHI G4–G5 or S4–S5 Species and Communities

MANAGEMENT IMPLICATIONS: Large regional natural area must not be fragmented or have its ecological processes disrupted. Subject parcel is evaluated in terms of its importance to the larger landscape. Portions of the subject parcel are likely to be restricted in use because of their role in providing resources, processes, or buffer to the larger natural community. Typically, a single large preserve is located adjacent to natural areas off-site.

Category D

Surrounding Landscape Includes Some Natural Area (generally less than 5,000 acres, and/or located on only one side of subject parcel) Supporting Native Species Assemblages, Including NHI G4–G5 or S4–S5 Species and Communities

MANAGEMENT IMPLICATIONS: Regional natural area must not be reduced below critical size or have its ecological processes disrupted. Subject parcel is evaluated in terms of its importance to the larger landscape. Portions of the subject parcel are likely to be restricted in use because of their role in providing resources, processes, or buffer to the larger natural community. Location of core preserve areas is constrained by their relationship to off-site features.

Category E

Surrounding Landscape Includes Smaller Patches of Marginally Connected Natural Area, Typically Supporting Partial or Remnant Native Assemblages

MANAGEMENT IMPLICATIONS: Evaluate subject parcel in terms of its ability to connect remnant patches or to provide "stepping-stone" habitat patches.

Category F

Surrounding Landscape Is Degraded or Developed, and Contains Few Native Species and Little Natural Community

MANAGEMENT IMPLICATIONS: Subject parcel will have few restrictions on development, and emphasis will be on restoration, demonstration, and education.

EXAMPLE 1

The property is about 1,000 acres in size and is primarily abandoned agriculture. Although it does contain remnant patches of jurisdictional wetlands and pine flatwoods, it is not considered to be a functional natural community, and it does not support any globally or regionally significant elements. These characteristics place it in *Class 4*.

The surrounding landscape is mainly degraded. An interstate highway borders one side, developments border two, and more agriculture borders the fourth. Although there are some natural remnant patches in the surroundings, they are neither intact nor permanent. This landscape is a *Category F*.

Because of its *4F* designation, this parcel has relatively few restrictions associated with its development. Audubon International recommends preservation and restoration of the jurisdictional wetlands and of the remaining patches of Upland Pine Flatwoods. A system of naturalized areas is designed to connect these natural areas and facilitate movement of birds and other small animals around the site. Elements in this naturalized network are demonstration and education pieces, such as butterfly and hummingbird gardens. To the extent possible, this network also provides connections to off-site natural patches.

EXAMPLE 2

The property is about 1,600 acres, including pasture, jurisdictional wetlands, and seminatural oak hammock natural community. Although partly degraded, about half of the property appears to function as a natural community and to support a native species assemblage that includes a variety of wading birds and gopher tortoises, all species of regional significance. These characteristics place it in *Class 2*.

The surrounding landscape is degraded on two sides and seminatural on a third. The fourth side borders the Myakka River, a significant natural feature in the regional landscape. This places it in a *Category B* landscape.

Because of its 2B designation, this parcel must be very carefully designed. Wading bird and gopher tortoise habitat is preserved and provided with buffer zones. Jurisdictional wetlands and remnant natural patches are connected to this natural network by corridors of native vegetation. A 500-foot vegetated buffer is set aside to prevent damage to the river, and this area too is connected into the natural network. There is a golf course included in this project, and it is placed immediately outside the river buffer to further isolate the river from more intense land uses. In total, approximately 50 percent of the property is set aside as undeveloped natural area.

CHAPTER 5

PLANNING AND DESIGNING NEW GOLF COURSES

Once the site for a new golf course development has been chosen, it is critical to plan the project and design the golf course in a manner that not only fits the chosen site but captures the special qualities of the site in a manner that facilitates the overall goals of watershed protection and enhancement. There are many books about golf course architecture and design. The purpose here, however, is to describe a process that should be incorporated into the design process.

As a golfer, I certainly understand the issues of "shot value," finishing holes facing into the sun, golfer safety concerns, and all the other topics that must be addressed by the course architect. Nevertheless, I am amazed at how many golf courses evidently ignored the normal (natural) flow of water on a property, only to find out later that fairways flood. Why do I see course designs that include greens in locations of excessive shade, which result in courses having to expend large sums of money on chemical products to keep the greens in playable condition? Why do I still see golf courses where the superintendent and crew have to spend hundreds of hours per year managing particular portions of courses (often nearly having to stand on their heads to fly mow) in areas that are not only environmental problems but are totally unsafe? (See Figure 5-1.)

The environmental design of a golf course is at least equal to the golf course design. A good environmental design doesn't just happen by itself. You cannot expect to just design some golf holes in accordance with standard golf design procedures, and then between the holes, and over here and over there, stick in some trees, tall grass, and some flowers and—ta da!—you have a environmentally friendly golf course! An effective environmental design requires a fundamental understanding of environmental concepts.

FIGURE 5-1. *Fly mowing is labor- and cost-intensive and can be dangerous to workers. Every effort should be made to find environmental and maintenance alternatives to such practices.*

Design Concepts

Design concepts should include the key elements of the property and take into account the area around and near the site and include the following:

- Identify resources on the property.
- Conduct a watershed scale investigation of the site.
- Identify environmental protection areas.
- Identify construction and management practices that will protect the property and include management zones, best management practices (BMPs), integrated pest management (IPM).
- Manage construction to minimize disturbance and promote revegetation programs.
- Implement a wildlife and habitat enhancement plan.

DESIGN IN CONTEXT WITH THE LANDSCAPE

By designing in context with the landscape, overall site disturbance is minimized. Minimizing disturbance is important because disturbance upsets ecological systems at the site, which negatively affects biodiversity, stability, and overall ecological health of the site. Even though the site can be revegetated so that it looks attractive, or perhaps as it once did, disturbance upsets the ecological functioning of the area. For example, nutrient recycling is impeded or impaired, and hydrological characteristics are altered. In the desert, for example, regrowth may require decades to replace the functioning of the system. Nondisturbance is positive and should be a priority of the development and construction team. Both site structure and function can be maintained by prudent clearing and construction practices.

DESIGN IN AN ECO-CENTRIC MANNER

By designing in an eco-centric manner, the basic ecology of the site is central to the overall design. This method ensures that ecological attributes will be given due consideration in the decision-making process.

DESIGN TO INCREASE THE ECOLOGICAL SENSITIVITY AND BIODIVERSITY OF THE GOLF COURSE SITE

Designing the site in consideration of existing, as well as potential, wildlife habitat will increase the biodiversity more than a design that does not consider wildlife needs. (See Figure 5-2.) Not unlike humans, the most basic elements all wildlife need for life are space, food, shelter, and water. Combining those elements when designing will not only help wildlife management efforts but will also ensure greater harmony between the golf course and the land in which it is situated. In addition, biologically integrating those elements throughout the property and allowing the site biology to dictate the design of the course will ultimately maximize the environmental and economic value of the site after development.

DESIGN IN AN ENVIRONMENTALLY PROACTIVE MANNER

Take a proactive approach to protecting and enhancing natural resources at the golf course. Proactive environmental approaches are more likely to be successful, and the probabilities of negative incidents can be significantly reduced.

FIGURE 5-2. SAND RIDGE GOLF CLUB, CHARDON, OH. *Biological diversity is often referred to as the web of life. Everything is connected to everything else. Remove one important part of the web and the entire web can unravel.*

Environmental Design Guidelines

In order to effectively develop and implement an environmental design, the following actions should be taken:

> ➤ Identify the biological, chemical, and physical resources at the property. Knowing the characteristics of the site facilitates informed decisions.

> ➤ Examine the golf course and its surroundings relative to its position in the watershed. Land and land-use changes must be understood in terms of the landscape.

> ➤ Identify environmental and ecological areas on the property that require protection. Identification allows protection of the sensitive areas or species.

> ➤ Implement a wildlife and habitat enhancement plan, giving consideration to the basic needs of wildlife and their habitat. This not only adds to the overall project but can benefit the economic bottom line as well.

IDENTIFYING BIOLOGICAL, CHEMICAL, AND PHYSICAL RESOURCES

In the process of environmental planning, existing site conditions and resources should be identified and measures to protect those resources should be deter-

mined. An assessment with Geographical Information Systems will facilitate inter-
pretation and use.

Physical Setting

The site location should be identified on county maps, United States Geological
Survey (USGS) topographic maps, and aerial photos. The site should be visited to
reconcile the maps with the proposed development. Each area should be examined
relative to roads, railroads, commercial centers, housing, water bodies, existing
vegetation, parks, and schools.

Topography

The property's topography should be identified on USGS topographic maps, or on
site-specific maps, if available. Other physical features are also evident on the topographic maps like streams, rivers, mining operations, towns, and railroads.

Surface Water

Surface water location, quantity, and quality should be identified. Jurisdictional
waters should also be identified. Movement of water onto and from the property
should be evaluated relative to quantity and quality.

Soils

Soils are of significance from a turf or integrated pest management perspective
because soil physical and chemical properties determine the nutritional requirements as well as the behavior of materials, such as pesticides, that are applied
during golf course maintenance. A complete soils analysis should be required.

Groundwater

Depth of groundwater and groundwater quality should be determined for the
property. Locations of any drinking water sources within the area need to be identified. Connections from the surface directly to the groundwater (e.g., seeps, sink
holes, etc.) should be managed to ensure that surface pollutants do not migrate to
the groundwater.

Climate

Understanding the weather is important to selecting and maintaining the right
turfgrass as well as native plant materials (see Figure 5-3). Average annual high
and low air temperatures, average time of first frost, and rainfall need to be determined for the site. Long-term weather records greater than 30 years are desirable.

FIGURE 5-3. LAKE PLACID CLUB, LAKE PLACID, NY. *Choosing appropriate turfgrasses for specific geographical locations and climatic conditions is essential to reduce unnecessary chemical applications while providing optimal playing conditions.*

Wildlife and Vegetation Analysis

Habitat types present on the property should be identified, and then the property should be surveyed for wildlife species. Wildlife are generally evaluated in terms of birds, small mammals, amphibians, reptiles, insects, and large mammals. It is essential to survey the property to identify where habitats are located and to identify essential elements to particular species. Habitat analysis can also help identify what is needed to discourage unwanted wildlife. Understanding habitat preferences not only helps increase beneficial wildlife but aids in the understanding and control of problem species as well.

Areas or Species of Special Concern

Areas on the property that are unique or provide special resources to inhabitants should be identified and protected, such as old-growth forest, a bog in a location where there would usually be none, or a tree that is a nest site. Likewise, unique or protected species should also be identified and protected. (See Figure 5-4.)

Golf Course Watershed

The golf course and surroundings should be evaluated relative to the watershed. Land and land-use changes should be understood in terms of the landscape, or

FIGURE 5-4. CORDILLERA VALLEY GOLF, EDWARDS, CO. *Allowing for some habitat areas to grow essentially unmanaged to what is often referred to as "old growth" is important to many species of wildlife that depend on this type of area in order to live.*

how a particular site functions relative to the surrounding land. Wildlife core areas, drainage patterns, and other land uses in the watershed are readily determined with this level of inspection. The watershed level of inspection is critical to managing water resources on the golf course. The watershed and water body that it drains to are inseparable. Water is the dynamic link between the land and water resources. One must manage the watershed to effectively manage water quality.

Environmental Protection Areas

Environmental protection areas are natural resource areas that are susceptible to change, and change may cause degradation of the resource. A plan to protect areas and species through correct design, and during construction and operation of the golf course, helps to ensure the preservation of habitats and species. Environmental protection may include many different areas, such as the following:

FIGURE 5-5. OLD MARSH GOLF CLUB, PALM BEACH GARDENS, FL. *Wetlands, whether natural or constructed, play valuable roles in regard to habitat for wildlife and as important components of water quality management.*

- The interface of the native or restored areas and turfgrass
- The interface of water resources (wetlands, ponds, riparian corridors) and the golf course
- Groundwater
- Threatened, endangered, or special-consideration species and their habitat

Protection of environmentally sensitive areas is achieved through the use of a number of different protocols, and depending on the location, several may be employed for any given sensitive area. These include construction management, conservation management zones, best management practices, and integrated pest management.

Best Management Practices for Drainage

The goal for all golf courses should be to protect water quality through proper treatment of runoff prior to discharge to surface waters or environmentally sensitive areas. BMP pollutant removal efficiency is improved by creating a "treatment train" of two or more practices (e.g., a roadside swale that collects runoff before discharging to a constructed wetland).

INLET CONTROL PRACTICES

There are a number of control practices to reduce the impacts of storm water on receiving water bodies. Inlet control measures are designed to protect water quality by managing runoff before it is collected in the drainage system. Under most circumstances, inlet controls must be selected in combination with one or more practices from the following list of golf course BMPs.

VEGETATIVE PRACTICES

Vegetation can be used to reduce the velocity of storm water, which helps promote infiltration into the soil and settling of solids. Plants also protect against erosion and remove pollutants through uptake.

Dry/Wet Swale

Swales are earthen channels covered with a dense growth of a hardy grass. Swales have a limited capacity to convey large volumes of runoff but are effective outlet devices or components of a BMP treatment train. (See Figure 5-6.) Swale effective-

FIGURE 5-6. GLENDALE COUNTRY CLUB, BELLEVUE, WA. *The use of grassy swales on golf courses as buffers are important components of a golf course water quality management practices.*

ness can be enhanced by adding small check dams (4 to 10 inches high) across the swale bottom, thereby increasing detention time.

Filter Strip/Outlet to Natural Area

Filter strips are typically bands of close-growing vegetation, usually grass, planted between pollutant source areas and a receiving water (e.g., pond, lake, or stream). They can also be used as outlet or pretreatment devices for other storm water control practices. Filter strips reduce pollutants such as sediment, organic matter, and many trace metals by the filtering action of the vegetation, infiltration of pollutant-carrying water, and sediment deposition.

Vegetated Buffer

A vegetated buffer is a natural or landscaped strip of land, including nontreated turfgrass, that protects the edges of water bodies and provides vegetative treatment of runoff.

INFILTRATION PRACTICES

Infiltration practices include treatment structures that promote water entering into the soil and recharging or replenishing groundwater. Infiltration devices include basins, trenches, and dry wells. If properly designed and maintained, infiltration devices can effectively remove pollutants through adsorption to soil particles.

Infiltration Basin/Trench

Infiltration trenches are excavations typically filled with stone aggregate used to capture and allow infiltration of storm water runoff. This runoff volume gradually exfiltrates through the bottom and sides of the trench into the subsoil and eventually reaches the water table. Infiltration systems are limited to areas with highly porous soils and where the water table and/or bedrock are located well below the bottom of the trench. Infiltration trenches are not intended to trap sediment and must always be designed with appropriate pretreatment measures to prevent clogging and failure.

Bioretention Area

Bioretention devices are shallow (6 to 9 inches) storm water basins or landscaped areas that utilize engineered soils and vegetation to promote infiltration and treatment of storm water. These areas are typically excavated and filled with a porous soil mixture and then planted. Soils should be suitable to drain the area within two days or less. Bioretention areas are best suited to treat small drainage areas, parking lots, roadways, and individual lots.

French Drain

French drains are systems of perforated pipe set in trenches. The trenches are filled with porous stone that allows runoff to percolate out of the drainpipes and into the surrounding soil. French drains are designed to infiltrate only small volumes of runoff. Pretreatment measures may be necessary to prevent clogging and failure.

OUTLET CONTROL STRUCTURES

Outlet control measures are designed to treat runoff collected and transported to them through the drainage system. These control practices treat runoff at the point of discharge through settling, biological uptake of substances, and infiltration.

Phytozone

A phytozone is a small pocket wetland at the edge of a lake designed to function as a combination forebay/wetland treatment structure (see Figure 5-7). Phytozones

FIGURE 5-7. RAPTOR BAY GOLF COURSE, BONITA SPRINGS, FL. *A phytozone is a shallow area that receives drainage from a portion of a golf course. It is built as a shallow area that actually holds runoff for a period of time. It allows any pollutants to settle, for uptake by plants, prior to being emptied into a deeper area of a lake or pond.*

are constructed to receive runoff directly from the storm water drainage system, where the runoff is detained and treated before flowing into the main body of the lake. The wetland system is defined by an earthen berm heavily vegetated with appropriate aquatic plants. Phytozones are typically sized to treat runoff from smaller, more frequent storm events through a combination of physical settling of solids and uptake of dissolved nutrients by aquatic plants. Phytozones can also be beneficial as habitat and feeding areas for wading birds and other wildlife.

Water Quality Pond

Storm water ponds can be designed and constructed to look like natural basins. The outlet structures, however, are engineered to retain a portion of runoff for treatment. Runoff from each rain event is detained in the pond and treated primarily through settling and biological uptake.

Constructed Wetland

Constructed wetlands are artificial wetland systems that behave like natural wetlands. These devices remove pollutants through settling and vegetative uptake. Wetlands can provide numerous benefits by reducing storm water flows, effectively filtering pollutants, providing wildlife habitat, and being attractive centerpieces to a development. (See Figure 5-8.)

FIGURE 5-8. STEVINSON RANCH GOLF COURSE, STEVINSON, CA. *While it is important to protect wetlands, it is also possible to construct wetlands that can mimic the function of a natural wetland.*

Vegetated Outlet Structures

Vegetated outlet control measures should have a minimum flow path length of 25 feet to effectively reduce pollutants entering a receiving water. These measures include grassed swales, filter strips, and buffer zones. Care must be taken to properly size the treatment area, to minimize slopes and velocities, and to prevent erosive scouring.

In-Line Filters

These filters are designed to treat water flowing through the runoff collection system. The in-line filters use a specific media (peat, sand, or granular activated carbon) to treat runoff in the drainage system prior to discharge. These devices require active maintenance and inspection.

Planning and Design Guidelines

The points listed in the following are offered as guidelines for planning and designing new golf courses, or for redeveloping or remodeling existing golf courses. Every site is different, however, and the techniques used to plan and design each project must be tailored to each individual site.

SITING

As indicated earlier, many topics should be considered in regard to choosing an appropriate site for a golf course. A range of ecological, economic, and social issues should be considered as well. Following are important concepts to keep in mind.

> Avoid developing in sensitive areas, including the buffer zones that are required to ensure protection of natural resources and habitats.

> Provide habitat links between open spaces.

> Place land uses with potential impacts to ecological resources away from the resource.

> Conduct cultural resource surveys. Integrate archaeological, historical, and current culturally significant features and facilities into the development. Protect sensitive resources.

Best Management Practices for Golf Course Drainage*

Inlet Control Practices
(not applicable to green drainage due to subsurface design)

There are a number of control practices to reduce the impacts of storm water on receiving water bodies. Inlet control measures are designed to protect water quality by managing runoff before it is collected in the drainage system. Under most circumstances, inlet controls must be selected in combination with one or more practices from the following list of golf course BMPs.

> Inlets located in natural/unmanaged area
> Inlet protection (e.g., inlet covers)
  - Protected inlets must be identifiable (e.g., different color or structure)
> Inlet management plan (e.g., 25′ diameter no-spray zones)
  - Pollutant reduction programs (e.g., minimize use and exposure)
  - Education programs (e.g., IPM instruction for golf staff)

Vegetative Practices

Vegetation can be used to reduce the velocity of storm water, which helps promote infiltration into the soil and settling of solids. Plants also protect against erosion and remove pollutants through uptake.

> *Dry/Wet Swale*—Swales are earthen channels covered with a dense growth of a hardy grass. Swales have a limited capacity to convey large volumes of runoff, but are effective outlet devices or components of a BMP treatment train. Swale effectiveness can be enhanced by adding small check dams (4–10 inches high) across the swale bottom, thereby increasing detention time.
> *Filter Strip/Outlet to Natural Area*—Filter strips are typically bands of close-growing vegetation, usually grass, planted between pollutant source areas and a receiving water (e.g., pond, lake, or stream). They can also be used as outlet or pretreatment devices for other storm water control practices. Filter strips reduce pollutants such as sediment, organic matter, and many trace metals by the filtering action of the vegetation, infiltration of pollutant-carrying water and sediment deposition.
> *Vegetated Buffer*—A vegetated buffer is a natural or landscaped strip of land that protects the edges of waterbodies and provides vegetative treatment of runoff.

(*continued*)

*From *Sustainable Resource Development Guidelines*, Audubon International, 2000.

Infiltration Practices

Treatment structures that promote water entering into the soil and recharging or replenishing ground water. Infiltration devices include basins, trenches, and dry wells. If properly designed and maintained, infiltration devices can effectively remove pollutants through adsorption to soil particles.

> ➤ *Infiltration Basin/Trench*—Infiltration trenches are excavations typically filled with stone aggregate used to capture and allow infiltration of storm water runoff. This runoff volume gradually exfiltrates through the bottom and sides of the trench into the subsoil and eventually reaches the water table. Infiltration systems are limited to areas with highly porous soils and where the water table and/or bedrock are located well below the bottom of the trench. Infiltration trenches are not intended to trap sediment and must always be designed with appropriate pretreatment measures to prevent clogging and failure.

> ➤ *Bioretention Area*—Bioretention devices are shallow (6–9 inches of ponded water) storm water basins or landscaped areas that utilize engineered soils and vegetation to promote infiltration and treatment of storm water. These areas are typically excavated and filled with a porous soil mixture and then planted. Soils should be suitable to drain the area within two days or less. Bioretention areas are best suited to treat small drainage areas, parking lots, roadways, and individual lots.

> ➤ *French Drain*—French drains are systems of perforated pipe set in trenches. The trenches are filled with porous stone which allows runoff to percolate out of the drain pipes and into the surrounding soil. French drains are designed to infiltrate only small volumes of runoff. Pretreatment measures may be necessary to prevent clogging and failure.

Outlet Control Structures

Outlet control measures are designed to treat runoff collected and transported to them through the drainage system. These control practices treat runoff at the point of discharge through settling, biological uptake of substances, and infiltration.

> ➤ *Phytozone*—A phytozone is a small pocket wetland at the edge of a lake designed to function as a combination forebay/wetland treatment structure. Phytozones are constructed to receive runoff directly from the storm water drainage system, where the runoff is detained and treated before flowing into the main body of the lake. The wetland system is defined by an earthen berm heavily vegetated with appropriate aquatic plants. Phytozones are typically sized to treat runoff from smaller more frequent storm events through a combination of physical settling of solids and uptake of dissolved nutrients by aquatic plants. Phytozones can also be beneficial as habitat and feeding areas for wading birds and other wildlife.

(continued)

➤ *Constructed Wetland*—Artificial wetland systems that behave like natural wetlands. These devices remove pollutants through settling and vegetative uptake. Wetlands can provide numerous benefits by reducing storm water flows, effectively filtering pollutants, providing wildlife habitat, and being attractive centerpieces to a development.

➤ *Dry Detention Basin*—Dry detention basins temporarily detain a portion of storm water runoff for a specified length of time, releasing the storm water slowly to reduce flooding and remove a limited amount of pollutants. These basins are designed to dry out between storm events. Pollutants are removed by allowing particulates and solids to settle out and limited uptake from vegetation.

➤ *Vegetated Outlet Structures*—Vegetated outlet control measures should have a minimum flow path length of 25 feet to effectively reduce pollutants entering the water. These measures include grassed swales, filter strips, and buffer zones. Care must be taken to properly size the treatment area, to minimize slopes and velocities, and to prevent erosive scouring.

➤ *In-Line Filters*—Filters that are designed to treat water flowing through the runoff collection system. The in-line filters use a specific media (peat, sand, or granular activated carbon) to treat runoff in the drainage system prior to discharge. These devices require active maintenance and inspection.

BMP pollutant removal efficiency is improved by creating a "treatment train" of two or more practices—for example, a roadside swale that collects runoff before discharging to a constructed wetland.

DESIGNING NATURAL SYSTEMS

For golf courses to move toward more sustainable operation, the entire design of all aspects of the golf course and surrounding landscapes should function ecologically (see Figure 5-9). An effort should be made to mimic what works in nature. A simple thought would be to remember that water runs downhill! Why try to make water run where it doesn't naturally want to run? We have the technology, and many companies seem to have the money, to make water run uphill, but that doesn't make economic or ecologic sense in the long run. Following are some basic considerations regarding protecting, enhancing, or restoring natural systems.

➤ Restore natural systems where lost or degraded by development. Create natural systems where feasible and where they can function naturally in perpetuity.

➤ Design open areas with native plants and varied plant communities that will provide cover, forage, and other habitat requirements for wildlife.

FIGURE 5-9. *Many species of butterflies have been more negatively impacted than birds and can benefit greatly from the creation of butterfly gardens.*

➤ Control or eradicate nonnative or invasive species.

➤ Use open space to protect natural resources and to provide a natural green framework for the community.

➤ Design open space with multifunctional uses, such as community gardens, passive recreation, wildlife viewing areas, wildlife corridors, water treatment facilities, and so on.

➤ Employ low-water-use, regionally appropriate plant communities. Incorporate native species where possible. Provide shade and pedestrian facilities and amenities to encourage outdoor use by residents. Do not include turfgrass in medians or in areas that are too narrow to effectively irrigate. Use appropriate ground covers.

➤ Use raw or tertiary-treated water for irrigation. Harvest rainwater where appropriate and legal.

➤ Develop a water budget based on prototypical landscapes and evaporative or infiltration water losses to maximize efficiencies of landscape irrigation, water features, and habitat restoration.

➤ Use drainage channels to create wildlife habitat, habitat linkages, and wetlands.

➤ Use native and regionally adapted plants. Place plants in appropriate microclimatic condition. Use mulch to retain soil moisture.

➤ Use a central irrigation controller and weather station. Efficiently design irrigation systems to avoid overspray and to apply water to root zone. Design irrigation systems to use raw water.

➤ Create varied ecological communities, avoiding monocultures. Provide vertical landscape layering for wildlife cover. Select species for wildlife value.

➤ Place trees and large shrubs relative to the solar objectives of structures. Require a minimum-percentage plant cover in landscape areas for heat island reduction.

➤ Design storm drainage systems to slow runoff times, to allow for infiltration, and to include best management practices that control erosion and clean runoff before entering primary waterways. This can be accomplished through minimizing underground piping and maximizing open drainage swales.

➤ Employ water quality ponds to trap sediment on-site. Ponds can be dry, natural basins or constructed wetlands and should be designed to trap and hold runoff from small storms and nuisance flows.

➤ Add detention ponds to on-site storm drainage system to protect against flooding, reduce sediment loading, and reduce outfall piping sizes.

BUILDINGS AND HARDSCAPE GUIDELINES

The primary use of development is focused on human use. A development is where people live, work, and recreate. A sustainable development is a development that also provides for functioning wildlife habitat areas, is energy-efficient, appropriately reduces and manages waste, and creates buildings and other "hardscapes" that are not only located in the correct locations but have sustainability built into the fabric of the buildings themselves (see Figure 5-10). Accepting and using sustainable guidelines for buildings is a way that a development can actually have a positive impact on the environment well beyond the borders of the specific development. Energy exploration, production, transmission, and use are at the root of many of our environmental problems. Air quality, for example, is impacted by power production. A commitment to energy efficiency in buildings will not only save money for the building owners but will reduce air quality impacts where the energy is generated. This is just good business no matter how we look at it.

Following are some suggested approaches to sustainable development for buildings and hardscapes:

FIGURE 5-10. COLLIER'S RESERVE, NAPLES, FL. *A maintenance facility is more than just a building. It should be a small complex of buildings. The plan of where these buildings go should be completely thought through so as to make it easy for people and equipment to move around with ease. The entire complex should be contained to prevent unnecessary impacts to the environment or to other property and community uses.*

➤ Locate footprint for the maintenance facility to minimize any adverse impacts between maintenance activities in and around the facility, but so there is easy access from the maintenance facility and the front and back nines of an 18-hole golf course.

➤ If residences are planned as part of the golf course development, locate residential uses near employment and commercial services, and balance relative quantities of each.

➤ Provide higher density than traditional suburban development.

➤ Provide numerous safe, common areas and walking/biking paths adjacent to or close to homes, providing a safe alternative to playing in roadways.

➤ Minimize road widths and share pavements with other uses in local situations.

➤ Provide a community garden and environmental education center. Include composting and recycling areas.

➤ Site buildings to take advantage of natural heating/cooling associated with its specific climate type.

➤ Reduce earthwork operations by minimizing cuts and fills.

➤ Specify maximum allowable slopes.

➤ Strip, stockpile, and reuse existing on-site topsoil. Store topsoil in shallow layers. Conduct soil fertility tests and amend deficient soils in place rather than importing soils.

➤ Phase grading operations to match the disturbed area with the immediate area of development.

➤ Specify materials that can be recycled.

➤ Avoid paving unless absolutely required. Gravel paths are accessible and preferable for walking and jogging. Stabilized road base and porous paving systems have proven to be effective surfaces for parking lots in some regions.

➤ Design pavements to minimum thickness required to support design loads. Limit types of maintenance vehicles on pedestrian/bike paths to carts or light-duty vehicles to avoid the need for thick pavements.

➤ Use bioengineering to stabilize channels, use sheet flow instead of concentrating flows, use bio-swales in parking areas, incorporate small detention/retention ponds on-site versus large regional facilities, and separate impervious areas with landscaped areas to filter runoff.

➤ Landscape to provide shade on paved surfaces. Share spaces with other uses to reduce paving quantity. Use light pavements to reduce heat storage. Consider parking shade covers with photovoltaics.

➤ Design irrigation pump stations with premium efficiency motors. Reduce pump sizes by designing for natural aeration of ponds versus mechanical. Define maximum street-lighting levels and types, and lighting policies in open spaces and parks. Specify shielded sources and maximum brightness levels, and eliminate light spillage.

➤ Design the site to minimize noise impacts on neighbors. Incorporate berms or noise barriers if necessary.

➤ Utilize alternative power or green power when appropriate and available (e.g., solar hot water, passive solar, wind power, etc.). See Figure 5-11.

➤ Install Energy Star-rated appliances.

➤ Employ heat reclaim systems, HVAC duct system design, evaporative cooling, attic fans, thermal mass, and nighttime air flushing.

➤ Include operable windows to use outdoor air for heating, cooling, and ventilation.

FIGURE 5-11. *Wind power is a growing source of energy around the world. Although there are concerns about possible adverse impacts by and on birds, a variety of energy options are necessary in a sustainable society.*

> Install energy-use measurement and verification equipment.

> Design paper recycling systems in offices and public spaces.

> Specify requirements for contractors to recycle construction waste.

> Utilize certified wood.

> Design dimensions to reduce material waste.

> Design the shell of the building and the mechanical systems with the end users in mind to maximize thermal comfort and performance.

> Use low-noise, low-vibration mechanical equipment, a building design to isolate noise generators, and sound-attenuating walls.

CHAPTER 6

SUSTAINABLE BUILDING DESIGN

Sustainable building design balances human needs with the carrying capacity of the natural and cultural environments, and strives to minimize environmental impacts, importation of goods, consumption of energy, and generation of wastes. The goal of sustainable building design and construction is to incorporate sustainable technologies and to heighten environmental awareness.

Buildings are one of the major direct and indirect contributors to most of our environmental problems, and accordingly they offer some of the most important opportunities for environmental improvement (see Figure 6-1). According to the Worldwatch Institute, buildings in the United States:

➤ Use 17 percent of the total fresh water flows

➤ Use 25 percent of harvested wood

➤ Produce 50 percent of all CFC production

➤ Use 40 percent of the total energy flows

➤ Generate 33 percent of CO_2 emissions

➤ Generate 40 percent of landfill material from construction waste

In addition, one-third of all buildings suffer from "sick building" syndrome

Sustainable buildings meet the challenge of providing for the needs of residential and commercial growth in a better way for the planet, humans and wildlife, and protection of natural resources. This is an important consideration. Over the next 40 to 50 years, the population of the planet is projected to double. In the United States, population trends are projected to spike upward in many of the most beautiful and popular areas of the country.

FIGURE 6-1. *Buildings are one of the major direct and indirect contributors to most of our environmental problems and offer important opportunities for environmental management.*

Energy Use in the United States

According to the U.S. Department of Energy, the United States comprises about 5 percent of the Earth's population and uses one-third of all resources consumed on Earth in a given year. Between 35 percent and 85 percent of community resources are used at the household level, but about 75 percent of that use is wasted through inefficiency.

From an energy perspective, in the year 2000 the total United States energy consumption was 98.5 British thermal units (BTUs) and represented about 25 percent of the world's energy use. Most of the energy for the nation is provided by fossil fuels consisting of petroleum (38 percent), natural gas (24 percent) and coal (23 percent). Other energy supplies include nuclear (8 percent) and renewable resources (7 percent). Industry is the largest user of energy in the United States with 38 percent of the total energy consumption. The transportation, residential, and commercial sectors account for 27 percent, 19 percent, and 16 percent, respectively. Expenditure for electricity is over $216 billion per year and is the second largest energy expense in the United States following petroleum. Approximately 70 percent of the energy used to generate electricity is lost because of heat loss and other inefficiencies in the generation, transmission, and distribution of electricity. The average efficiency of power plants is less than 33 percent. Of the 19 percent total U.S. energy use in the residential component, 44 percent goes for heating and cooling; 33 percent for lighting, cooking, and other appliances; 14 percent for water heating; and 9 percent for refrigeration.

For every golf course, there is a long list of simple actions that can be taken to save energy and money. Every golf course should conduct a simple energy audit of its entire facility. It is not necessary to wait for some expensive technological development; a simple step of installing energy-efficient lightbulbs can make a big difference. What is essential is to assess energy use and develop a plan to reduce that use.

Energy Resources

There are many assistance programs throughout the United States, including programs through the U.S Department of Energy (DOE), the U.S. Small Business Administration (SBA), state energy offices, energy service companies (ESCOs), and local utilities.

U.S. DEPARTMENT OF ENERGY

DOE programs relating to energy efficiency originate in the Office of Energy Efficiency and Renewable Energy (EERE). This office has responsibility for demand and supply technologies in four areas: utilities, transportation, industry, and buildings. Their website is http://www.doe.gov/.

ENERGY EFFICIENCY AND RENEWABLE ENERGY

The office of Energy Efficiency and Renewable Energy provides answers to the public's questions on energy efficiency and renewable energy. Their website is http://www.eere/energy.gov/

EERE Regional Offices

The Regional Offices of EERE are the primary vehicle through which EERE develops state and local partnerships to promote the use of its technologies. Consult the following list to determine which regional support office serves your state.

Southeast Regional Office
75 Spring Street, S.W., Ste. 200
Atlanta, GA 30303
(404) 562-0555
(AL, AR, FL, GA, KY, MS, NC, PR, SC, TN; Territory: VI)

Midwest Regional Office
One South Wacker Drive, Ste. 2380
Chicago, IL 60606
(303) 353-6749
(IA, IL, IN, MI, NM, MO, OH, WI)

Mid-Atlantic Regional Office
The Wanamaker Building
100 Penn Square East, Ste. 890 South
Philadelphia, PA 19107-3396
(215) 656-6950
(DC, DE, MD, NJ, PA, VA, WV)

Central Regional Office
1617 Cole Blvd. MS 1521
Golden, CO 80401
(303) 275-4826
(CO, KS, LA, MT, ND, NE, NM, OK, SD,
TX, UT, WY)

Northeast Regional Office
JFK Federal Building
15 New Sudbury, Ste. 675
Boston , MA 02203
(617) 565-9700
(CT, MA, ME, NH, NY, RI, VT)

Western Regional Office
800 Fifth Avenue, Ste. 3950
Seattle, WA 98104
(AK, AZ, CA, HI, ID, NV, OR, WA)

WEBSITE RESOURCES

http://www.dsireusa.org is a useful database of state incentives for renewable energy (DSIRE) and provides information about state, local, utility, and selected federation incentives that promote renewable energy.

http://www.energystar.gov is a government-backed program that helps businesses and individuals protect the environment through energy efficiency. This website offers information about making your existing home or business more energy efficient, building for efficiency, and finding energy efficient products.

http://www.sbaonline.sba.gov/ is the website for the U.S. Small Business Administration that offers a variety of financial and technical services for small businesses. In addition, there are 57 Small Business Development Centers throughout the country, many of which provide assistance on energy savings to small businesses.

Approaches to Creating Sustainable Buildings

Golf courses should consider two approaches to sustainable building design. In the first, they would identify environmental strategies appropriate for the project by: (1) conserving natural resources (energy, water, materials) within the community; (2) identifying and using strategies to reduce environment impacts; and (3) developing architectural solutions that embody the sustainable building practices. In the second, they would use full-cost accounting to identify direct, indirect, and external benefits by: (1) reallocating design strategies with budgets (direct cost); (2) applying marketing, branding, and financing benefits (indirect costs); and (3) considering global environmental benefits, such as CO_2 reductions and possible global warming benefits (full cost). Full-cost accounting involves the evaluation of the benefits and liabilities of all stages in building design, construction, and ownership. This process is accomplished through an economic process that combines front-end costs, operating costs, indirect costs, liability costs, and global environmental costs. Full-cost accounting considers the full technological, regulatory, and financial issues of project design and requires thinking about a wide range of areas in the design process. This makes use of building systems, products, and technologies that offer increased project value beyond conventional code-driven design.

Establishing Design Goals

A number of strategies should be adopted for commercial and residential buildings and include energy, waste, water resources, "green" materials, and indoor air quality. The building standards for each site are unique to that site, but the overall goals remain consistent. The basic design goals for each area are summarized in the following.

> *Energy*
> *Design Goal:* Energy savings of 30 percent over a typical structure or Model Energy Code for the area, and for residential, become recognized as Environmental Protection Agency Energy Star Homes. (See Figure 6-2.)

> *Solid Waste Planning*
> *Design Goal:* Reducing landfill contribution during both construction and building operations by 50 percent over typical construction and operating costs; encourage recycling, reduction, and reuse.

FIGURE 6-2. *While we work for or wait for new technologies that will make things more energy-efficient, we can take simple steps right now, including the use of more energy-efficient lightbulbs. Source: Jean Mackay.*

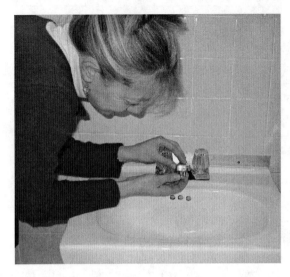

FIGURE 6-3. *Simply installing low-flow faucets or flow restrictor devices in existing faucets can save thousands of gallons of water per year and the users will not even notice the fact that they are saving water. Source: Dan Mackay.*

➤ *Green Materials*
Design Goal: Use of green materials that are more energy-efficient and less toxic to manufacture, make more efficient use of resources, encourage forest preservation, and encourage recycled-content use.

➤ *Indoor Air Quality*
Design Goal: To provide healthy indoor air quality and reduce toxicity of materials during manufacture and disposal.

➤ *Water Resources*
Design Goal: Reduce water usage by 30 percent or more relative to a typical building in the area, and reduce utility costs for water and sewage. (See Figure 6-3.)

Guidelines for Green Buildings

In a well thought out building design, establishing priorities for green buildings can make the difference between a good building and a great one. The following guidelines for establishing priorities for green buildings should be incorporated wherever possible into new developments and renovations. It also serves as a useful evaluation tool for current green practices of existing facilities.

Environmental Building News is a publication of BuildingGreen and we highly recommend it as a source of valuable information for those dedicated to sustainable building practices. BuildingGreen helps building industry professionals broaden their expertise with authoritative, independent information about environmentally responsible design and construction. Their online and print resources include *Environmental Building News*, a monthly newsletter, the BuildingGreen site online information service, and GreenSpec® Directory, featuring information about more than 1,750 green building products. They can be reached at www.BuildingGreen.com or at 1 (800) 861-0954.

Establishing Priorities with Green Building*

It is rarely possible to do everything we would like to reduce the environmental impact of building projects. It takes time to research alternative design and construction systems; new materials may not have proven track records; higher costs may be an impediment; or clients simply might not be interested. Therefore, it makes sense to figure out where our efforts will do the most good. Where should we focus most of our attention in designing and building structures that will have minimum impact on the environment?

Some designers and builders who emphasize sustainability have picked out just one aspect of green design—often it's recycled-content building materials—and hold that up as their flag. Material selection is one of the most visible green building strategies and often the easiest to point to—but it is usually not the most important. Deciding which measures are most important is no simple task. Here we take a look at some of the factors to consider and suggest a listing of priorities in green design. This sort of list can never be considered final—we look forward to an ongoing discussion of priorities that we might all learn from.

FINDING A BASIS FOR ESTABLISHING PRIORITIES

Several related factors should be considered in making objective decisions about where our investments of time and money will do the most good in reducing environmental impact. First, we need an understanding of what the most significant environmental risks are. These may be global in nature, or more specific to your particular region or site. Prioritizing these risks is difficult because often they occur in unrelated fields, with no way to make direct comparisons. Which is worse: the release of toxic waste, destruction of an endangered species' habitat, or stratospheric ozone depletion? Interestingly, scientists often come up with very different priority rankings than the general public on these issues.

The second critical factor is an understanding of how our buildings contribute to these risks, and how significantly the measures we adopt can help the situation.

We may decide, for example, that ozone depletion, a global problem, is more important than the survival of a particular bird species. But if a building project we're working on could eliminate the last remaining habitat of that species—a major contribution to its demise—that's probably a higher priority than reducing our use of HCFCs, which are contributing incrementally to ozone layer damage.

The third factor has to do with the specific opportunities presented by each individual project. On some projects one can dramatically affect a building's performance in one particular area with very little investment, while addressing other impacts might prove very expensive and only minimally effective. Energy performance, for example, can sometimes be improved by simply adjusting a building's orientation, while using a recycled-content floor tile might increase cost significantly for relatively little gain.

Finally, we have to consider the available resources and agenda of the client. There are often measures that can be taken at no additional cost—some may even save money—to reduce environmental impacts. Implementing such measures should be a "no-brainer." Other measures might increase the first cost of a building, but save money over time. How far we can go with such measures, in length of payback and size of initial investment, depends a great deal on the resources and willingness of the client. In some cases a third party can be found to finance such measures, and share in their savings. There are also measures that are important environmentally but don't offer the building owner any direct financial reward. Pursuing these strategies depends on the client's good will, environmental commitment, and interest in some of the less tangible benefits that may result, such as good public relations.

Given all these factors to consider, deciding which environmental goals to pursue on a given project might seem overwhelming. To provide a more concrete starting point, we've come up with a list—*EBN*'s priority ranking of measures to reduce the environmental impact of buildings. Clearly the order is arguable, and for specific projects and climatic regions a different order will apply. All the measures listed below are important, and one should definitely implement any that are feasible within the constraints of a particular project.

This list—a builder's dozen—reflects our sense of where you might look to get the most bang for your buck.

1. Save Energy—Design and Build Energy-Efficient Buildings. The ongoing energy use of a building is probably the single greatest environmental impact of a building, so designing buildings for low energy use should be our number one priority. Decisions made during the design and construction of a building will go on affecting the environmental performance of that building for decades to come—perhaps even centuries—through energy consumption. An integrated design approach often presents energy savings that result from interactions between separate building elements, such as windows, lighting, and mechanical systems.

> In buildings with skin-dominated energy loads, incorporate high levels of insulation and high-performance windows, and make buildings as airtight as possible.

> Minimize cooling loads through careful building design, glazing selection, lighting design, and landscaping.

> Utilize renewable energy resources to meet energy demand.

> Install energy-efficient mechanical equipment, lighting, and appliances.

> Assure the quality of both materials and equipment installation.

Energy efficiency measures are likely to increase first cost, but significant savings in operating cost can often be achieved. Reduced heating and cooling loads may reduce first cost of HVAC equipment, offsetting some of the expense.

2. Recycle Buildings—Utilize Existing Buildings and Infrastructure Instead of Developing Open Space. Existing buildings often contain a wealth of material and cultural resources, and contribute to a sense of place. In some cases the workmanship and quality of materials that has gone into them is almost impossible to replicate today, making the restoration all the more valuable.

> Do not ignore priority #1, above. When restoring or renovating buildings, maximize energy efficiency.

> Handle any hazardous materials appropriately (lead paint, asbestos, etc.).

Usually—but not always—restoration is less expensive than building new. These projects can be difficult to budget.

3. Create Community—Design Communities to Reduce Dependence on the Automobile and to Foster a Sense of Community. To reduce environmental impacts, we must address transportation. Even the most energy-efficient, state-of-the-art passive solar house will carry a big environmental burden if its occupants have to get in a car each morning and commute 20 miles to work. Since the 1940s, zoning and land-use planning have, in general, been impediments to, rather than supporters of, responsible transportation patterns. Effective land-use planning can also help to foster strong communities.

> Design communities that provide access to public transit, pedestrian corridors, and bicycle paths.

> Work to change zoning to permit mixed-use development so homeowners can walk to the store or to work.

> Incorporate home offices into houses to permit "telecommuting."

> Site buildings to enhance the public space around them and maximize pedestrian access.

Smaller and shorter roads, services lines and storm sewers reduce infrastructure costs. Obtaining zoning variances can be time-consuming.

4. Reduce Material Use—Optimize Design to Make Use of Smaller Spaces and Utilize Materials Efficiently. Smaller is better relative to the environment, and no matter what the materials, using less is almost always preferable—as long as the durability or structural integrity of a building is not compromised. Reducing the surface area of a building will reduce energy consumption. Reducing waste both helps the environment and reduces cost.

> ➤ Reduce the overall building footprint and use the space more efficiently.

> ➤ Simplify the building geometry to save energy and materials.

> ➤ Design building dimensions to optimize material use and reduce cut-off waste. For example, design buildings on a 2′ or 4′ (600 mm or 1,200 mm) module. With light-frame construction, use 24″-on-center framing and headers sized to each opening.

Additional design time may be needed, but overall this strategy should save money, particularly with larger projects and multiple-building developments. Increasingly, we need to consider not only the cost of buying materials but also the cost of disposing of what's left over—by reducing waste we save both ways. A 4 × 10 (1,200 mm by 3,000 mm) sheet of ⅝″ (15 mm) drywall, for example, which costs about $8 to buy, now costs more than $4 to landfill in some areas!

5. Protect and Enhance the Site—Preserve or Restore Local Ecosystems and Biodiversity. In fragile ecosystems or ecologically significant environments, such as old-growth forests or remnant stands of native prairie, this might be the highest priority.

> ➤ Protect wetlands and other ecologically important areas on a parcel of land to be developed—on some sites you should reevaluate whether development should be carried out.

> ➤ On land that has been ecologically damaged, work to reintroduce native species.

> ➤ Protect trees and topsoil during construction.

> ➤ Avoid pesticide use—provide construction detailing that minimizes the need for pesticide treatments.

> ➤ With on-site wastewater systems, provide responsible treatment to minimize groundwater pollution—there are several innovative new wastewater treatment systems that do a better job at nutrient removal than conventional septic systems.

Some of these measures cost less than standard practice, others cost more. Maintenance costs with natural landscaping are often much less than for conventional practice.

6. Select Low-impact Materials—Specify Low-environmental Impact, Resource-efficient Materials. Most—but not all—of the environmental impacts associated with building materials have already occurred by the time the materials are installed. Raw materials have been extracted from the ground or harvested from forests; pollutants have been emitted during manufacture; and energy has been invested throughout production. Some materials, such as those containing ozone-depleting HCFCs and VOCs, continue emitting pollutants during use. And some materials have significant environmental impacts associated with disposal.

> Avoid materials that generate a lot of pollution (VOCs, HCFCs, etc.) during manufacture or use.

> Specify materials with low embodied energy (the energy used in resource extraction, manufacturing, and shipping).

> Specify materials produced from waste or recycled materials.

> Specify materials salvaged from other uses.

> Avoid materials that unduly deplete limited natural resources, such as old-growth timber.

> Avoid materials made from toxic or hazardous constituents (benzene, arsenic, etc.).

Some resource-efficient products are available at no extra charge; others may cost more. Installation may differ from standard practice, raising labor cost if an installer is unfamiliar with a product.

7. Maximize Longevity—Design for Durability and Adaptability. The longer a building lasts, the longer the period of time over which the environmental impacts from building it can be amortized. Designing and building a structure that will last a long time necessitates addressing how that building can be modified to satisfy changing needs.

> Specify durable materials—this is usually even more important than selecting low-embodied energy materials.

> Assure quality installation that enhances service life and, hence, resource-efficiency.

> Design for easy maintenance and replacement of less durable components.

> Design for adaptability—particularly with commercial buildings.

> Allocate an appropriate percentage of building funds for ongoing maintenance and improvements.

> Consider aesthetics during design, and whether a particular style is likely to remain popular—the idea of "timeless architecture."

Though not necessarily more expensive in all cases, building for durability usually does require a larger initial investment. Preventative maintenance also requires ongoing investment, though it is generally cheaper over the long term than repairs due to insufficient maintenance.

8. Save Water—Design Buildings and Landscapes That Are Water-efficient. Although this is generally a regional issue, even the Pacific Northwest has experienced droughts and water issues associated with endangered salmon species. In some parts of North America, reducing water use is much higher on the priority list.

> ➤ Install water-efficient plumbing fixtures and appliances.
>
> ➤ Collect and use rainwater.
>
> ➤ Provide low-water-use landscaping (xeriscaping).
>
> ➤ Separate and use graywater for landscape irrigation where codes permit.
>
> ➤ Provide for groundwater recharge through effective stormwater infiltration designs.

Most of these measures will add to the cost of a project. Some savings in lower water and sewage bills and longevity of on-site septic systems can offset the additional costs. Designs that promote stormwater infiltration are usually less expensive than storm sewers.

9. Make the Building Healthy—Provide a Safe and Comfortable Indoor Environment. Though some people tend to separate the indoor environment from the outdoor environment, the two are integrally related, and the health of the building occupants should be ensured in any "sustainable" building. With many clients, this is the issue that first generates interest in broader concerns of environmentally sustainable building.

> ➤ Design air distribution systems for easy cleaning and maintenance.
>
> ➤ Avoid mechanical equipment that could introduce combustion gases into the building.
>
> ➤ Avoid materials with high rates of VOC offgassing such as standard particleboard, some carpets and adhesives, and certain paints.
>
> ➤ Control moisture to minimize mold and mildew.
>
> ➤ Introduce daylight to as many spaces as possible.
>
> ➤ Provide for continuous ventilation in all occupied buildings—in cold climates, heat-recovery ventilation will reduce the energy penalty of ventilation.
>
> ➤ Give occupants some control of their environment with features like operable windows, task lighting, and temperature controls.

Most of these measures will increase construction costs, but they often are easily justified based on the increased health, well-being, and productivity of building occupants. Failure to pursue these measures can lead to expensive "sick-building" lawsuits.

10.   Minimize C&D Waste—Return, Reuse, and Recycle Job-site Waste and Practice Environmentalism in Your Business. For more and more materials, sorting and recycling job-site waste is paying off economically, and it can certainly generate a good public image.

> ➤ Sort construction and demolition waste for recycling.
> ➤ Donate reusable materials to nonprofit or other community groups, where they can be used to build or improve housing stock.

Additional labor to sort and recycle waste is often offset by the savings in disposal costs, though these vary by region. Sorted material can sometimes be sold for a profit. Some low-value materials can be ground and recycled on-site; for example, clean wood waste can be used as an erosion-control material, and drywall as a soil amendment.

11. Green Up Your Business—Minimize the Environmental Impact of Your Own Business Practices, and Spread the Word. In addition to creating buildings with low environmental impact, you should practice environmentalism in your own business, thus serving as a model for other design or construction firms.

> ➤ Purchase fuel-efficient company vehicles and promote use of public transportation and carpooling by employees.
> ➤ Use this priority list in the operation of your own business.
> ➤ Use the design process to educate clients, colleagues, subcontractors, and the general public about the environmental impacts of buildings and how they can be mitigated.

Carpooling and public transportation can save money for employees, while reducing the number of parking spaces the business must provide. Greening your business practices will help demonstrate your convictions to your clients.

FINAL THOUGHTS

In deciding which measures to pursue on specific projects, consider the relative benefits of the different measures. You might begin by customizing the list for your region. In an arid climate, for example, water conservation would go near the top, while in a city prone to smog inversions, transportation alternatives might be the most important. Then refer to your list as you consider each project, and identify the areas where you can do the most for the environment.

Pick the low-hanging fruit first, and go after the tougher issues as time and resources allow. Return to buildings you've completed to see which systems are working and which aren't, and how occupants have modified your work to fit their needs. When possible, use your buildings to strengthen the link between occupants and the global environment through education and direct interaction.

Finally, if you are incorporating environmental features into your work, take advantage of that fact in your marketing efforts.

Like most lists and categories, this list serves a purpose but also carries the risk of compartmentalizing the design and construction process. Often the most significant opportunities for benefiting the environment come from a careful integration of the design, taking advantage of synergies between building elements. The most elegant design solutions—those that reduce complexity while solving multiple problems—won't be found by considering each item on this list in isolation. We hope that this ranking will serve to inspire others who regularly think about environmental impacts of building to offer their opinions. Let us know your thoughts.

—*Alex Wilson, Nadav Malin, and Peter Yost*

FIGURE 6-4. *Geni-G, short for Generation Green, is a green model home built as part of the WCI Evergrene Community development in Palm Beach Gardens, Florida. Geni-G's green features include insulated concrete form walls that provide superior energy efficiency and noise reduction, an air filter system that uses ultraviolet light to reduce dust, germs, mold, and bacteria, and conventional-looking and feeling products produced with recycled materials, including carpeting made from plastic soda bottles.*

CHAPTER 7

CONSTRUCTING NEW GOLF COURSES

Now that you have selected an appropriate site, you have developed an environmental and course design that truly fits the site, and you have received all your permits, you are ready to construct the course. Construction is not a process for the faint of heart. It is big. It is rough. And it takes a lot of room just to move the equipment around to accomplish the feat. This part of the process also follows principles associated with sustaining golf.

The key is to find and hire contractors who have demonstrated by past projects that they care about their work and that they follow the rules as established by the developer and landowner. The overall goals associated with the project in regard to water, wildlife, and habitat and the clean, neat, and orderly appearance of workplaces need to be clearly spelled out in the bidding documents. In addition, prebid meetings need to be held and the rules of the road need to be clearly stated at the start. Potential contractors need to clearly state that they understand what is expected of them. They also need to know what penalties will be in place if the guidelines are not followed. And after contractors are hired, an education and training program needs to be conducted to make sure that everyone that drives equipment on a day-to-day basis understands too. This may sound a bit overboard, but because so many people are involved in the construction process, an approach such as this is critical. A tree that has been identified as one to be preserved may have taken hundreds of years to grow; yet it takes only a few seconds to kill it.

Construction Management

Managing site disturbance during clearing and construction is an important step in minimizing ecological damage to the site. Moving earth should be minimized but,

FIGURE 7-1. CYPRESS RIDGE, ARROYO GRANDE, CA. *The construction of golf courses takes equipment and energy, and often looks very intrusive. Properly planned and coordinated, the process can have fewer negative impacts on the land and environment.*

if the course is extremely flat, undulations make it more marketable, which is part of sustainability. One of the goals is to allow the golf course to reflect natural site conditions; consequently, extensive reshaping should not be necessary (see Figure 7-1.)

Minimizing disturbance is important because disturbance upsets ecological systems at the site, which, in turn, negatively affects biodiversity, stability, and the overall ecological health of the site. Even though the site can be revegetated so that it looks attractive or perhaps even as it once did, disturbance upsets the functioning of the area. Nutrient recycling can be delayed or impaired, and hydrological characteristics can be altered. In the desert, for example, regrowth may require decades to replace the functioning of the system. Non-disturbance is positive and should be a priority of the development and construction team. Both site structure and function can be maintained by prudent clearing and construction practices.

The following are components of a construction management program. When followed, they should minimize site disturbance and provide the foundation for enhancement of the habitat and wildlife on the property.

> *Clearly identify all jurisdictional limits.* This may include wetlands, wildlife management or protection areas, pipelines, or other right-of-ways.

> *Protocols for clearing vegetation for golf course construction should be defined on a site plan.* Areas should be identified for the following: storage area for wood chips; storage area for soil; area for removal of all vegetation between the marked limits; area for removal of all undesirable vegetation; service roads; limits of second phase clearance; and wooded zones, wetlands, buffers, and corridors.

➤ *Areas for soil storage and burn/rubbish piles should be identified.* Service roads to the storage areas should also be identified.

➤ *All areas designated for clearing should be marked and defined.* They can be identified by the golf course project manager with input from appropriate personnel, including the natural resource manager, golf course architect, landscape architects, and associated consultants. Marked areas should employ color-coding that is consistent throughout the project.

➤ *Clearing should be iterative (repetitive).* The first phase of clearing generally includes the initial centerlines and an approximate 100-foot-wide strip, with 50 feet cleared on either side of the centerline. The second phase includes selective clearing. The third phase includes selective removal of remaining vegetation, depending upon the requirements of each golf hole. Throughout the clearing process, all specimen trees that have been marked remain. For smaller areas like a home lot or a pocket park, clearing should occur only after the significant site elements have been provided adequate protection.

➤ *Clearing lines should be identified with a uniform color coding.* Care needs to be taken so that flagging does not fade, and so that the different colors do not fade or become indistinguishable. The following is an example of color coding:

Clearing	Color Coding
Jurisdictional limits	Blue tape
Perimeter edges of clearance	Red and white tape
Perimeter edges of clearance with no motorized vehicles	Orange tape
Areas of access denied to everything	Orange "snow fence"
Edges of haul routes	Red tape
Protected specimen trees	Yellow tape

➤ *An attempt should be made to preserve specimen trees, significant sites, or other important features wherever possible.* In many cases, the final determination of what can be preserved successfully is not made until clearing begins. This is the heart of incremental planning, in which decisions are made based on the results of previous actions. To ensure the greatest opportunity for the successful retention of these features, the following practices should be employed:

■ Areas to be retained should be clearly marked prior to the onset of clearing within an area. (See Figure 7-2.)

■ Grading and any vehicular movement should be kept to an absolute minimum within the areas to be preserved. For example, the drip-line of the

FIGURE 7-2. THE OLD COLLIER GOLF CLUB, NAPLES, FL. *Clearly marking off areas to protect from construction activities is an important action to take to protect trees and habitat areas during the construction phase of development.*

base of trees should be preserved. This can be achieved by the placement of temporary construction fencing (orange "snow fence") around such areas.

- In maintaining these areas, emphasis should be placed on vegetation that produces food, or provides appropriate habitat.

➤ *Edge conditions should be maintained, restored, or created.* This is particularly important with clearing that is proposed within and adjacent to wooded areas. Construction activity (actual clearing as well as haul road activity) should be kept within the specified boundaries and follow the prescribed pattern of clearing. Regrading should be kept to an absolute minimum within these transitional areas. Where minor regrading is necessary, native topsoil should be reinstated. Native topsoil contains a seed bank that will encourage the development of a natural edge. Plantings along these edges should allow for the rapid establishment of appropriate native species.

➤ *Haul routes should be identified and the roads should be followed at all times.* Unacceptable environmental damage may occur if the vehicles deviate from the haul roads. For example, soil compaction may occur and cause stress to plants; habitat may be destroyed; foraging and nesting sites may be damaged. (See Figure 7-3.)

FIGURE 7-3. CYPRESS RIDGE GOLF COURSE, ARROYO GRANDE, CA. *It is important to carefully plan construction haul routes to maximize efficient movement of construction equipment while minimizing impact to habitat. Ideally, haul routes should be located in areas that are already impacted by past human activities and that may later be restored to functioning habitat.*

➤ *An erosion control plan should be prepared and implemented.* The plan should be used each time the golf course undergoes any type of construction or reconstruction.

➤ *The use of vegetated swales, or buffers constructed from native plant materials, to direct runoff waters are effective in minimizing the effect from the direct input of drainage waters.* "Soft" engineering (e.g., grassy swales) is preferred over the use of concrete or "hard" piping where this is appropriate for storm water management.

➤ *An education program for construction workers should be developed.* A 15- to 20-minute session with the contractor, including the supervisors and operators, provides a common vision for the property. The contractor and everyone else involved should be made aware of all expectations. An effective way to present this is with an 8½-inch × 11-inch brochure. It should highlight the major protection areas and what the contractors should and should not do in particular areas. Some key points should be:

■ Respect all wildlife as an important part of the ecosystem.

■ Avoid harming wildlife, both plants and animals.

- Call for help in removing animals you are not comfortable with.

- If threatened or endangered species are identified on-site, do not disturb.

- Have workers sign off on the training session, for accountability purposes.

➤ *Surface and subsurface drainage from greens should be directed over vegetative buffers, through vegetative swales, or into sumps or similar devices before discharging to water.* The use of swales, sumps, or other devices that retain or move drainage water away from surface waters are meant to protect surface waters from unwanted chemical inputs. There are many ways to accomplish the goal of not putting synthetic chemicals directly into water in a way that makes the most sense for the specific property. (See Figure 7-4.)

➤ *Drainage from fairways should be routed away from direct input to surface waters.* This is to protect the resource from unwanted inputs, and it also protects the property owner. Best management practices can be used effectively to accomplish this goal.

➤ *Maintenance facility footprint should be established.* The location should be maximized for efficiency and safety of operations. Focus should be placed on correct sighting of wash pads, pesticide storage and mixing areas, fuel islands, and equipment maintenance to minimize the potential for negative incidents and ease of deliveries.

FIGURE 7-4. LOST KEY GOLF COURSE, PREDIDO KEY, FL. *All greens have drainage. The water that travels through these green drain lines should be day-lighted to vegetative areas before the drain water enters a stream, creek, wetland, or other water body.*

FIGURE 7-5. ASPEN GLEN CLUB, CARBONDALE, CO. *It is important not to fragment habitat areas. Habitat corridor areas should be bridged to provide safe passageways for wildlife from one habitat area to another.*

➤ *Bridge crossings must be built so that the impact to the environment is minimized during construction.* Erosion barriers (silt fence with hay bales and sedimentation ponds where needed) should be in place for bridge crossings. Bridge construction should be conducted so that construction equipment does not enter a stream, wetland, or other water body; rather, only the location of the footings will disturb the bottom areas. The bridges are built with the bridge itself as the work platform. Clearing should be by hand to avoid damaging the wetland or water body with heavy equipment. (See Figure 7-5.)

➤ *Clearing for the cart path should follow the guidelines for the clearing of the golf course.* The cart path should be routed to avoid sensitive areas and areas that have been identified for protection (e.g., specimen trees). Erosion barriers should be in place for construction. Construction should be conducted so that construction equipment does not enter sensitive areas or disturb areas that are otherwise undisturbed.

➤ *A nursery should be established on the site.* Natural vegetation that is removed from the site should be appropriately potted and held in the nursery until it is time to revegetate the property. The nursery needs to be in an area that has electricity and water, and that is convenient to revegetation locations. This should be supplemented by retaining the services of someone experienced with native plants.

FIGURE 7-6. *This is an example of what a construction fuel-up area should* not *look like. Although construction yards are temporary, they should be clean, neat, and organized. All fuel-up areas should be located away from any significant habitat areas such as wetlands and contained to prevent any spills beyond the fuel-up area.*

> ➤ *Polices should be established concerning construction fueling containment and spill notification and cleanup requirements.* The overall appearance of the construction yard should be clean, neat, and orderly at the end of each work day. Trash should be contained and removed to an approved disposal site. (See Figure 7-6.)

Conservation Management Zones

The process of constructing and managing a golf course in an environmentally sensitive and responsible manner involves establishing management zones throughout the golf course. Management zones are areas on the course that have distinct management practices that coincide with their position in the watershed and are based on the drainage basin analyses conducted for the watershed. Management zones work hand in hand with establishment of best management practices and integrated pest management. Management zones include the following.

REGULATORY ZONES

All areas that are governed by applicable rules and regulations must be identified. Activities within these zones must be specified so that management activities are consistent with the applicable rules.

NO-SPRAY ZONES

No-spray zones should be established around each resource identified for protection (see Figure 7-7). For example, no-spray zones should be established 25 feet landward from the normal water elevation or edge of moist areas. No synthetic pesticides should be used in these areas, and only controlled release fertilizers should be used. Additionally, when wind speed is greater than 10 mph, a shroud should be used on spray equipment to avoid drift. No-spray zones should be established around habitat areas, corridors, or in areas of shallow groundwater.

LIMITED-SPRAY ZONES

Limited-spray zones are established 25 to 50 feet landward from the normal water elevation or edge of moist areas. A limited set of pesticides should be used in this zone, and controlled release fertilizers or "spoon feeding" should be used. Pesticides that can be used should be identified and selected with appropriate risk assessment techniques. Additionally, when wind speed is greater than 10 mph, a shroud should be used on spray equipment to avoid drift. Limited-spray zones should be established around habitat areas, corridors, or in areas of shallow groundwater.

FIGURE 7-7. STEVINSON RANCH, STEVINSON, CA. *Various management zones should be created on golf courses including areas established as no-spray zones around water features.*

HAND CLEARING AND MAINTENANCE OF SENSITIVE AREAS

Sensitive areas (e.g., wetlands, streams, etc.) should be repaired using only hand tools, unless a mechanical tool "arm" can reach into the wetland or sensitive area to perform a task. No mechanical leaning should occur. Damage to sensitive areas may include such things as siltation, erosion, and compaction, or trampling by golfers. Accumulated silts should be removed, eroded channels should be filled, and compacted areas should be raked. Channels, which form within the buffer filter strips, should be filled and immediately reseeded. Trash, golf balls, and other debris should be removed from wetlands and buffers. (See Figure 7-8.)

PLANT MATERIALS POLICIES AND GUIDELINES

If quality landscape material is available on-site for transplanting, a nursery should be established. Natural vegetation that is removed from the site should be appropriately potted and held in the nursery until it is time to revegetate the property. The nursery needs to be in an area that has electricity and water and that is convenient to revegetation locations.

FIGURE 7-8. MURPHY CREEK GOLF COURSE, AURORA, CO. *Often turfgrass and habitat areas should be maintained by hand. This includes hand pulling weeds as opposed to spaying chemical products. This can save money and protect sensitive environmental areas.*

An attempt should be made to preserve specimen trees, significant sites, or other important features wherever possible. In many cases, the final determination of what can be preserved successfully will not be made until clearing begins. This is the heart of adaptive management, in which decisions are made based on the results of previous actions. To ensure the greatest opportunity for the successful retention of these sites, the following practices should be employed:

> Areas to be retained should be clearly marked prior to the onset of clearing within an area.

> Grading and any vehicular movement is to be kept to an absolute minimum within the areas to be preserved. For example, caution should be used near the drip-line of the base of trees to be preserved. This can be achieved by the placement of temporary construction fencing (orange "snow-fence") around such areas.

> In maintaining these areas, emphasis is placed on vegetation that serves as a filter for storm water management and produces food as well as appropriate habitat for wildlife.

CHAPTER 8

WILDLIFE HABITAT

Introduction

Developing a wildlife enhancement and management plan is a process that relies on understanding the wildlife and vegetation currently using the site, and the basic principles of wildlife biological requirements and interactions with the environment. Once the basics of the process are defined, an enhancement and management program can be developed. The development of the program is an incremental process. The stepwise process is required because of the interdependency of the various tasks that must be completed by various individuals. So, for example, vegetative structure, a very important component of habitat, is a given for the property as it is; but enhancement of the structure depends on the golf routing, plant selection and placement, and human and wildlife needs.

In the design and preconstruction/construction phases of the project, understanding the basics of wildlife requirements is an important first step in the process. When the basic requirements of wildlife are understood, the design process can factor in those needs from the beginning of the design process.

Key Wildlife Concepts

All wildlife species require four basic things to survive: food to eat, water to drink, cover or shelter to protect them, and the necessary space to carry on the basic requirements of life. In plans to attract or sustain wildlife, food availability is often the first element that comes to mind. Food resources can be manipulated by adopt-

FIGURE 8-1. *All living creatures need food, shelter, and water to live. Making sure that all wildlife can move from one of these components to the others without facing danger or death is critical to a good wildlife management plan.*

ing a landscape plan that includes plants of high food value to a variety of wildlife species. (See Figure 8-1.)

The availability of water is often the most important factor in sustaining and attracting wildlife (see Figure 8-2). Birds, for instance, not only use water for drinking but need a water source to keep their feathers clean in order to retain body heat. Managing water resources should be a primary commitment in sustaining and enhancing the value of property for wildlife.

Cover is a general term applied to any aspect of an animal's habitat that provides protection for the animal to carry out life functions such as breeding, nesting, sleeping, resting, feeding, and travel. Anticipating the need for cover is related to planning food sources because animals often will not come to food if there is not a protected place for them to eat it. Hedgerows and taller grasses will be used as safe travel corridors by wildlife seeking food or water. Strive to landscape with a variety of flowers, grasses, shrubs, and trees to accommodate a diversity of wildlife, from ground-dwelling species to those who prefer living in treetops. Dead trees (*snags*), provide important shelter and nesting sites for many insect-eating mammals and birds. When snags pose no safety hazard, consider leaving them in place. Forest understory also provides cover for safe travel and nesting. (See Figure 8-3.)

Adequate space is the foundation of the balance of nature. An animal will not tolerate an over-abundance of its own kind within its space. This area may be a few square feet for a mouse or a few thousand acres for a grizzly bear. Within the spa-

FIGURE 8-2. WILDERNESS COUNTRY CLUB, NAPLES, FL. *Clean water is key to abundant wildlife and the cycle of clean water will be passed along from species to species.*

FIGURE 8-3. *All living things need shelter. Some species will use shelter created by people. Building and placing nest boxes is not only an educational opportunity for those who place and monitor them but also plays a significant role in bringing some species back to plentiful numbers.*

tial restrictions for a species, all other basic requirements (food, water, and cover) must be met or the species will not exist in that area. Each species has different requirements. Additionally, at any given time, there is a fixed limit for the kind and number of animals that may live in a habitat. This is called the "carrying capacity."

Within the area of space, physical makeup and location will determine the numbers and types of wildlife to be present. This physical makeup is referred to as "habitat." A complete habitat is an area that fills the four basic needs of any particular species. Some habitats are obvious. A running stream is habitat for fish and a woodlot is habitat for songbirds. But habitat requirements can be very specific. For example, the stream "fish habitat" can be further divided into "bass habitat" and "trout habitat." Habitat is the single most important influence on wildlife.

Food, water, and cover should be interspersed (interspersion) throughout the space so that wildlife can get all necessary elements for survival without traveling too far. Certain species require "pure" habitat, but the greatest diversity of wildlife species is at the "edge," where one vegetation type meets another. For instance, the border between a marsh and a meadow, or the border between woods and a field provide "edge effect." This "edge" supports more wildlife than pure woods, pure meadow, or pure marsh.

The first step in developing an integrated resource management approach is to determine what habitat is present on your property and then to survey the property for wildlife species presently using the property. Finally, an assessment of present interspersion is essential. Interspersion analysis requires that you survey the property to identify where habitats are located. It also requires that you identify the elements important to a particular species that are missing within habitat areas. Interspersion analysis can also help identify what is needed to discourage unwanted wildlife. Understanding habitat preferences not only helps increase beneficial wildlife but aids in the understanding and control of problem species as well.

Wildlife Design Basics

Proposed developments should build on the natural heritage values of the site. While there is a corresponding desire to maintain existing natural areas, this must be balanced with the creation of a viable and attractive golf course community that introduces residents, guests, and golfers to the natural beauty and heritage of the site.

One way to achieve this effect is to consider how wildlife inhabiting the property might use it. Not unlike humans, the most basic elements all wildlife need for life are space, food, shelter, and water. Combining those elements when designing the golf course will not only help wildlife management efforts but will also ensure greater harmony between the golf course and the land. In addition, biologically integrating those elements throughout the golf course and allowing the site biology to dictate the design of the course will ultimately maximize the environmental and economic value of the site after development.

Vegetation selection not only impacts wildlife management but also impacts the economic maintenance of the completed course, as well as environmental issues of pesticide use and water conservation. Four primary areas should be taken into consideration when addressing issues of vegetation selection.

NATURAL LANDSCAPING

Retaining and enhancing areas of vegetation that are already part of the natural habitat of the property makes both environmental and economic good sense. Such areas will not only continue sustaining wildlife already inhabiting the property but will contribute to lower maintenance costs by allowing self-sustaining vegetation in out-of-play areas.

NATIVE PLANT SELECTION

Choosing plants that are native to a particular area will not only contribute to wildlife enhancement but will lower maintenance costs. (See Figure 8-4.)

FIGURE 8-4. BIG CEDAR LODGE, RIDGEDALE, MO. *Choosing plants that are native to the region where they are planted will decrease the need for maintenance and provide the most value to wildlife of the region as well.*

TURFGRASS SELECTION

The key traits desired in turfgrass species used on golf courses include rapid recuperative ability, adaptability to required cutting heights, tolerance to soil compaction, and turfgrass wear. The turfgrass selected for use should have a low spreading or creeping growth habit so that it can tolerate close mowing heights and achieve rapid healing, and it should be well adapted to the area. (See Figure 8-5.)

BIOFILTERS

It is important that transition zones be established between areas of high golf course maintenance and sensitive environmental areas. Not only will these areas provide transition buffers between maintenance activity and environmentally sensitive areas, but it will provide cover for wildlife.

FIGURE 8-5. BRIDGES AT CASINO MAGIC, BAY ST. LOUIS, MO.
Choosing the appropriate turfgrass for use on the golf course is critical. This not only includes appropriate cultivars for the region, but cultivars that are resistant to heat, drought, salt, and insect pressures.

Wildlife Management Planning

The development of a wildlife management plan is predicated on understanding and using several basic components of wildlife habitat. When these components are used as a foundation, decisions can be made relative to placement and distribution of habitat patches based upon the specific site for which a wildlife management plan is being prepared. The key to maintaining wildlife populations on the site is providing appropriate habitat. The goal of wildlife planning is to maximize biological diversity of the site. (See Figure 8-6.)

CHOOSE APPROPRIATE SITES TO PRESERVE AS WILDLIFE HABITAT

A central principle in the process of choosing habitat preserves is that it is far better to maintain existing habitat patches than to try to create new ones. Despite the advances made in ecological restoration in recent years, supplementing existing habitat is a more successful (and less costly) strategy than trying to create new habitat from scratch. The first step in creating a functional network of wildlife habitat

FIGURE 8-6. RAPTOR BAY GOLF COURSE, BONITA SPRINGS, FL. *Planning for and implementing a habitat restoration project can not only add beauty to the golf course but can increase wildlife use and save money in the long run in regard to course operations.*

is to identify the core areas that already exist on the property. These areas should include existing bodies of water (wetlands, ponds, streams, shorelines) and substantial buffer zones surrounding them. Core habitat areas should also include any special plant communities on the site, such as old-growth forests, rare-plant assemblages, unusual geological features and their associated floras, and the habitats of any animal species that have been identified as having special interest. Finally, core areas should include the best (most undisturbed, largest, most complete) examples of the common plant communities on the site, such as forests, prairies, and dunes.

SUPPLEMENT EACH CORE HABITAT TO MAXIMIZE ITS WILDLIFE VALUE

Once wildlife core areas are identified, each should be examined from a variety of perspectives and modified as needed to ensure the maximum value to wildlife. Areas to be considered include the following:

1. Size and Shape

Particularly with regard to forested core areas, it is important to maximize interior habitat. Many native species, such as certain songbirds, require continuous habitat away from clearings. Because the forest edge extends into the forest at least as far as the height of the trees, a forest habitat core must be twice as wide as the trees are tall before it starts to include any forest interior at all. Thus, it is important to make sure that habitat areas are big enough to house interior species. Sometimes this means combining small areas into bigger patches. Another way to ensure interior habitat is to alter the shape of a core area. A long, slender habitat area would contain less interior habitat than a circular one of the same size. Habitat core areas can be enlarged and modified by selective planting of appropriate vegetation adjacent to the existing habitat. Frequently, the plants needed for such projects can be salvaged from other areas of the property and maintained in "transplant gardens" on the site until needed. It is wise to maintain transplants for two years after the project is completed so that they are available for replacements and for unanticipated landscaping changes.

2. Habitat Structure and Resource Availability

Each core habitat must also be examined to ensure that it provides appropriate food, water, and shelter for wildlife. Leaving the natural vegetation in an area usually provides shelter. (See Figure 8-7.) Standing dead trees, for example, provide

FIGURE 8-7. BELLVILLE, ONTARIO. *Core habitat provides valuable food, water, and cover for wildlife but can also be enhanced to provide structural layers of vegetation, gradual transition zones, and buffers from chemicals and human activity.*

sites for species that need nesting cavities, while fallen vegetation provides shelter for ground dwellers. If it is impossible to provide sufficient cover naturally, artificial supplements can be added in the form of nest boxes or brush piles. Additional types of shelter, along with living space and food resources, can be provided by good habitat structure. A typical forest, for example, has four layers of vegetation: canopy trees, understory trees, shrubs, and ground covers. Each provides for the needs of a variety of animals. To maximize the number of animals that can be supported, one should maximize the number of structural layers provided. Add understory, shrub, and ground cover layers wherever they are missing, and do not remove them when they are present. Finally, consider the presence of suitable water sources. Virtually all wildlife need a place to drink, and many use water for other purposes such as breeding sites. All wildlife core areas should include access to permanent, shallow water. If a given area does not include a water body, access to one should be provided. This can frequently be accomplished through the creative routing of storm water or through the creation of corridors between core habitats and water bodies. In certain instances, specialized needs can be met with artificial sources such as bird baths and bird feeders, but be aware that these are very limited in their usefulness to other wildlife.

Characteristics of a Good Core Habitat Area

> Is as large as possible

> Is round in shape

> Contains snags, brush piles, and other shelter

> Has multiple layers of living vegetation, including shrubs and ground covers

> Contains or has access to a source of water

> Includes only native plants

> Contains food plants: nuts, berries, cones, fruits, nectar

> Includes gradual transition zones around edges that blend into surrounding vegetation type

> Is buffered from chemicals and human activity

3. Plant Species Composition

Even in the best cases, wildlife core areas are likely to start out with relatively few plant species, and in some cases, they will be dominated by invasive exotic species like loosestrife, kudzu, tamarisk, or Asian honeysuckle. In contrast, the best wildlife habitat contains as wide a variety of native plants as possible. Each type of animal has its own preferred plants for nesting, feeding, and so forth, and so the greatest variety of plants will support the largest number of different animals. Likewise, because wildlife evolved together with the native flora, native plant species are the best match for the specific needs of the animals. The first step to restoring a plant community is to eliminate the invasive exotics. This can be a very complicated task, best driven by specific knowledge of the pest species in question. The second step is the introduction of the missing native plants, especially those with cones, berries, fruits, nectar, and nuts. The *Landscape Restoration Handbook* (Harker et al., Boca Raton, FL: Lewis Publishers, 1999) contains species lists for an exhaustive number of plant communities.

4. Protective Buffers and Edges

The final step in establishing each wildlife core area is to provide it with an appropriate edge. This serves two purposes: first, it provides habitat for edge species and second, it isolates the wildlife core area from the impact of surrounding human activities. Natural habitat edges, or "ecotones," typically change gradually from one type to the next. A forest, for example, has a transition zone consisting of small trees and shrubs before it opens onto grassland. This gradual transition provides

FIGURE 8-8. *Establishing buffer areas between maintained turfgrass and water features is an important component of establishing a water quality management program. A buffer zone can be an area of turf or tall native vegetation that is between managed turfgrass and water. The buffer zone will give surface water runoff a chance to both "dam up" as water comes into contact with taller vegetation, and therefore slow the speed of water and increase opportunities for vegetation to help clean-up water.*

important habitat for a variety of animals that prefer such edges to either interior forest or open grassland. Thus, the edge can increase biodiversity on the site. In addition, it is important to provide a buffer to keep both chemicals and human activity away from wildlife core areas. The specifications for the buffer zone will vary with the type of wildlife and the type of human activity involved, but in general, the buffer should be as wide as possible. (See Figure 8-8.)

CONNECT THE CORE AREAS

At this point in the process, we have a series of wildlife core areas. Each was chosen because it represented some important feature of the natural history of the site. Each has been supplemented so that it is an appropriate shape and size; has good vegetative structure, shelter, food, water, and plant species composition; and has good edge structure and buffering from disturbance. Now it is time to step back and look at how the pieces fit together, both on-site and in the surrounding region. (See Figure 8-9.)

FIGURE 8-9. NICKLAUS NORTH GOLF COURSE, WHISTLER, BRITISH COLUMBIA. *Some species require large areas of "core" habitat and will utilize a golf course as a passageway from the core preserve areas to other needed habitats.*

This is a very important step. With the exception of very small animals, like soil mites, an individual core area is not likely to be big enough to support an entire population of any animal species. Each individual animal requires a certain amount of space to supply the resources (food, shelter, living space) it needs. This is called the animal's "home range." In order to support enough individuals to have a genetically viable population, able to mate and reproduce for generations, the larger habitat must contain literally thousands of appropriate home ranges. Thus, it is critical to make sure that each core area, containing maybe one or five or ten home ranges, is connected to other suitable habitat areas.

The first step in this process is to connect the wildlife core areas on the property together with habitat corridors. Corridors should be composed of the same type of vegetation as the core areas they are connecting. Two forest core areas, for instance, should be connected by a forest corridor. Ideally, the corridor would itself be large enough to serve as good habitat. That is, a forest corridor would be more than twice as wide as the height of a tree; would contain canopy trees, small trees, shrubs, ground cover, water, and shelter; and would be buffered by a gradual ecotone into its surroundings. In practice, this is seldom possible. Rather, the rule is to come as close to this ideal as possible. Some animals will cross corridors consisting only of tall grass, while others will refuse to cross anything short of ideal habitat. The closer you can come to the ideal, the more animals will use the corridor.

The next step is to look at the surrounding landscape beyond the site to be developed. Are there surrounding natural areas in the neighborhood that can be connected to the on-site network? The same principles apply to the region as to the site itself. Many times it is possible to connect your site to a larger green space network including such places as schools, cemeteries, parks, and playgrounds. In many communities, corridors already exist, sometimes following streams, for example. Other times your project can be the catalyst that starts a neighborhood discussion about creating such a network of open spaces.

THE CONSERVATION AND ENHANCEMENT PLAN

With the basic principles of biodiversity and habitat management in place as a foundation, the next step is to develop an individual conservation plan for the specific property in question. Although this process may take a variety of forms, it most commonly includes the following elements:

> Assemble all available imagery of the project site, including topographic maps, soil maps, and aerial photography. Use these to develop a geographic inventory of the major habitat types on the property. A good property manager can usually predict the plant community found at many of these sites without even visiting them.

> On the ground, visit each area identified in the preceding to determine what plant community is present in each location. This may require more or less effort depending on the complexity of the property. Verification of major communities may be quite easy, while in-depth investigation of rare and specialized communities may require outside expertise.

> Obtain an evaluation and map of wetlands on the site, and also conduct a survey for species of special status under state or federal law. Both of these tasks are typically accomplished through the use of local consultants with specific expertise in these areas.

> Conduct surveys of key animal species of management interest. These can be determined by membership interest, by consultation with state or local conservation groups or colleges, or by a variety of other means. (See Figure 8-10.)

> Combine the information obtained in the preceding four steps to identify a series of wildlife core areas that will be preserved as the backbone of the green space network on the site.

> For each core area identified, conduct an analysis of size and shape to determine boundaries of the core area.

> For each core area, prepare a list and timetable of management activities, including plant removals and additions, and habitat enhancements.

FIGURE 8-10. OLD MARSH GOLF CLUB, PALM BEACH GARDENS, FL. *Golfer, wildlife conservation groups, students, and others can and should be involved in continuous surveys of wildlife that are utilizing the golf course. This not only provides data but also informs people of the values a golf course can provide to wildlife.*

> For each core area, determine edge and buffer zones. Block off entire areas for protection during construction, and determine any other protective measures that may be required for each specific area.

> Evaluate the entire property to determine how habitat core areas can be connected together by corridors. Where existing habitat can be utilized for corridors, block it off for protection during construction. Where new corridors are required, reconcile them with other site plans and integrate them into the landscape design.

> Develop habitat enhancement plans for all bodies of water on the property, and make sure that they are connected by corridors to the green space network on the site.

> Evaluate landscape plans for the site amenities, such as garden areas and landscaping along roadways and around buildings. Be sure that all plantings are consistent with native and naturalized design guidelines, and that all naturalized areas are connected to the green space network of the site.

> Obtain large-scale maps of the region, showing any existing green space networks, and consider how the internal habitat network of the property might be connected to them. Identify potential regional wildlife corridors, and contact other property owners whose cooperation might be required in order to complete them.

CHAPTER 9

WATER QUALITY AND CONSERVATION

Introduction

Water is the most significant issue facing the future of golf. As populations grow and the demands on clean, abundant water become greater, everyone and every agency in the United States is focused on water conservation and water quality management. If the golf course industry does not aggressively address water quality and conservation issues in a very proactive manner, golf courses around the country will begin to see their water taps being turned off, or at the very least turned significantly down. Many organizations, such as the United States Golf Association, have spent millions of dollars over the past several years researching the topics associated with water-use efficiency. New cultivars of turfgrass have been bred to be drought-tolerant or salt-tolerant. New or improved cultural practices have been promoted, and test after test has been done to document the actual water-use rates of golf courses and to document actual, rather than perceived, water quality impacts being made by golf courses. In addition, a growing number of golf courses are being irrigated with wastewater and have actually become part of the community wastewater treatment system. (See Figure 9-1.)

Water will be one of the primary limiting factors to the future of the game of golf. Overwatering golf courses just doesn't make sense—environmentally or economically. Overwatering costs money, not only for the water, but for the electricity to move the water. Overwatering is also a prime cause for many of the turf management issues that superintendents face, and then must figure out how to fix, often turning to the use of chemical products to fix the problems they have caused themselves! Golf courses should only water exactly what needs water, only in the

FIGURE 9-1. THE VENETIAN GOLF & RIVER CLUB, VENICE, FL. *The water quality goal of all golf courses should be to prove that water leaving the golf course property is cleaner than it was when it entered the course property.*

amount that is needed, and only at the correct times. This is the foundation for what is called a "prescription irrigation system."

People often say, "Wait a minute, our planet is nearly covered in water. What is the big deal about water conservation—there is plenty of water!" Let's take a look at our "watery" planet and see what the facts say. Of the 100 percent of the water on Earth, only 2 percent of the total supply is fresh water that is available to supply our needs. The rest is either saltwater or locked up in places that we simply can't access. Of the 2 percent of the fresh-water supply, we are presently using 25 percent, with the remaining 75 percent remaining in streams, lakes, and aquifers. Of the 25 percent that is being used, following is a breakdown of how it's being used:

> 79 percent—Agriculture

> 8.5 percent—Industrial power

> 4.3 percent—Domestic

> 3.2 percent—Livestock

> 2.9 percent—Landscape

> 1.9 percent—Golf courses

Of the 4.3 percent that is used to meet domestic needs, following is a breakdown of how it is being used:

> 34 percent—Showers and baths

> 29 percent—Toilets

> 19 percent—Kitchen/cleaning

> 3 percent—Outdoors

> 1 percent—Miscellaneous

Water use on golf courses is highly visible to the public, and it is a use of water that appears wasteful, especially to those who do not play golf. In addition to water quantity, golf courses must face the fact that everyone cares about the quality of water, and there is a perception that golf course management adversely impacts water quality. For golf courses to be sustainable, water quality and quantity management must become a central focus of course management.

Coupled with a prescription irrigation system is a written and implemented integrated pest management (IPM) plan. A good IPM plan is the foundation for using cultural practices first and limiting chemical use to the least toxic materials available and only on a curative (not a preventative) basis. The combination of a water management plan using a prescriptive irrigation system and a good IPM program will provide the foundation for a golf course management program that is truly aimed at keeping water clean and abundant.

Watersheds

Making decisions about how a golf course is managed from a watershed perspective is a key factor to managing water quality. This is the first step in taking responsibility not only for the quality of the water on a specific golf course but for the quality of water in a region. To accomplish this, golf course management must understand what makes up the specific watershed within which the golf course is located.

The term *watershed* describes an area of land that drains downslope to the lowest point. The water moves by means of a network of drainage pathways that may be underground or on the surface. Generally, these pathways converge into a stream and river system that becomes progressively larger as the water moves downstream. However, in some arid regions, the water drains to a central depression, such as a lake or marsh, with no surface-water exit.

Watersheds can be large or small. Every stream, tributary, or river has an associated watershed, and small watersheds join together to become larger watersheds. It is a relatively easy task to draw a map of watershed boundaries using a topographical map that shows stream channels. The watershed boundaries will follow the major ridgeline around the channels and meet at the bottom where the water flows out of the watershed, commonly referred to as the "mouth" of the stream or river.

The way the various streams are connected is the primary reason why aquatic assessments need to be done at the watershed level. *Connectivity* refers to the physical connection between tributaries and a river, between surface water and groundwater, and between wetlands and all of these various water sources. Because the water moves downstream in a watershed, any activity that affects the water quality, quantity, or rate of movement at one location can change the characteristics of the watershed at locations downstream. For this reason, everyone living or working within a watershed needs to cooperate to ensure good watershed conditions.

Best Management Practices

Best management practices (BMPs) are those drainage facilities or cultural approaches to golf course management that act to prevent the movement of storm water, sediments, nutrients, or pesticides into environmentally sensitive areas. Through the use of best management practices and management zones, turfgrass management can coexist in harmony within a natural setting. The goals of BMPs are (1) to reduce the off-site transport of sediment, nutrients, and pesticides, generally by controlling water movement; (2) to control the rate, method, and type of chemicals being applied; and (3) to reduce the total chemical load by use of integrated pest management.

The quantity and quality of water, both surface and groundwater, from a golf course watershed can be protected by appropriate watershed controls and management practices. Because water is the primary movement mechanism for contaminants, protection of water resources also provides protection for sensitive areas and species. Surface water is the focus of watershed protection because recent research on the environmental impact of nutrients and pesticides applied to golf courses has indicated that for the majority of the acreage under turf management, surface runoff is a much greater concern than leaching. Surface-water runoff occurs from rain events or from irrigation. While leaching of certain materials does occur at low levels and under specific environmental and climatic conditions, more materials are transported in surface runoff than through leaching (*USGA Turfgrass and Environmental Research Summary*, 1995, 1996, 1997, 1998). Preventative measures offer a measure of protection against potential contaminants from creating environmental problems in surface waters. (See Figure 9-2.)

BMPs include preventative and structural controls that constitute the building blocks of the watershed protection program. The watershed protection plan includes water (surface, subsurface, and groundwater), vegetation, and wildlife.

> ➤ *Preventative measures* include nonstructural practices that minimize or prevent the generation of runoff and the contamination of runoff by pollutants; for example, using controlled-release fertilizers instead of those that are

FIGURE 9-2. UNITED STATES GOLF ASSOCIATION, TURFGRASS & ENVIRONMENTAL RESEARCH
COMMITTEE. *The USGA has spent millions of dollars to research the environmental issues
facing golf, as well as providing funding that has led to the creation of new resistant varieties
of turfgrass.*

highly soluble. Preventative measures are considered the first line of defense
in an integrated storm water management system. A system of preventative
measures, if properly implemented, offers an effective means of storm water
management and of enhancing habitat for humans and wildlife.

➤ *Structural controls* are capital improvements designed to remove, filter,
detain, or reroute potential contaminants carried in surface water. The most
effective way to manage surface water is by using a comprehensive systems
approach that includes integration of preventative practices and structural
controls.

This comprehensive systems approach should be used throughout the golf
course and community, and it stresses optimum site planning and the use of natural drainage systems. A storm water management system should be considered as a
"best management practices train" in which the individual BMPs are considered
the cars. The more BMPs incorporated into the system, the better the performance
of the treatment train. The first cars in this treatment train might include BMPs to
minimize generation of runoff (e.g., irrigation management) and use of pollutants
(e.g., IPM), and the final car may include retention in a pond.

1. *Source Prevention BMPs for Golf Courses.* Source prevention BMPs can be generally divided into those related to construction management and those related to course management.

2. *Construction Management BMPs.* Construction management BMPs include erosion control, haul road, clearing, cart path, bridges, composting and chipping management, and staging-area management. The construction management BMPs are discussed in another section.

3. *Course Management BMPs.* Course management BMPs are many and varied; common BMPs are, for example, use of resistant crop varieties, cultural control of pests, irrigation water management, soil testing and wet lab analysis to determine fertilizer requirements, timing and placement of fertilizers, use of slow release fertilizers, biological control of pests, pesticide selection, rotation of pesticides, correct application of pesticides, and correct pesticide container disposal.

4. *Land-Use Control BMPs.* Land-use control BMPs can be divided into two broad categories: vegetative and structural. Both types of land-use controls work effectively, and each must be used and designed with the proper engineering protocols and practices. In many locations, local, county, or state government specifies land-use controls for storm water protection.

With proper design and landscaping, a proper balance between aesthetics and function can be achieved. Most BMPs can be incorporated into the routine maintenance practices for the golf course or community common areas, resulting in nominal costs for effective management.

VEGETATIVE PRACTICES

A variety of vegetative practices can contribute to the quality of water by filtering sediments and chemicals on golf courses. As many of these methods as possible should be included as part of the design of a new golf course, and they should be incorporated wherever possible on any existing golf course. These practices include (1) vegetative filtration, (2) grassed swales, (3) vegetated filter strips, (4) buffers, and (5) turfgrass.

1. Vegetative Filtration

Vegetative filters act as natural biofilters to reduce storm water flow and pollutant load, and appropriately managed turf areas can be effective filters. Vegetated filter strips remove sediment and attached chemicals, organic material, trace metals, and nutrients such as nitrogen and phosphorus. If appropriately managed, sediment removal rates are generally greater than 70 percent and nutrient removal are gener-

FIGURE 9-3. ROBERT TRENT JONES GOLF CLUB, GAINESVILLE, VA. *Vegetation of different types and heights play important roles in filtering water.*

ally greater than 50 percent according to studies done by the United States Environmental Protection Agency. The length, or width, of the vegetated filter strip is an important variable influencing effectiveness, because contact time between runoff water and vegetation in the filter strip increases with the length or width of the filter strip length. Some sources suggest a minimum of 50 feet of vegetative buffer for maximum effectiveness, and other studies have shown that 15 to 25 feet of turf is an effective filter. Length of the buffer is site-specific and should take into account such things as buffer vegetation, slope, location, and quantities of water that require treatment. (See Figure 9-3.)

Maintenance of vegetative filters requires active cultural management to achieve dense, hearty vegetation. Turfgrass can be an effective filtration medium, and to maintain its effectiveness, cultural activities should focus on producing healthy turf with a minimum of maintenance activities. The height of the turf should be allowed to grow to the highest end of the optimum range for more effective filtration; fertilization in these areas should occur, but at a reduced rate.

2. Grassed Swales

Grassed swales are designed to carry storm water runoff to either a treatment pond or to carry treated runoff from a treatment pond to a wetland or watercourse.

FIGURE 9-4. BLACK LAKE GOLF CLUB, ONAWAY, MI. *Grassy swales properly located can add a challenge to the game and can also provide both connections for wildlife management and links in the water management system for the course.*

When combined with other structural storm water measures, swales can substantially improve the quality of storm water (see Figure 9-4). In order to be used as an effective BMP, a typical grassed swale may have the following design criteria, but each swale should be developed for the particular site:

> Swale slopes should be graded as close to zero as drainage will permit. Side slopes should be no greater than 3:1 (height:vertical).

> A water-tolerant, erosion-resistant grass should be established.

> Soils should have a percolation rate of >0.5 inches/hour. The soil should be tilled before the grass cover is established to maximize infiltration capacity.

> Swales should be planted with a dense growth of water-tolerant grass (such as tall fescue) that is maintained at the highest end of the optimum range for more effective filtration and reduced maintenance requirements.

Swales should also be designed to generate sheet flow. The grassed swales should be constructed initially as part of the erosion control plan. After site stabilization, the grassed swales should be regraded and seeded to maximize infiltration capacity. An example of their use is the routing of water from the under-drains of greens. Filtration can be greatly increased by carefully choosing the route of water from the under-drain. If space is limited, drainage water could be directed to flow along a path that maximizes the distance of contact with vegetation, rather than be directly routed to the lowest point.

3. Vegetated Filter Strips

Filter strips are man-made or naturally occurring flat areas that are established at the perimeter of the disturbed or impervious areas to intercept runoff as sheet flow and remove particulates and contaminants. Either grassed or wooded (forested) areas can function as filter strips. Effective filter strips include dense growing turf filter strips, which should be incorporated into golf course roughs and the perimeter of the impervious areas. In order to be an effective BMP, filter strips should be a minimum width of 25 feet, with slopes not to exceed 10 percent.

4. Buffers

The most sensitive portions of watercourses are the areas immediately adjacent to the water. Disturbance within and adjacent to watercourses can degrade water quality by increasing the availability and transport of pollutants. The retention of vegetated buffers along watercourses is, therefore, one of the most effective practices used to protect water quality. Buffer areas should be a minimum of 25 feet in width when adjacent to fairways and tees, and 50 feet in width when adjacent to greens. In areas where nonplay buffers are less than 25 feet, roughs can be maintained as buffers. Management zones for these buffers also help protect the water. (See Figure 9-5.)

FIGURE 9-5. GRAND HARBOR CLUB, VERO BEACH, FL. *Terrestrial and aquatic vegetation can help provide water cleaning properties, as well has provide habitat for wildlife.*

5. *Turfgrass*

One of the most effective BMPs for protection of surface water is use of turf as a vegetative filter in swales and filter strips. Compared to other crop systems, turfgrassed areas are extremely effective in reducing soil losses. Turf uses the natural processes of infiltration, filtration, and biological uptake to reduce flows and pollutant loadings. The effectiveness of turf is related to the architecture of the turf canopy and the fibrous nature of the turf root system. Turf density, leaf texture, and canopy height are physical factors that restrain soil erosion and sediment loss by dissipating impact energy from rain and irrigation water droplets, providing a resistance to surface movement of water over turf. Turfgrasses have an extensive fibrous root system, with 80 percent of the root mass found in the upper 2 inches of the soil profile. Therefore, it is a combination of the turf canopy and root mass that has a strong soil stabilizing effect in regard to holding and filtering water.

STRUCTURAL BEST MANAGEMENT PRACTICES

Structural best management controls are capital improvements designed to remove, filter, detain, or reroute potential pollutants carried in surface water. Common types of structural BMPs include (1) extended detention basins, (2) wet ponds, (3) biofilters, (4) peat or charcoal filters, (5) water quality inlets, (6) infiltration controls, and (7) storm water diversions, but there are many more that work well. Maintenance of the structural BMP is critical to its success, and each site-specific BMP should have a maintenance program as part of general operations.

1. *Extended Detention Basin*

This BMP is a storm water detention pond that also provides water quality benefits by capturing the "first flush" runoff and detaining it for an extended period of time to allow for settling and removal of particulate pollutants, as well as peak attenuation. A low-flow opening is incorporated into the multistage primary outlet structure for the slow release of storm water in order to achieve the required extended detention times for the "first flush" runoff from the tributary watershed. In most instances, minimum extended detention time is established by regulation, and this is often 24 hours.

The benefits of extended detention include (1) a high removal rate of sediments, biochemical oxygen demand (BOD), organic nutrients, and trace metals; (2) removal of soluble nutrients because of natural biological processes occurring within the pond; (3) creation of new wildlife habitat; and (4) erosion control.

Storm Water Pollutant Removal Efficiencies, Urban BMP Designs*

BMP/Design	Total Suspended Sediment (TSS)	Total Phosphorous (TP)	Total Nitrogen (TN)	Zinc (Zn)	Lead (Pb)	Biological Oxygen Demand (BOD)
Extended Detention Pond						
Design 2	75%	50%	35%	55%	55%	40%
Design 3	80%	70%	55%	75%	75%	50%
Wet Pond						
Design 4	55%	35%	25%	25%	45%	25%
Design 5	75%	55%	40%	40%	70%	40%
Water Quality Basin						
Design 7	70%	50%	50%	50%	50%	70%
Filter Strip						
Design 11	40%	20%	20%	40%	40%	20%
Design 12	90%	50%	50%	90%	90%	70%
Design 12A	80%	40%	40%	80%	80%	60%
Grassed Swale						
Design 13	20%	20%	20%	10%	10%	20%
Design 14	30%	30%	30%	20%	20%	30%

Extended Detention Basins

Design 2	"First flush" runoff volume produced by 1.0 inch, detained for 24 hours.
Design 3	Runoff volume produced by 1.0-inch storm, detained for 24 hours or more with shallow marsh added in bottom stages.

Wet Pond

Design 4	Permanent pool equal to 0.5 inches of runoff per watershed acre.
Design 5	Permanent pool equal to 2.5 times the volume of runoff from the mean storm (0.5 inches).

Water Quality Basin

Design 7	Infiltration basin that filtrates "first flush" of 0.5-inch runoff/impervious acre.

Filter Strips

Design 11	25- to 50-foot turf strip.
Design 12	100-foot wooded strip.
Design 12A	25- to 50-foot turf strip.

Grassed Swale

Design 13	High slopes with check dams.
Design 14	Low gradient (less than 5%) with check dam.

*Sources: Schueler, T. R. 1987. *Controlling Urban Runoff: A practical manual for planning and designing urban BMPs*. Department of Environmental Programs, Metropolitan Washington Council of Governments (MWCOG); NYS Dept. of Environmental Conservation. *1993. Reducing the Impacts from Storm Water Runoff from New Development*, 2nd Edition.

2. Wet Ponds

Wet ponds have substantially higher pollutant removal efficiency rates than conventional dry detention basins (see Figure 9-6). As with any standing water body, the water column concentrations of incoming particulate pollutants (e.g., nutrients, heavy metals) will initially be reduced as a result of the settling of the heavier, course-grain particulate matter (i.e., total suspended solids). Studies have shown that the majority of suspended particulate pollutants will settle out of the water column during the first 6 to 12 hours. Most wet ponds are designed to store water from storm events of a given magnitude.

Unlike most conventional structural storm water measures, wet ponds can also remove significant amounts of dissolved pollutants, especially soluble nutrients, from the water column. This occurs because of bacterial, algal, and aquatic plant uptake of dissolved constituents. Biological assimilation of dissolved pollutants and soluble nutrients represents an important removal pathway, since these types of pollutants are not greatly affected by water column settling processes. Once assimilated, the nutrients are either trapped in biomass and sequestered in the sediments or microbial activities remove the nutrients from the system. This combination of the settling of total suspended solids (TSS) and the assimilation of soluble forms of nutrients, such as phosphorus and nitrogen, make wet ponds a very effective means of reducing storm-water-related pollutant loading.

FIGURE 9-6. THE VENETIAN GOLF AND RIVER CLUB, VENICE, FL. *Providing and managing "wet-pond" areas for storm water runoff, or as receiving bodies for golf course irrigation, is important in the overall project design and management.*

3. Biofilters

Biofilters are capable of achieving pollutant-removal efficiencies of the magnitude associated with wet ponds (see Figure 9-7). *Biofilter* is a broad term used to encompass BMPs designed specifically to detain and treat storm water runoff. The fact that the biofilter is designed to meet specific hydrologic criteria distinguishes it from wetlands created for mitigation or the creation of wildlife habitat. Most biofilters have a broad, gently graded (1 to 2 percent) bottom and are designed to accommodate and treat the runoff volume of the one-year storm event (i.e., largest amount of rainfall to occur in a one-year time period) through the use of specially designed outlet control structures or check dams. Most are planted with a dense assortment of vegetation capable of existing in saturated or temporarily standing water conditions. Small standing pools of water, interspersed within the dense vegetation, also characterize some biofilters.

In essence, biofilters are intended to function as a shallow wetland. That is, pollutant removal is achieved as a result of settling, filtering, and bio-uptake. When properly constructed, the detention time of storm water required for exceptional pollutant removal efficiency will be experienced, especially in respect to nutrient removal.

FIGURE 9-7. TURNING STONE CASINO, SHENANDOAH GOLF COURSE, VERONA, NY. *A biofilter is an area of vegetation that is used to retain water for a period of time and allow for the vegetation to capture any possible water contaminates. These areas then become living water filters.*

4. Peat or Charcoal Filters

Peat filters or charcoal filters utilize a peat/sand or charcoal/sand filter media to treat storm water runoff (see Figure 9-8). They can be designed with or without a presedimentation chamber. The general concept of their operation focuses on the infiltration of collected runoff through an approximately 18-inch-thick peat layer, into a sand/peat layer, and eventually to an under-drain system that either conveys the treated runoff to another BMP or discharges it off-site. The peat element of the filter is intended to function in a manner similar to a biofilter, with pollutants being removed as a result of the combination of filtration, adsorption, and bio-uptake processes.

5. Water Quality Inlets

Water quality inlets are catch basins with an outlet invert pipe raised approximately 2 feet from the bottom. By the raised outlet pipe, a retention volume is created within the basin. This sump helps to trap sediments by slowing storm surges

FIGURE 9-8. BRIDGES AT CASINO MAGIC, BAY ST. LOUIS, MO. *Where more "natural" forms of water filtration can't be utilized, the creation of more "mechanical" forms is acceptable, such as the use of peat or charcoal filter systems.*

and reducing the velocity of water from the inflowing runoff. Slowing storm water flow allows for the settling of coarse and medium-sized sediment particles.

In addition to trapping sediments, water quality inlets have the added effect of removing other pollutants such as heavy metals, petroleum hydrocarbons, and to a lesser extent, nutrients. These pollutants are removed because of their tendency toward binding with sediment particles. Water quality inlets are unobtrusive and are compatible with standard storm drain networks.

6. Infiltration Controls

Infiltration controls are a general category of structural BMPs that maintain or enhance the ability of water to percolate through the soil profile. Infiltration generally improves water quality by allowing natural physical, chemical, and biological processes to remove pollutants. Pollutant removal in the artificial media or soil profile occurs through filtration, absorption, and oxidation by soil microorganisms. Examples of structural infiltration BMPs include infiltration basins, infiltration trenches, dry wells, and porous pavement. In general, infiltration BMPs require more frequent maintenance than detention basin or wet pond BMPs in order to eliminate clogging of sand and gravel filter media.

7. Storm Water Diversions

For highly urbanized watersheds or areas where soil and climatic conditions are poorly suited for conventional detention and infiltration BMPs, storm water diversions may be the only acceptable alternative. In some cases, poor land-use planning may preclude the opportunity to retrofit the natural drainage system with wet ponds or dry detention basins. The cost for diversion projects is usually much higher than other structural BMPs because of their larger scale, greater complexity, and requirements for right-of-way easements.

Water Management and Monitoring

Maintaining water quality at the golf course includes the processes described in the siting, design, and construction chapters of this book. Cultural practices, including careful selection of materials for use on the golf course, were identified to provide protection to water quality. The environmental monitoring program is an important aspect of the overall water protection program. (See Figure 9-9.)

An environmental monitoring program should do the following:

1. Establish a baseline of water and sediment quality prior to construction.
2. Provide data that will establish environmental conditions, thus providing a basis for measuring compliance with environmental regulations.
3. Ensure that integrated pest management is functioning properly.

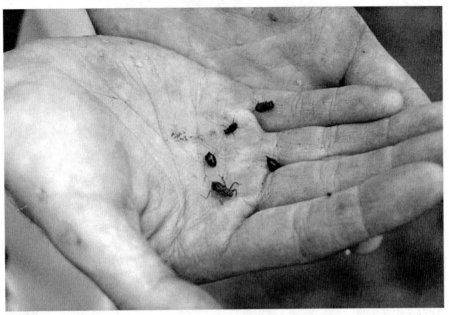

FIGURE 9-9. *It is important to monitor the quality and health of the aquatic systems on and around the golf course. Both water chemistry and biological diversity, such as the macroinvertebrates shown here, and health are important components of a water quality monitoring program.*

The management program at the golf course is evaluated based on the results of the monitoring program. Based on this evaluation, the management plan may need to be revised and adjusted. This kind of adaptive management is key to successful conservation management.

The environmental monitoring program is usually established in three phases that coincide with golf course development. Phase I is background; Phase II is con-

Components of an Environmental Monitoring Program

➤ Establish a baseline.
➤ Provide data to assess compliance.
➤ Provide information on management practices.
➤ Develop in phases.
➤ Include surface water and groundwater data.
➤ Identify **where** samples are taken, **how often** they are taken, **what** should be **analyzed**, and **what actions** should be taken if established criteria are exceeded.

struction and development; and Phase III is the postdevelopment, operational golf course. During each phase, samples are collected and analyzed, and the results are evaluated.

There are several steps to setting up a water monitoring program.

> *Identify what will be sampled.* It is important to sample both surface water and groundwater resources because of the geologic connection between them. Consideration should also be given to sampling shallow sediment. Sediment generally accumulates material and is considered a good indicator of environmental quality.

> *Identify the sample locations.* To determine sample locations, survey the water bodies on the golf course. If there are only a few, you may choose to sample each. Golf courses with many water features may choose to sample representative water bodies. How many sample locations you choose is highly site dependent. For groundwater, sample locations are chosen based on the projected flow of groundwater. Three or four sample locations are the minimum number required to assess water quality. When establishing the program, remember that sampling the same location over time is important so that comparisons can be made.

> *Determine sampling frequency.* Identify how often each location will be sampled over a year's time. It is important to sample during different seasons because the environment responds differently during each season.

> *Determine the variables that will be sampled.* This should include general water characteristics (temperature, pH, conductance, dissolved oxygen) as well as nutrients (primarily phosphorus and nitrogen) and pesticides. Select pesticides for analysis based on their aquatic toxicity, water solubility, and adsorption coefficient, using the procedure for selecting pesticides to reduce adverse water quality impacts. Pesticides may also be selected based on an ecological risk assessment.

In addition to the previous steps, it is essential to establish a formal protocol for the entire water-monitoring process. This protocol should include the following:

1. *Identify the sampling field methods.* Clearly identify the methodology for taking samples.

2. *Identify the laboratories to perform the sample analysis.* Make sure that these labs are certified and have strong quality assurance and control practices in place. Also, make sure that the lab can detect variables at appropriate concentrations, as this is often a concern with pesticides.

3. *Determine the data storage techniques.* Storage of data should be determined in the beginning of the monitoring program. Storage should be both on a computer diskette and on paper. The computer storage allows you to easily analyze and use the data to help better manage the course.

4. *Establish criteria for management response.* There should be specific criteria against which the sampling results can be compared. If a criterion is exceeded, then a problem is occurring and a management response is required. Specific, step-by-step responses that will be undertaken if the criteria are exceeded should be identified in Phase I of the monitoring program.

IRRIGATION MANAGEMENT AND WATER CONSERVATION

Water management, through irrigation practices and conservation techniques, is important for successful golf course management. As noted earlier, too much water or too little water leads to maintenance problems, contributing to the need for pesticide or fertilizer applications. Water is the mode of transportation for contaminants into surface and groundwater resources, including springs, so the use of water on the course is important. Additionally, excessive water withdrawal for irrigation can impact water levels in aquifers below the golf course. (See Figure 9-10.)

The overall management plan for a golf course should address irrigation and water conservation practices, with one of the goals being to reduce the golf course demand for water. To assist in this effort, a number of BMP strategies can be used. Initially, the various golf areas should be prioritized in terms of whether irrigation

FIGURE 9-10. ALTA SIERRA GOLF & COUNTRY CLUB, GRASS VALLEY, CA. *It is important to only put water where water is needed and only in the amounts that are needed. This is particularly important if fertilizer is applied through the irrigation system.*

will be necessary, and what level of irrigation will be required. Greens, for example, would receive the highest irrigation priority, while roughs or out-of-play areas would receive the lowest priority. This prioritization will help in the design of an appropriate irrigation system, as well as help managers determine what should be watered in times of water restrictions or drought. Reducing the amount of irrigated turf areas where possible can help. Where appropriate, use of effluent water for irrigation should be considered.

Irrigation patterns and control systems should be planned and programmed to meet the needs of the plant and turf species. Using the right plants initially can reduce irrigation requirements, so wherever possible, use native, naturalized, or specialized drought-tolerant plant materials. Choose turf species that are well suited to the local climate and soils. Additionally, make sure that the irrigation system distributes the water uniformly over the designated area and only as fast as the soil can absorb it. Regularly inspect the irrigation system, and quickly fix any leaks or operational problems. Water only at the appropriate time to minimize evaporation and to reduce disease potential. Avoid watering at peak evaporation periods. Automatic irrigation systems reduce unnecessary watering and should include a shutoff mechanism if it begins to rain.

Water demand can be reduced through the use of BMPs like those identified previously. These practices can also be combined with cultural techniques (mowing practices, cultivation/aeration, and cutting heights) to maximize the effectiveness of water on the course. These types of practices can also lead to an associated economic benefit—energy cost savings can result from reducing the use of pumps.

OVERSIGHT AND ONGOING EVALUATION

Oversight and ongoing evaluation of the golf course is a major building block for golf course management. Periodic site evaluations provide a means to assess the operations of the golf course with field observations and review of monitoring and IPM data. An annual on-site review should be conducted. This review should include pesticide, fertilizer, and irrigation records; the IPM program; BMPs; special management zones; the maintenance facility; and cultural management practices.

The annual review should be conducted by a nationally recognized golf course certification program. Often, local governments do not have sufficient in-house expertise to evaluate plans, potential construction impacts, and operations of golf courses, or to conduct an annual review. By having golf courses enrolled in a nationally recognized certification program, such as Audubon International's Signature Program for newly constructed or remodeled courses, and Audubon International's Cooperative Sanctuary Program for existing courses, the technical expertise is available to evaluate the operations of the golf course and monitoring data, and to educate golf course superintendents about, for example, research results for practices or new pesticides that may be appropriate for the golf course. Enforcement of the plan rests with maintaining certification in the nationally recognized certification programs.

Coordination and communication with local governments is important in this process, whether for a golf course that will be constructed or an existing course. Field observations, monitoring, and IPM data should be communicated to the local government via an annual report. Should remedial actions be required, those actions are specified, and follow-up site visits are conducted to determine completion and compliance.

According to James T. Snow, National Director, United States Golf Association Green Section:

> Among the most important issues facing the future of the game of golf is that of water use. In many parts of the country, golf courses require large amounts of water to irrigate the landscape on which the game is played. Often, golf courses are highly visible features in communities and are targets for criticism during periods of drought when homeowners and others are restricted in their use of fresh water.
>
> For several decades the golf industry has recognized its responsibility to reduce water use and become less reliant on potable irrigation sources, and has taken many steps to achieve that goal. The industry has taken a multifaceted approach to the problem, including the development of (1) new grass varieties that use less water or can tolerate poor quality water; (2) new technologies that improve the efficiency of the irrigation system; (3) best management practices in golf course maintenance that result in less water use; (4) alternative water sources that reduce or eliminate the use of potable water; (5) golf course design concepts that minimize the area maintained with grasses that require considerable use of water; and (6) programs that educate golf superintendents and other water users about opportunities for ongoing water conservation. (*Water Conservation on Golf Courses*, USGA Green Section Web page)

The future of the game of golf is directly connected to how seriously the golf course industry takes its responsibilities regarding water quality and quantity management. The industry must think beyond the borders of a specific golf course and must continue with and expand on the leadership expressed by Jim Snow. This is not only critical to the game of golf but to all life on Earth.

CHAPTER 10

OUTREACH AND EDUCATION[1]

When you invest in environmental improvement projects on your property, it's wise also to invest in outreach and education activities to help build support and ensure the long-term success of your efforts. Outreach and education are designed to help you accomplish three primary goals:

> Improve your ability to communicate your commitment to environmental stewardship and implement conservation activities.

> Educate patrons, staff, decision makers, and community members about programs and projects that improve environmental quality.

> Provide opportunities for people to be involved in environmental projects in the community.

Forming a resource advisory group is a good first step in creating a successful outreach and education program. Resource advisory groups can be made up of fellow employees, golfers, and residents who can provide technical expertise. The primary role of resource people is to aid in communicating a commitment to environmental stewardship and implementing conservation activities.

Identifying Support

The first logical step is to designate at least one staff person or resource advisory group member who will take primary responsibility for communicating your envi-

[1]The following is adapted from Audubon International's Audubon Cooperative Sanctuary Program materials with permission.

FIGURE 10.1. SCHUYLER MEADOWS GOLF CLUB, LOUDONVILLE, NY. *While helping wildlife on golf courses is important, sharing information with golfers about these projects and what they can do to help is an important part of overall golf course management.*

ronmental goals, objectives, and projects to patrons, staff, decision makers, and community members. This person should be someone in a respected position who can comfortably communicate with a variety of people. (See Figure 10.1.)

Start by contacting residents in your community. Inform them of your involvement in conservation projects, and invite their participation. A newsletter article or announcement on the bulletin board requesting help from individuals to assist with projects, such as wildlife surveys, nest box construction, or monitoring, may result in more positive responses than you may think.

Prepare a list of organizations, agencies, and people from the community who might be interested in helping with conservation projects on the property. This list could include a local schoolteacher, scout leader, or garden or bird club member. For larger projects, consider college interns, local Fish and Wildlife Agency personnel, cooperative extension agents, or members of your town conservation committee or local board.

Education

There are many ways to let people know about your commitment to conservation. Education projects can inform people about your efforts or teach people how they can support environmental practices. Try one or more of these ideas. All have been successfully implemented on a number of properties across the country.

CREATING A DISPLAY

Creating a display in your community center, restaurant, or clubhouse can help to educate residents and staff about wildlife species, natural areas, water conservation, and integrated pest management (see Figure 10-2). The purpose of a display is to promote the positive efforts you have undertaken to maintain a high degree of environmental quality in your community. The following information will help you set up an attractive display that draws people's interest and encourages their support.

Step 1: Choose the best style and format for your display.

Before deciding *what* you want to include in your display, determine *how* information would be best presented. The display could be formal or informal; you may want to design it in such a way that you can periodically change information, or simply create a permanent display. Determine what style and format will best suit your needs.

Step 2: Determine how you want to present information.

There are many ways to present information about your environmental efforts. The display could be instructional, interactive, or simply a collection

FIGURE 10-2. WINCHESTER COUNTRY CLUB, WINCHESTER, MA. *Information about course management actions should be made available to golfers and the general public when appropriate. This is one way to gain support for planned management actions.*

of artwork or photographs of the wildlife and natural features on your property. An instructional display might explain the needs of wildlife, or tell how the property is maintained. For a more interactive presentation, invite participation in creating a wildlife inventory, or present questions to test residents' knowledge about the natural history of the property.

Step 3: Present information to encourage interest.

While there are many things you might want your display to say, remember that pictures speak a thousand words. Choose a combination of pictures and text for the best results.

There may be people in your community who would enjoy volunteering their time or expertise to help create a display. Someone with knowledge of birds or wildlife may be interested in writing wildlife descriptions. Others may be talented artists. Let people know of your plans, and invite the help, talent, and suggestions of interested residents or staff.

DISPLAY FEATURES

The following features could be incorporated into your display to create interest and inform people about your golf course:

> Photographs, artwork, or awards

> Information about wildlife and habitats on the course

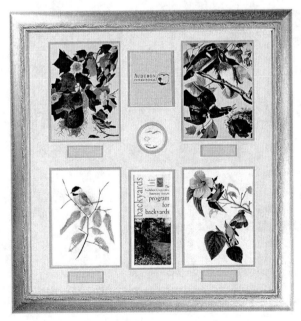

FIGURE 10-3. *Any awards or recognition that are given to the golf course should be prominently displayed as evidence of third-party verification of the efforts being taken on the course.*

➤ Information about conservation projects

➤ Wildlife inventory

➤ List of resource advisory group members

➤ Upcoming events and activities

➤ List of what residents can do to support environmental stewardship on the course

➤ Various maps of the property/habitat

➤ List of special plants on the property

WRITING NEWSLETTER ARTICLES

Newsletter articles in your community are a natural. Promoting your stewardship efforts doesn't only include writing about wildlife or habitat management. Best management practices, water quality testing, dealing with problem wildlife, and water conservation measures are just a few topics to address.

MOUNTING SIGNS

Mounting signs is a simple way to educate the public about different projects you are doing. They also can be used to protect areas of special concern or to create a display garden. The primary objective of any sign is to communicate your message concisely to all who will see it. (See Figure 10-4.)

Following are sample statements for educational signs

➤ Natural Area.

➤ This area is being (has been) naturalized to improve wildlife habitat and environmental quality.

➤ Environmentally Sensitive Area—*Please keep out.*

➤ Shoreline Naturalization.

➤ Vegetative "buffers" provide important sources of food and cover for wildlife and improve the environmental quality of ponds.

➤ Critical Nesting Habitat—*Please keep out.*

➤ [Community Name] is committed to environmental quality.

➤ Wildflower Meadow: Once meadow flowers are established, we hope you'll enjoy the beauty and variety of native flowers and grasses in this area.

FIGURE 10-4. QUAIL RIDGE COUNTRY CLUB, BOYNTON BEACH, FL. *There are many opportunities on the golf course for providing not only information about the golf course but environmental education as well.*

DEVELOPING AN EDUCATIONAL BROCHURE

An educational brochure is an excellent way to inform people who use your site about your general environmental efforts or specific conservation projects. A brochure doesn't have to be elaborate, with fancy text, color, or graphics—though if you have the budget, you can certainly choose to go that route. A simple layout that is easy to read can be just as effective. It can even be produced on a home or office computer with little expense.

Step 1: Determine for whom the brochure is geared.

Before producing a brochure, determine the kinds of people who are likely to read it. If they have specific needs or concerns, you can address them right in the brochure.

Step 2: Figure out how the brochure will be distributed.

You also need to decide how to distribute the brochure. Is there a central location where it can be displayed? Do you want to mail the brochure to everyone who regularly uses your course? Keep in mind that without a good method for distribution, your brochure will be useless. In addition, consider how many copies you are likely to use. If you are having the brochure professionally printed, the price per copy generally decreases as the number of copies increases.

Step 3: Include basic information.

The brochure layout can follow a fairly standard format. Usually a three-fold brochure will be large enough to communicate your message. Your brochure should include the following components:

What: Write a paragraph that describes your commitment to stewardship. List the environmental aspects of the program that you will focus on. Use larger headlines to communicate key words or phrases, such as "Committed to Stewardship," "Environmental Projects," or "What golfers can do."

Why: Clearly and concisely state the benefits of good stewardship for residents and your community. You may want to bullet this information to make each benefit stand out.

How: You may want to include a section about how you will implement particular projects. Tell *how* residents can help.

Who: Describe who is involved. If you have formed a resource advisory group, list each member's name.

For More Information: Tell people whom they should contact with questions or to get involved. Make sure your address and phone number are included.

The best rule to follow in creating any educational brochure is to *keep it simple.* This allows the reader to understand the message. Another helpful hint is to gather other educational brochures you've received and look at them carefully. Ask yourself these questions: "Why am I attracted to this brochure?" or "Why is this brochure hard to read and confusing?" Learning from other's mistakes and successes will help you design a great educational piece.

WRITING A PRESS RELEASE

A press release is a useful vehicle for announcing your environmental plans or projects. Because it is designed to attract media and public attention, it must spark interest and conform to the style of layout and writing used by the media.

Though some news sources may publish your press release exactly as you wrote it, most will rewrite the information to fit the style of their publications. They'll use the basic information you've provided, including quotes, but build a story around it. Therefore, one of your primary goals is to spark interest in your subject. Second, you must be concise, while giving enough detail to explain your project.

Your press release must include the following information:

> Use letterhead stationery or type your organization's name and address at the top of the page.

> Include a contact name and telephone number.

> Type the words "PRESS RELEASE" and indicate when the information can be released, for example, "FOR IMMEDIATE RELEASE" or "OCTOBER 5, 2004."

> Include a short title to introduce the subject of the release.

> Begin your first paragraph with the CITY and STATE.

> Explain WHO, WHAT, WHY, WHEN, and WHERE in the first paragraph. If the newspaper were to print only this paragraph, it should say enough to tell the basic details of your story.

> Use quotes in the second and third paragraphs to spark interest and embellish the story.

> Keep the press release to one to two pages of double-spaced copy.

> Check your spelling, dates, and contact information carefully. There should be no mistakes in your release.

> End with the following notation: ####.

WORKING PROACTIVELY WITH NEIGHBORS

Working with homeowners may be essential to the success of your stewardship efforts. Sometimes homeowners tamper with sensitive habitats, cut back natural buffers between their homes and common or recreational areas to improve the view, or add trees or shrubs that are inconsistent with the ecological region of the property. (See Figure 10-5.)

To address concerns effectively or avoid problems from the outset, it is critical to inform residents of landscape changes that may affect them and develop strategies for dealing with problems. By working together in a positive way, property managers and community association members or neighboring homeowners can find common goals and work to achieve them. Flexibility on both sides is often the key to effective communication.

If a homeowner association exists, introduce yourself and communicate your commitment to environmental stewardship. Let people know about management practices that protect water quality, minimize chemical use, or provide wildlife habitat. Make yourself available as a community resource.

Sometimes it's effective to communicate with individual landowners directly. This is especially important if changes in common or recreational areas will alter

FIGURE 10-5. *Keeping people who live on or around the golf course informed of course management activities and encouraging them to participate in environmental stewardship can add to successful course operations as well as motivate others to follow the lead of well-managed golf courses.*

views or manicured aesthetics. A straightforward letter sent *before* naturalizing along property boundaries will be far more effective than a letter sent *after* homeowner complaints are registered. (See Figure 10-6.)

STEPS TO INTEGRATING HOMEOWNER LANDSCAPES WITH NATURAL AREAS

There are a number of ways in which you can work positively with homeowners affiliated with the golf course to educate and guide them in making landscaping decisions that are consistent with the other natural areas on the property. Communicating with homeowners, educating them, and structuring decision-making opportunities are essential.

1. Appoint a project management team or design review committee made up of a planning or development engineer, landscape coordinator, community manager, golf course manager, design review manager, or other qualified personnel.

2. Mail a formal policy letter outlining the guidelines for habitat maintenance or removal to residents and property managers. Ask several managers to sign the policy letter. Remail the letter each year.

FIGURE 10-6. TREESDALE GOLF & COUNTRY CLUB, GIBSONIA, PA. *It is important that golf course management communicate with homeowners that live on and around the course. The way homeowners maintain their homes and yards should be integrated into the overall management system for the entire property and this needs to be communicated to them.*

3. Establish an approved vendor list for landscape maintenance.

4. Develop a recommended landscape plant list for trees, shrubs, and perennial flowers that are native to your site. Distribute the list to homeowners.

5. Promote a unified effort by informing all staff of your habitat maintenance policy.

6. Encourage residents to call for an appointment, and make a drawing of their plan for habitat maintenance or removal before the committee meets with them.

7. Use the community newsletter to communicate the policy to residents.

8. Make no exceptions. Consider an appropriate penalty that may be applied for infractions against the policy.

9. Bring in two or three local experts (e.g., botanist, ornithologist, game commissioner) to speak five to seven minutes each on the impact of this endeavor. Arrange for a comfortable meeting place with appropriate equipment and lighting to help make the message more impressive.

Providing opportunities for people to be involved in environmental projects in your community can help to ensure an understanding of your stewardship activities. It also helps the maintenance crew share the work of conservation activities, such as nest box monitoring, inventorying wildlife, or developing a display, which are often viewed as "nonessential" projects. Spreading the work and enjoyment among many people builds a broader base of support for conservation activities and best management practices.

Inviting participation in stewardship activities can begin when you form a resource advisory group. This gives staff, patrons, decision makers, and community members an opportunity to become involved in planning and implementing stewardship projects right from the start. There are many stewardship activities that can include an outreach component. By simply inviting patrons or their children or community members to participate, you will spread goodwill and communicate good stewardship.

Choosing Outreach Projects

It goes without saying that every property is different, but this is especially true when it comes to choosing outreach activities that are best suited to each community. What works for one may not be appropriate for another. Some communities may have greater flexibility in inviting residential participation, while others may be bound by labor union contracts or community regulations that prohibit certain types of activities. (See Figure 10-7.)

FIGURE 10-7. EAGLE KNOLL GOLF CLUB, HARTSBURG, MO. *Some wildlife conservation projects are very visible, provide great benefits to wildlife, and provide motivation to those individuals who participate in the conservation measure taken. Just seeing that an action has been taken by the course management sets an environmental example.*

Listed in this section are a variety of outreach activities that have been successful on a number of properties across the country. Your resource advisory group can help determine which activities will be most appropriate for your property.

➤ *Request help with nest boxes.* As a good starter project, nest boxes may also serve as a catalyst for residents' involvement. Here are a few suggestions:

  ■ Invite residents to "adopt-a-box" by donating money for one or more boxes and agreeing to check and maintain them throughout the spring and summer.

  ■ Make a few extra birdhouses every year. Donate the boxes to golfers, schools, or the local cemetery association to stimulate interest in your stewardship activities.

  ■ Invite a local scout troop or Eagle Scout to make and monitor your nest boxes.

  ■ Sponsor a workshop for children or guests to make nest boxes for the golf course. Extra boxes can be given away.

  ■ Place a few nest boxes within view of your property border. These boxes will subtly communicate a message that the community is concerned about local birds and wildlife.

➤ *Create a garden.* If you choose to create a garden for butterflies, hummingbirds, or songbirds, invite gardeners in the community to help with planting. A local school class, scout troop, or after-school program may also like to help. You can expand garden activities to include a brief lesson about connections between plants and wildlife. Invite a local newspaper to visit on planting day to garner positive publicity.

➤ *Inventory wildlife.* A great way to get people involved in inventorying wildlife is to provide wildlife inventory cards. You can even encourage people to fill out these cards by creating a raffle. Each filled-out card can serve as one raffle ticket. Alternately, you can simply post a wildlife inventory list in the community center, pro shop, restaurant, or locker rooms. Provide books on natural habitat, building nest boxes, butterflies, bird identification, or environmental issues as a service to residents.

➤ *Create a nature guide.* Create a simple hole-by-hole environmental guide for golfers. At each stop, you can point out interesting natural features or environmental projects. This can include native plants, nest boxes, unique trees, habitat areas, common wildlife, IPM practices, and water conservation measures.

➤ *Host nature walks.* Ask residents who are knowledgeable about birds to host an early morning walk to look for birds and other wildlife species in the community. People who attend can add their sightings to the community's wildlife inventory. Providing refreshments is a nice way to conclude the walk. (See Figure 10-8.)

> *Lead a golf course tour.* Very basic golf course tours have a great impact on public perception. A successful outing demonstrates goodwill and will spread by word of mouth. Consider hosting an outing once per year for members or regular golfers, or extend the invitation to specific golfing groups (e.g., juniors, seniors, ladies), grade school children, young adults, biology clubs, scout groups, college students, local golf course superintendents, or even local media. Your tour should showcase various aspects of your stewardship efforts.

> *Use tournaments to showcase environmental aspects of the course.* If you are hosting a tournament, use the opportunity to educate people about the environmental quality of your course. For example, highlight your involvement through the media or put up a simple display to show some of the environmental projects you've undertaken. Create a media fact sheet that highlights stewardship accomplishments and key natural features of the course. (See Figure 10-9.)

FIGURE 10-8. WCI PELICAN PRESERVE BOARD WALK, BONITA SPRINGS, FL. *Golf is a game played in nature, but it can also provide opportunities for experiences in nature that are not connected to golf. In many cases, a short field trip into the natural areas around a golf course is as close as some people ever get to an experience in nature.*

FIGURE 10-9. 2002 UNITED STATES OPEN GOLF CHAMPIONSHIP, BLACK COURSE, BETHPAGE STATE PARK, LONG ISLAND, NEW YORK. *Golf tournaments, especially televised professional-level golf tournaments, are excellent opportunities for golf to serve as an environmental model. Television commentators should include information about the environmental actions taken by courses and not just about the game of golf.*

> *Teach good stewardship to golfers.* If your course offers golf lessons or has a junior golf program, include lessons on how golfers can support good environmental stewardship while they play. Repairing ball marks and divots are just the beginning of what golfers can do. Discuss how golfer demands for fast greens and perfect conditions can stress turf and pose risks to turf health and the environment. Encourage people to view natural areas as integral to the nature of the game and to respect wildlife and natural habitats on the property.

> *Encourage neighborly stewardship.* Write a letter to residents to encourage participation in environmental stewardship activities in their own backyards. This may tie in well with nest box giveaways, providing garden or lawn care tips, or conducting a seasonal tour of natural areas in the community. This type of outreach serves as a catalyst for more environmental activities, spreads the word regarding environmental stewardship, and extends environmental quality improvements beyond the property itself. (See Figure 10-10.)

> *Host kids' projects.* Get kids involved by making bird feeders or houses for common areas or their own backyards, hosting a fishing derby, or leading a

FIGURE 10-10. MOUNT JULIET GOLF COURSE, COUNTY KILKENNY, IRELAND. *Inviting people to visit the golf course and having a program to inform people about how the course is managed is an important part of total golf course management.*

school tour. You can also get kids involved with planting gardens, creating nature guides, or tracking wildlife on the property. Getting kids involved in environmental activities helps establish a life long environmental ethic, pulls parents into stewardship activities, and helps people begin to see the property as a whole as a natural community asset.

Environmental Code of Ethics for Golfers[2]

The American golf community is dedicated to preserving golf's treasured links to nature. We recognize our historic tradition of integrating the game with the natural heritage, character, and challenges of the landscape on which it is played. As golfers, we accept our responsibility to ensure that golf courses are managed in harmony with the environment.

[2]Adapted from "Environmental Principles for Golf Courses in the United States," March 1996, Golf & the Environment Summit, Pinehurst, North Carolina.

We commit to

- Use and protect natural resources on the golf course in an environmentally responsible way.
- Foster wildlife and natural habitats in nonplay areas of the golf course.
- Respect designated environmentally sensitive areas within the course.
- Support golf course management decisions that protect and enhance the environment.
- Encourage maintenance practices that promote healthy turf.
- Plan long-range conservation efforts on the golf course.
- Educate others about the benefits of environmentally responsible golf course management for the future of the game and the environment.

CHAPTER 11

MANAGING GOLF COURSES THROUGH THE ENVIRONMENTAL MANAGEMENT PLAN

Whether you are managing a golf course that is brand-new or one that is a hundred years old, you need an environmental management plan for your golf course. The environmental management plan is essentially the "owner's manual" for the golf course. Can you imagine purchasing a car and not having an owner's manual? Even if you don't intend to do one bit of mechanic work on your own vehicle, you still expect there to be an owner's manual in the glove compartment.

The environmental management plan is both a "statement of fact" and a plan for the future. It is a living document, and as such, it should be put into a three-ring binder so that new items can be added and revisions can be made to it over time. The environmental management plan is a reference document, but it may also serve as an "insurance policy" should someone ask questions about your management actions. If properly developed, the environmental management plan will be of historical value as well as provide a foundation for comparisons and data over time.

For proposed golf courses, all environmental management plan documents should be compiled by specialists or consultants trained to address complex environmental issues. Because various portions of it may be used during the site selection, planning, and design phases, the well-written environmental management plan can be a valuable asset during the permitting stage of new golf course planning and development. Many parts of the environmental management plan are sufficiently complex, time-consuming, and critically important that they should be completed by those who have demonstrated past experience in writing them.

For existing golf courses, I believe that a well-educated superintendent can develop a credible version of the environmental management plan him- or herself, with some technical assistance. In fact, participants in Audubon International's Cooperative Sanctuary Program for Golf Courses are expected to develop and implement a site assessment and environmental plan that is an abbreviated version of the environmental management plan. While it is designed to help the superintendent become familiar with the completed golf course he or she is managing, as well as to develop appropriate management practices for the future, it does not address the complex issues associated with planning, design, and construction of new courses. Its focus is to serve as an introduction to environmental management practices that are tailored to that already existing course.

This chapter is written for all golf courses, new or old, as there are always management practices that can be learned and applied. However, for the most part, it is aimed at courses that have not yet been built, and its focus is on establishing baselines and designing and planning all aspects of the golf course, including the maintenance facility. This chapter also addresses agronomic issues such as turf selection and grow-in, as well as future management of the property. However, every aspect of the environmental management plan is important, and to the extent possible, even a 100-year-old course would benefit from developing such a plan.

Summary of Environmental Topics

The environmental management plan is designed to encourage landowners to assess and develop strategies related to a variety of natural resource issues during the planning and construction of developments. The environmental management plan is the means by which environmental issues are addressed. The following is a summary of the environmental topics the environmental management plan should address.

1. Site Description and Evaluation
2. Wildlife Habitat Management
   a. Establishing and Maintaining a Naturalization Plan
   b. Habitat Protection and Restoration Measures
   c. Wildlife and Habitat Management Plan
3. Water Quality Management and Monitoring
   a. Management Zones
   b. Water Quality Monitoring Program

4. Water Conservation
5. Integrated Pest Management
6. Agronomic Considerations
7. Maintenance Facility
   a. Pesticide Storage and Mixing
   b. Wash Pad
   c. Fuel Island
8. Waste Reduction and Management
9. Energy Management
10. Outreach and Education
    a. Signage
    b. Written Materials
    c. Training

General Overview

The environmental management plan assists landowners and developers who are committed to designing and implementing a project that promotes sound land management and natural resource conservation. Creating and implementing the environmental management plan will help the landowner or land manager to address a variety of environmental and natural resource issues including compiling essential baseline information and establishing effective strategies to enhance habitat, protect wildlife, conserve natural resources, and ensure the safety of the environment.

After construction is completed and all of the consultants and architects are gone, it is the golf course superintendent, staff, members of the club, and others who utilize the property who will be left behind to care for and manage the land. Therefore, the environmental management plan must be tailored to incorporate the goals and realities of use and maintenance.

To make the plan a useful and effective document, rather than something that merely gathers dust on someone's shelf, it must not only provide details about the site and its resources that establish the environmental context, but it must also be considered a living document. Over time, monitoring results, changes in the structure of the golf course itself, or possible renovations may dictate changes to the environmental management plan. The process of planning, monitoring, and adjusting management practices as necessary is the best insurance investment that those associated with golf courses can make.

Components of the Environmental Management Plan

The purpose of the environmental management plan is to detail how the golf course design, construction, and maintenance will protect natural resources and the environment, focusing on the areas of water quality (including a water quality monitoring program), water conservation, integrated pest management, waste management, and wildlife habitat management. As a general matter, the level of detail in the plan must be sufficient to identify scientifically based environmental approaches to be used in design, construction, and management. The plan must integrate prevention, control, and detection in golf course design, golf course cultural practices, best management practices, integrated pest management, environmental monitoring, and maintenance facility planning and operations. For that reason, the environmental management plan should only be prepared by individuals or organizations that have proven technical ability by virtue of previous experience or technical expertise. Every environmental management plan should be tailor-made for each golf course. However, following are some environmental issues and questions that should be addressed in any environmental management plan.

1. SITE DESCRIPTION AND EVALUATION

Gathering and analyzing baseline information will help to identify the natural assets and constraints of the property, define goals, and guide decisions concerning the possibilities and limitations for naturalizing the site. The end result will be the identification and description of naturalized landscapes to be protected, created, restored, or enhanced.

A site survey should be conducted that includes biological resources and an analysis of the light, moisture, soils, slope, altitude, wind, and microclimate. This information is then used to select appropriate ecological communities as landscape models. The plant and animal data are especially useful to help identify the potential of existing communities for preservation, restoration, or enhancement.

Baseline information forms the framework of the environmental management plan. Some types of baseline information to be included on the base map are features such as property boundaries; easement boundaries; above- and below-ground utility and communication rights-of-way; existing trees, shrub borders, meadows, water bodies, and other natural features; and buildings, paved roads, and other permanent structures, with access and service corridors noted. Symbols may be used to identify orientation, predominant seasonal wind patterns, and seasonal changes in the angle of sunlight. Information on existing local ordinances governing vegetation, minimum setbacks, and other restrictions should be included.

A series of landscape surveys may be needed to obtain accurate baseline data, especially when knowledge of measurable quantities and qualities of the site is desired. Surveys are often a compilation of existing data from architectural drawings, maps, and aerial photographs, combined with on-site inventories of physical, biotic, and visual characteristics. Survey results are presented as drawings, photographs, and written documentation.

Physical survey data on soils, geology, topography, and hydrology can often be compiled from U.S. Geological Survey topographic and geologic maps, and county-based soil surveys. Soil survey data can be misleading in areas disturbed by past construction activities, in which case, samples from test holes can be used to plot topsoil and subsoil layers across a site. Soil tests, available through local Cooperative Extension Service offices, analyze soil fertility and acidity. Examine the site relative to environmental characteristics, including location of surface waters and proximity of environmentally sensitive areas to golf hole locations. The following should be included:

> Physical setting

> Topography and how it protects resources

> Surface water resources (lakes, ponds, streams, wetlands, and other types, natural and man-made) and susceptibility to adverse construction and management impacts from golf course development

> Existing water quality data

> Groundwater resources and their susceptibility to adverse construction and management impacts from golf course development

> Climate, temperature ranges, frost dates, rainfall

> Areas of special protection (e.g., habitat that supports a rare, threatened, or endangered species; areas particularly valuable because of maturity, density, or diversity of plant or animal species; highly productive habitat; areas of special commercial, economic, or recreational value)

At a minimum, this part of the plan should include maps or drawings with the following information:

> Map of the golf course

> Topographic map of the site

> Vegetation and habitat map of the site

> Soils map of the site

> Surface water map of the site

> Groundwater map of the site

2. WILDLIFE HABITAT MANAGEMENT

All living species (including humans) need food, cover, water, and space in order to survive. The key is to blend the needs of wildlife and plants with the wishes of human beings. Many sites have been seriously degraded by previous human activities. Other sites are as nearly pristine as one can find. Therefore, a site survey must be completed to determine the true, present condition of the site. The ecological region of the property must be determined, and the types and condition of soils on the property as well as its geological makeup must be assessed. It is from these basic facts that one can determine what kind of vegetative habitats are native to the area. It is this native habitat we are striving to encourage. Plants that are native to an area will not only require the least amount of maintenance but will benefit the greatest amount of wildlife. (See Figure 11-1.)

The overall goal of a wildlife habitat plan should be to determine how to create the most native habitat possible given the economic goals associated with the property. Both an economic and environmental perspective are essential. From an environmental perspective, appropriately minimizing impervious surfaces and exotic plant and animal species will maximize the value of the property for species that need the most help in terms of conservation. It will also cut down the need for maintenance activities that sometimes puts undue stress on the quality of the environment. From an economic perspective, the property will require less expensive

FIGURE 11-1. BONITA EAST GOLF COURSE, NAPLES, FL. *Some species add drama to the course and can also be potentially dangerous to humans. The interface between the game and habitat and wildlife needs to be carefully managed.*

maintenance procedures, less use of water, and less wear and tear on equipment. As the world becomes more populated, more complex, and more hectic, people are becoming increasingly interested in spending more time where they live, work, and recreate in areas that are designed with the environment in mind. The "feel" of a sanctuary is something people enjoy and value.

At the very least, a wildlife habitat management plan should include the following information:

> Specific identification of varieties of birds, mammals, reptiles, amphibians, and insects on the site and detailed courses of action for the conservation and management of those species. Special emphasis should be placed on any species listed by governmental agencies as endangered, threatened, or of special concern. Specific plans for the protection of migratory bird habitat are essential.

> Specific courses of action for the provision of appropriate and adequate space, water, food, and shelter for each species should be included, as well as details regarding how the species will be managed during and after construction.

> Detailed assessment of the types of habitats presently found on the property, plans for habitat protection and conservation, and specific procedures for habitat enhancement of the site relating habitat enhancement to wildlife conservation efforts should be included.

> A natural landscaping plan utilizing appropriate vegetation that are native to the site ecological region should be included.

Establishing and Maintaining a Naturalization Plan

Any effort at developing a plan for naturalizing areas of a golf course should include a detailed description, with maps and drawings, of the site and its vicinity, placing the site in a regional context, including its eco-region and watersheds. (See Figure 11-2.) In addition, the plan should include the following information.

> Identify the natural vegetation "zone" for the site (the latter is available from the *Landscape Restoration Handbook*, Harker et al., published by Lewis Publishers, or other similar reference materials). Identify all habitats and existing vegetation communities on the site. Of those habitats and species (wetlands, stream corridors, listed species, etc.), identify all that are endangered, threatened, or otherwise mandated by any local, state, or federal agency for protection (including critical habitat for protected wildlife). Identify all other existing habitat patches, terrestrial and aquatic flora, exotic and invasive plants, and plants native to the site's eco-region.

> Identify existing wildlife (avian, terrestrial, and aquatic) on the site. Identify all of those that are endangered, threatened, or otherwise mandated by any

FIGURE 11-2. HANSEN NATURE CENTER, HENRIETTA, NY. *Planning and planting gardens for wildlife are great projects that golfers or other community groups can participate in.*

local, state, or federal agency for protection. Identify any exotic, nonnative species of wildlife on-site.

> Identify all habitat centers, as well as corridors that connect the habitat centers, including those on land adjacent to the site. Identify all water sources for wildlife and significant sources of food or shelter for particular species of wildlife.

> Provide a plan for removal or control of exotic and invasive species of plants and animals, and for use of native species in plantings on the golf course, including both naturalized areas and actively managed portions.

Habitat Protection and Restoration Measures

Develop a habitat protection and restoration plan for the site, using government-mandated protection areas, coupled with identified conservation or restoration zones and the creation of connections or wildlife corridors to maximize habitat that is naturally occurring and native to the eco-region of the site. Identify key habitat and species and measures to protect them or mitigate impacts on them from construction through management. Explanations of how habitat corridors will be maintained or created to ensure access of these wildlife species to water, food, and

FIGURE 11-3. RIVER RUN GOLF CLUB, BERLIN, MD. *Diverse plantings add beauty to the game, help water quality management, and provide habitat for wildlife.*

shelter are essential to your plan. Aquatic habitat (e.g., ponds, streams, wetlands) and terrestrial habitat should both be included in the plan, paying special attention to areas where the managed golf course meets the aquatic environment. In those areas, provide for both vertical and horizontal habitat and design course water features to maximize wildlife value and to ensure that chemical products used on the course do not cause environmental impact to water and wildlife. (See Figure 11-3.)

Wildlife and Habitat Management Plan

Develop a wildlife and habitat management plan to maximize biological diversity for species of wildlife during various times of the year (e.g., provide nesting opportunities for breeding birds, but also provide food, water, and shelter for birds that may be found on-site only in nonbreeding seasons or just during migration). In preparing this plan, address both aquatic habitat and terrestrial habitat. Wildlife planning should include not only birds but also mammals, reptiles and amphibians, native pollinators, fish, and so forth. As part of the wildlife and habitat plan, include details for a wildlife and habitat monitoring program for the property by identifying the locations, types of habitat and species, number of sample transects, and data analysis methods for the property.

3. WATER QUALITY MANAGEMENT AND MONITORING

This part of the management plan should include identifying best management practices (BMPs), management zones, and fertilizers and pesticides that may be used at the golf course. BMPs are those drainage facilities or cultural approaches to golf course management that serve to prevent the movement of sediments, nutrients, or pesticides into water resources and other environmentally sensitive areas.

Preventative and structural controls should be clearly identified, and all construction, storm water management, and other types of BMPs should be included on site plans or drawings. BMPs should be detailed for each green, tee, fairway, out-of-play area, and other area of the golf course. The types and effectiveness of BMPs should be identified, and information regarding watershed size, pollutant reduction, and other relevant information should be included. All maintenance practices, short or long term, potentially affecting water resource quality should be identified and evaluated for their impacts.

Measures to protect surface waters during construction and grow-in should be described, along with plans to control runoff from impervious surfaces by filtering through vegetative covers. Use of sod on slopes (with staples) near wetlands or other water bodies is very effective in preventing soil erosion and potential pollution. Appropriate maps or drawings should be included with the plan. All subsurface drainage should be directed into buffer areas, or other vegetative filters, and not directly into water and a map of the entire drainage system for the golf course should be part of the environmental management plan. In addition, an active wetland/littoral area management program should be developed and implemented. The plan should include: (1) regular periodic monitoring, (2) maintenance of vegetative conditions, (3) restoration or repair of damaged areas, and (4) record keeping.

Management Zones

The environmental management plan should also establish and identify with appropriate maps or drawings the following management zones on the golf course property:

> No-spray zones. No-spray zones should be established around each water body (e.g., ponds, wetlands) extending to a minimum of 25 feet landward from normal water elevation. No synthetic pesticides should be used in these areas, and only slow-release fertilizers should be used in them. (See Figure 11-4.)

> Limited-spray zones. Limited-spray zones should be established around each water body, beginning from the outer edge of the no-spray zone (at least 25

FIGURE 11-4. OREGON GOLF CLUB, WEST LINN, OR. *Various heights of vegetation, planted in the right places, can add to the beauty of the course, and serve important functions in the overall conservation management plans for the course.*

feet landward from normal water elevation) and extending to at least 50 feet landward from normal water elevation. A limited set of pesticides may be used in this zone, and only controlled-release fertilizers or "spoon feeding" may be used. Additionally, when wind speed is greater than 10 mph, a shroud should be used on spray equipment to avoid drift.

> *Bridge Construction Zones.* Cart and foot bridges that cross environmentally sensitive areas must be built from the deck with only pilings disturbing the sensitive areas. Postconsumer recycled plastic is the most desirable material to use. Conventional wood treated with preservatives might be toxic and wash into nearby water bodies.

Water Quality Monitoring Program

A water quality management and monitoring program should be established and include plans for regularly scheduled monitoring of surface water, pond sediments, and groundwater (see Figure 11-5). The monitoring plan should

> Establish a baseline of water and sediment quality prior to construction

> Provide data that will establish environmental conditions, thus providing a basis for measuring compliance with environmental regulations

> Ensure that integrated pest management is functioning properly and that no health hazards have developed

FIGURE 11-5. ROBERT TRENT JONES GOLF CLUB, GAINESVILLE, VA. *Monitoring water chemistry is essential to not only the future of the game of golf but to the overall health of all living things that depend on clean water to flourish.*

Results of the monitoring program provide feedback to the golf course superintendent and thus provide a useful management tool.

The monitoring program should be established in three phases that coincide with golf development. Phase I defines predevelopment water and sediment quality conditions and is terminated when construction begins. Phase II is the construction and development phase and immediate post-development time frame. Pesticides and fertilizers are not applied to the course during this phase of monitoring. Phase III is the post-development, operational golf course and begins with golf course turf grow-in.

Obtaining water samples from the same location over time is imperative. Temporal changes in water quality can be interpreted with confidence only if the same location is consistently sampled. Sample stations should be located and permanently marked in the field, identified on maps, and photographed so that stations are easily located during subsequent sampling efforts.

A water quality management and monitoring plan should include the following for each phase of development and management:

> Description of specific *station location and number* of sampling locations for surface water, groundwater, and sediment.

> Description of *frequency of sample* at each surface water, groundwater, and sediment sampling station.

> Description of the *analytes* for which surface water, groundwater, and pond sediments will be analyzed (in addition to pH, temperature, dissolved oxygen, etc.)

4. WATER CONSERVATION

Water is one of our most precious resources. But still we waste it, abuse it, and misuse it. An environmental goal is to plan for the use of water, to allow for human recreation and use, while not diminishing the ability of other humans and wildlife species to maintain adequate supplies of clean water.

Central to this topic is the selection of vegetation for the property. In the past, many people have selected vegetation for sites that do not belong in the region of the country in which they are attempting to grow it. This translates into enormous use of water, fertilizer, and other substances that not only waste resources and money but are often wastes of time.

It is of paramount importance to utilize vegetation that is proven to fit biologically into the region of the country where the property is located. This includes not only the selection of the turfgrass for tees, greens, and fairways, but landscaping materials and habitat enhancement vegetation as well.

In addition, a well-planned irrigation system is crucial. When you are planning and designing the system, water should be placed where you need it and be easily available when you need it This will translate into using less water, using water pumps less, using less energy, and reducing irrigation maintenance costs. It means

FIGURE 11-6. *To minimize waste and maximize efficiency in the use of water for irrigation, a system that provides the correct amount of water at the proper time and only in the proper places is a critical aspect of water conservation on golf courses.*

healthier plants, which translates into saving resources and saving money. (See Figure 11-6.)

To minimize waste and maximize efficiency in the use of water for irrigation, a system that provides the correct amount of water at the proper time and only in the proper places is important. Use of the proper turfgrass is also critical for this purpose. Following is some of the information to include in a water conservation plan:

> Type of greens to be used

> Information concerning the irrigation system and the layout, including estimated number of acres to be irrigated

> Effluent water system and how it works

> Surface water management, including areas of the property to be irrigated and frequency

> Water source and alternative sources for irrigation, landscaping, and facilities

> Efforts to capture and reuse water from roofs and parking lots

> Efforts to reuse equipment wash water at the maintenance facilities

> Plans to conserve water within all structures

> Plant palette of proposed buffer area plantings

The design of all buildings should include simple, cost-effective devices to conserve water. This includes simple aerators on faucets, flow restrictor devices in showers, low-flow toilets, and numerous other practices, such as infrared or on/off motion detectors, that can save both money and water.

5. INTEGRATED PEST MANAGEMENT

Integrated pest management is a management plan that uses a variety of control measures to keep turfgrass pest populations below levels that are economically and aesthetically damaging, without creating a hazard to people and to the environment. It is a concept that utilizes cultural, biological, and chemical pest control strategies. An IPM program does not seek to discontinue use of pesticides completely but to reduce dependency on them as much a possible. (See Figure 11-7.)

In order to prevent nonpoint pollution problems, close attention must be paid to the managing pesticide applications. This involves a decision-making process to determine when, where, and what pest control measures are most appropriate in a given situation. Setting thresholds for pest populations allows tolerance and acceptance of certain detrimental species in order to minimize injury to nontarget beneficial organisms.

FIGURE 11-7. RIVERBEND GOLF COURSE, MADERA, CA. *After appropriate cultivars are chosen, practicing sound cultural management practices is the key in reducing costs associated with golf course management—costs that are increased when courses become overly dependent upon chemical solutions.*

The primary cultural practices that produce and sustain a healthy turf are mowing, irrigation, fertilization, and cultivation. These, if done properly, have a strong positive effect on turf performance. Thus, it is essential that these practices are executed in a proper and timely manner to ensure turfgrass quality and playability. The best deterrent to weed, insect, and disease infestation is a healthy turf. Thus, maintaining hearty grasses will minimize the need to apply pesticides.

The IPM Approach Includes the Following Six Basic Components:

1. **Monitoring** potential pest populations and their environment

2. **Determining** pest injury levels and establishing treatment thresholds

3. **Decision making,** developing and integrating all biological, cultural, and chemical control strategies

4. **Educating** personnel on all biological and chemical control strategies

5. **Timing** and spot treatment utilizing either the chemical, biological, or cultural methods

6. **Evaluating** the results of treatment

The environmental management plan should include detailed information about mowing, fertilizing, irrigation, and cultivation, and include a basic annual maintenance plan.

Integrated pest management is a program that uses information about turfgrass pest problems and environmental conditions that may precipitate these problems, and integrates these with turfgrass cultural practices and pest control measures to prevent or control unacceptable levels of pest damage. It is within itself a best management practice. IPM is not a new idea, as these practices have been an integral part of general agriculture for almost 40 years. However, as concern over the protection of natural resources has increased, it has become more refined and taken more of a systematic approach. This approach integrates a number of efforts including the following:

> Developing a healthy turf that can withstand pest pressure

> Judicious and efficient use of chemicals

> Enhancing populations of natural, beneficial organisms

> Effective timing of handling pest problems at the most vulnerable stage, often resulting in reduced pesticide usage

It is an ecologically based system that uses both biological and chemical approaches. As with BMPs, IPM strategies should be incorporated into every aspect of the environmental management plan for the golf course.

As a component of IPM, the golf course superintendent must make decisions about pest problems and develop control recommendations, including the judicious use of pesticides. Strategies should include identifying an anticipated pest complex and understanding the biology of the pest. Thresholds should be set for each specific local pest problem and then adjusted as necessary based on the effectiveness of IPM options. As part of the strategy, an approved pesticide list based on the pesticide risk assessment should be compiled for each specific pest problem.

Integrated pest management programs rely on six basic approaches for plant and environmental protection. These include the following:

> *Regulatory.* Using certified seed and sod to prevent unwanted weed contamination, and selecting the best adapted turfgrass species.

> *Genetic.* Selecting improved grasses that perform well in specific areas and demonstrate a resistance to pest problems.

> *Cultural.* Following recommendations made for proper primary and secondary cultural practices that maintain the healthiest turf and influence its susceptibility and recovery from pest problems. Practices such as aerification, vertical mowing, topdressing, maintaining proper soil nutrient levels, sound irrigation management, and proper mowing techniques should produce a high-quality turf.

> *Physical.* Cleaning equipment to prevent spreading diseases and weeds from infected areas.

> *Biological.* For a limited number of pest problems, biological control can be used whereby natural enemies are introduced to effectively compete with the pest.

> *Chemical.* Pesticides are a necessary and beneficial approach to turf pest problems, but use can be restricted in many cases to curative rather then preventive applications, thus reducing environmental exposure. Pesticides selection is based on a risk assessment approach. Pesticides selected for use on specific pest problems identified in the environmental management plan should be limited to those that have demonstrated a high degree of effectiveness, are not toxic to nontarget species, act quickly and degrade quickly, are not soluble, and not persistent. Few pesticide applications will be made on a regularly scheduled basis. Exceptions may include preemergence herbicides and fungicides used to control certain diseases. Additionally, materials should be applied strictly in accordance with label instructions, at labeled rates, under appropriate environmental conditions (i.e., no spraying on windy days or when rain is forecast), with a low-volume sprayer to reduce the possibility of drift, and materials use should be rotated. This will deter the development of resistant strains of pests that may require more frequent and/or higher rates of pesticide applications.

One of the most critical components to IPM programs is monitoring. A well-trained and experienced golf course superintendent will scout, or designate and train an individual to scout, to detect symptoms of a pest problem on a daily basis. This approach, coupled with compiling a site-specific history and consulting with other superintendents in the area and with specialists in turfgrass management, make it a successful program. The IPM scouting and monitoring plan relies on a number of tenants. In developing the program, there are specific items that need to be addressed in order to ensure the program will be successful. The superintendent must ensure that the following steps are followed:

1. Assign individuals to conduct the scouting, record the results, evaluate the information, and make the decisions once the information is recorded. This may be done in a team approach, with the scout consulting with specific members of the staff, or it may be an individual IPM specialist.

2. Provide proper education and training to all involved in any aspect of the IPM program. This should include formal seminars, workshops, conferences, short courses, and other IPM training opportunities. In-house training sessions for the maintenance crew should be held to inform them of IPM strategies.

3. Review, at least annually, the complete program and evaluate its effectiveness. Changes will constantly be made as the golf course matures, as changes

in design are made, or as new information concerning handling of turf management or pest problems becomes available.

The objective of the IPM program is to use information about turfgrass pest problems and environmental conditions that may precipitate those problems to establish a management system that integrates turfgrass cultural practices and pest control measures to prevent or control unacceptable levels of pest damage and minimize application of pesticides. A high-quality IPM program is essential to minimize the potential risk of contamination of water resources and to conserve water resources.

6. AGRONOMIC CONSIDERATIONS

Consideration of the impact of the golf course design, turfgrass selection, and grow-in on the management of water quality is of critical importance. The natural characteristics of turfgrasses limit movement of pesticides and fertilizers into underlying soils and groundwater. Thatch produced by the turf acts as organic filter to chemically bind pesticides that might otherwise enter the local surface and groundwaters. Producing healthy turf has the added benefit of immobilization and microbial degradation of pesticides retained in the thatch layer. In addition, turfgrass root systems are quite extensive and fibrous, and are able to absorbed applied pesticides that might penetrate the canopy and thatch and reach the roots. Thus, a healthy turf results in effective nutrient and pesticide retention and control. (See Figure 11-8.)

It is important that greens are constructed with surface and internal drainage that will maximize the playability even immediately after rainfall or irrigation. Construction techniques will ensure that surface runoff is directed to adjacent filtration areas and that materials that provide good drainage and resist wear and compaction will be used for constructing the playing surface. The following items should be included in the environmental management plan for new golf courses and can also be used in developing an environmental management plan for existing courses:

> Detailed drawings of putting greens and tees, including drainage systems, are essential. Greens should be constructed based on the United States Golf Association method as detailed in "USGA Recommendations for a Method of Putting Green Construction" (*USGA Green Section Record,* 1993). Detailed information about soil mixes and amendments to be used should also be included.

> Identify locations and numbers of soil samples that will be obtained on fairways, roughs, and driving ranges. Identify locations and numbers of soil samples that will be obtained. Obtain soil samples from as many locations as necessary and

FIGURE 11-8. *The United States Golf Association has funded more than 290 university research projects since 1983 in an effort to develop turfgrasses and cultural systems with better stress tolerance and reduced water requirements and pesticide use.*

have them analyzed to provide a proper analytical basis for preplanting fertilization decisions that will minimize fertilization requirements.

➤ Turfgrasses should be scientifically selected to ensure that they are properly suited for the eco-region of the golf course, to minimize irrigation requirements, fertilization needs, and pesticide use.

➤ Identify turfgrass to be used on greens, tees, fairways, and roughs, and include a detailed explanation of the suitability of the selected turfgrass.

➤ Identify techniques and practices to reduce soil erosion and reduce water use.

➤ A basic growing-in program should include information about the following:

  ▪ Techniques and practices to reduce water use and fertilizer loss

  ▪ Mowing heights for putting greens, tees, and fairways

  ▪ The rolling program

  ▪ The cultural practices to be used on tees and putting surfaces

  ▪ Pest inspections during the growing-in period

➤ After grow-in, mowing practices and heights for putting greens, tees, and fairways should be identified.

> Describe the approach to nutrient management to be used, including management measures to minimize or eliminate any threat to groundwater or surface water from fertilizers. Identify types of fertilizers to be used.

> For greens, tees, fairways, and roughs identify with tables: (1) each type of fertilizer to be used, (2) the recommended amounts for fertilizers, and (3) the timings of fertilizer applications. Show information for nitrogen, phosphorus, and potassium.

> Describe the management programs for turf, including spiking, vertical mowing, aerifying, topdressing, and rolling.

> Select pesticides for use at the golf course using U.S. Environmental Protection Agency (EPA) established procedures for assessing the risk of pesticide use to human health and the environment. Use the U.S. EPA-approved screening models for pesticides. Specific local problems, including disease management, insect and nematode control, turf weed control, and lake and pond weed management should be addressed. For each area, you should

  ■ Identify diseases, pests, or weeds to be controlled.

  ■ Identify measures to be taken to reduce the potential, manage, or control the problem.

  ■ Prioritize the management strategies.

  ■ Establish thresholds.

  ■ List pesticides to be used and a risk assessment for each.

> Develop a scouting and monitoring program for identifying developing problems with diseases, insects and nematodes, turf weeds, and pond weeds. The scouting and monitoring program should be detailed by day, week, month, and year and by greens, tees, fairways, roughs, water bodies, wetlands, and other out-of-play areas. Identify the specific information that will be collected. Include record-keeping requirements and copies of forms to be used for record-keeping purposes.

> Develop a plan explaining the storage, handling, disposal, and record-keeping practices for pesticides to be used at the golf course. Include forms to be used and a detailed spill prevention and response plan that includes prevention measures, containment measures, and training programs and activities.

7. MAINTENANCE FACILITY

The maintenance department is responsible for irrigating, mowing, fertilizing, applying pesticides, and generally maintaining the golf course and grounds. The maintenance area is where pesticides are loaded into application equipment, mowers, and other pieces of equipment are serviced, and pesticides, fuel, fertilizer, and cleaning solvents are stored. This is where there is potential for polluting the soil, surface water, or groundwater. Contamination can occur when pesticides are spilled, containers or equipment are cleaned and the rinse water dumped on the ground or discharged into surface water, or improperly cleaned containers are stockpiled or buried. Proper management of the maintenance area is an important part of responsible chemical and pesticide use (see Figure 11-9).

Maintenance and management activities that occur at the maintenance facility have the potential for causing serious environmental contamination. Steps taken to minimize potential contamination center on the pesticide storage/mixing/washing areas, the wash pad, the fuel island, and operations at the mechanics center.

Management practices should be implemented at these maintenance areas that will prevent contaminating natural resources by the materials that are stored or handled at these sites. The general approach to management of golf course maintenance facilities involves three principles:

> *Isolate all potential contaminants from soil and water.* Identify all the materials stored or handled at the golf course maintenance area, along with current practices that could cause environmental contamination. The next step is to develop management practices that isolate those materials from soil and

FIGURE 11-9. COLLIER'S RESERVE, NAPLES, FL. *Clean, neat, and orderly should be the standard for equipment storage areas at all golf courses. By putting equipment in the same location each day, potential accidents and maintenance problems, like leaking hydraulic lines, can be identified before the leak takes place on the turf surfaces of the course.*

water during storage, handling, and disposal. Storing these materials in covered, lockable storage areas; handling them over impermeable surfaces; cleaning up spills promptly and properly; recycling these materials where possible; and otherwise properly managing wastes will keep these materials from contaminating soil or water.

> *Do not discharge any material other than clean storm water onto the ground or into surface water bodies.* Preventing contamination of storm water and eliminating the discharge of materials such as equipment wash water to ground or surface waters. Discharges to surface or ground water should be eliminated through the containment and collection of equipment wash waters and proper management of collected material.

> *Minimize irrigation, fertilizer, and pesticide use requirements through use of integrated pest management and native or naturalized vegetation wherever practicable.* Minimizing fertilizer, pesticide, and irrigation use through use of native vegetation and integrated pest management directly impacts the amount of material handled annually, reduces the annual maintenance budget, and encourages good environmental stewardship.

Pesticide Storage and Mixing

Pesticide storage and mixing should be in a separate room or building designated for these materials only, and located away from water sources (wells, ponds, streams). (See Figure 11-10.) The building should have a concrete floor with a poured concrete lip extending upward into the concrete block walls. The center of the building should be the lowest, and the floor should be sloped to the center. A concrete sump should be located at the low point. This area is for mixing and should provide excellent containment for any inadvertent spills. The building should be kept locked and posted.

Continuous circulation fans should provide good ventilation, and chemicals should be kept away from direct contact with the concrete floor. Storage should be on nonwooden shelving. Other features to include are switches for lights and the fuse box on the outside of the building, explosion proof lights and fans, and a "lip" at the entrance that moves rainwater away from the interior of the facility. All pesticides should be stored in their original containers, with visible labels.

To be prepared for spills or leaks, absorbent floor-sweep materials, sawdust or cat litter, and activated charcoal should be kept on hand. An inventory of pesticides and other chemicals should be kept, and labels for each pesticide used should be readily accessible. An emergency equipment box should be located on the outside of the building. Typically this is a wooden box (perhaps 3 feet by 3 feet with a sloping roof) that stores items for emergency use. Such things as a fire extinguisher, respirator, first-aid supplies, goggles, respirators, gloves, rubber boots,

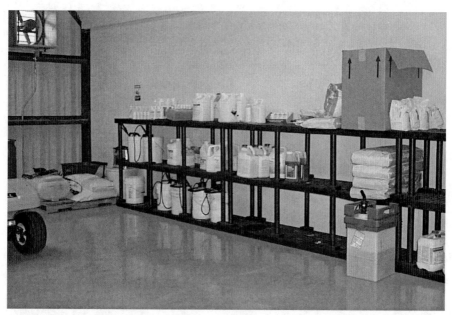

FIGURE 11-10. WEST BAY GOLF CLUB, ESTERO, FL. *All chemical products should be stored in locked and secured buildings that are separated from other buildings. Dry materials should be stored above liquid materials.*

and a coverall (perhaps a Tyvek® suit) should be provided. These items are placed in the locked box on the outside of the building so they are readily available in case they are needed. Water should be available for both routine and emergency chemical removal, including showers and eye wash facilities.

Mixing and loading should be done in the pesticide storage building near the center area where the sloping concrete should provide excellent containment for any inadvertent spills. A sump should be located at the base of the sloped area, thus facilitating cleanup of spills or overfill. A number of different options exist for the removal of excess water from the filling or rinsing of pesticide equipment, or for mixing pesticides. These include the following:

> Filtration systems that physically filter water.

> Filtration systems that physically filter water and provide for biological water cleansing. These may also degrade pesticides with the use of microorganisms.

> Reuse of water. One system that works well is to use rinse water tanks to store excess water from the filling or rinsing of sprayers. The rinse water is pumped into the holding tanks and reused as makeup water the next time that type of material is applied. Three different tanks are used—one for herbicides, one for insecticides, and one for fungicides. The rinse water from herbicide applications is pumped to the herbicide tank, rinse water from insecticide applications is pumped to the insecticide tank, and rinse water from fungicide

applications is pumped to the fungicide tank. The tanks are located above the mixing/wash area on metal or nonabsorbent shelves.

Care should be taken to mix only the amount of pesticide needed for the application. As soon as pesticides are loaded, all equipment and apparel used will be washed, rinsed, and air-dried. Water used in the cleaning process should be dumped into the spray tank.

After the pesticide is applied, the sprayer tank, boom, and nozzles should be washed in the designated area where the tank will be refilled with water; and this material (which will have an extremely low concentration of pesticide) should be handled with an appropriate system as described previously.

Additional Considerations

In addition to the preceding, the following activities should be taken relative to the maintenance facility and pesticide storage and mixing.

> The pesticide storage facility should have a complete alarm system, with battery backup, for burglary and fire.

> Locks and bolts used at the control center should be of the highest quality materials available.

> Materials used inside the control center should be composed of high-quality durable plastic, aluminum, or concrete to avoid absorbing chemical residues or vapors.

> An explosion-proof fan and explosion-proof light should be installed.

> A ventilation design should be an integral part of the control center.

> All pesticides stored on nonabsorbent shelving should be located at least 6 inches off the floor.

> All pesticides should be segregated by liquid, powder, or granular class.

> All powders and granules should be stored above liquids.

> All shelving should be sturdy and secured to avoid sagging and falling.

> The entire floor of the control center should be sloped to the center of the room, with a recessed sump located at its center.

> A light and fan switch should be located outside of the door entering the control center.

> A sink with potable water and spigot and hand blower (not paper towels) should be installed, with the drainage funneled back into the sump.

➤ A mixing table should be attached to the sink at a slightly higher elevation to allow overspill to be washed into the sink.

➤ Plastic pesticide containers may be recycled and turned into plastic pallets or other usable materials.

➤ A portable eye wash bottle should be located over the sink; immediately outside, an eye wash/shower station supplied by potable water should be installed.

➤ A refill hose should be located above the sump to allow proper and timely filling of spray tanks with water.

➤ Only qualified personnel should be allowed access to the control center.

Wash Pad

Equipment wash areas have the potential to cause environmental problems—particularly the runoff associated with wash water and debris. Pesticides can be a serious concern to the environment, but by washing the pesticide spray equipment in the pesticide storage area, many of those concerns will be avoided.

Washing equipment other than pesticide application equipment should take place at a specially constructed wash pad. The wash pad is a concrete pad that is covered and sloped to a center collection area. Grass clippings and sediments are collected in the central collection area. Water should be passed through an oil/water separator and then recycled or discharged to an area for appropriate treatment.

If pesticide equipment is washed in the same location as the other equipment, then an oil/water separator should not be used and filtration through natural areas should not be a treatment option. In all cases, it is best to recycle the water from all washing activities.

Treatment may include any one of the following:

➤ Filtration systems that physically filter water.

➤ Filtration systems that physically filter water and provide for biological water cleansing. These may also degrade pesticides with the use of microorganisms.

➤ Filtration through natural areas including turf swales or biofilters (wetlands) after passing through an oil/water separator (a management plan should be developed for maintenance of the natural area to maintain its effectiveness over the years).

Examples of how treated water may be reused could include irrigation of practice areas or the mixing of filtered water in an irrigation lake for future use through the course irrigation system.

Additional Considerations

In addition to the preceding, the following actions should be taken relative to the wash-down area:

> - All water used to wash equipment should be recycled, and contaminating materials such as grease, oil, and gasoline should be filtered from this recycled water.
> - Only water recycle systems with a proven track record should be utilized.
> - Pesticide equipment should not be washed off in this area.
> - A roof should cover the wash-down area to keep rain off the pad and prevent excessive water from going into the recycling system.
> - The wash-down pad should be elevated along the outer edges to direct rainwater away from the area, but the center area should be recessed from normal ground level to allow for wash water to be collected for recycling, and the roof should be high enough to allow golf course equipment the proper amount of clearance, yet low enough to meet any aesthetic requirements (e.g., visibility to homeowners).
> - Several air hoses attached to posts prior to the wash-down pad can be used to remove excessive grass residue off equipment prior to moving onto the wash-down pad, which will reduce the amount of grass clippings or debris entering the water recycle system.
> - The pad should have double- or triple-screen baskets, weighing less than 40 pounds each, to prevent an excess of grass clippings and debris from entering the recycling system. Grass clippings should be composted and recycled on the golf course.
> - Hoses with attachable spray bottles of liquid wax at the wash-down pad can be utilized so valuable equipment can receive a brief application of liquid wax (cut with water) after each use.
> - Concrete in the pad should be impermeable to prevent leaching of any contaminates.
> - Installing lightning protection in this area is vital for worker and equipment protection.

Fuel Island

The fuel island has the potential for spills or accidents. Several steps should be taken to avoid problems (see Figure 11-11):

> - Cover the fuel island to minimize the effect of sunlight on the equipment as well as possible increased evaporation of fuel and provide protection for

FIGURE 11-11. COLLIER'S RESERVE, NAPLES, FL. *It is important that fuel areas be covered, secured, and constructed in such a manner to prevent and contain any spills that may occur.*

employees. The roof should be high enough to allow golf course equipment the proper amount of clearance, yet low enough to meet any aesthetic requirements (e.g., visibility to homeowners).

➤ Install adequate lighting around and beneath the roof to allow for operation during periods of darkness or inadequate light.

➤ Install lightning protection on the fuel island roof.

➤ If possible, all fuel storage and carrying mechanisms should be above-ground devices.

➤ Fuel should be stored in above-ground, double-vaulted tanks from a reputable manufacturer.

➤ The pad should be elevated along the outer edges to direct rainwater away from the area, but the center area should be recessed from normal ground level to allow for containment in the event of a fuel spill. The recession should be deep enough to contain a few hundred gallons of spillage but not so severe that it presents difficulty for equipment entering and leaving the fuel island.

➤ Concrete in the pad should be impermeable to prevent leaching of any contaminates.

➤ Prior to construction of the fuel island, the fire marshal and other appropriate authorities should review the specifications.

8. WASTE REDUCTION AND MANAGEMENT

The generation of waste products is a central environmental issue faced by everyone. Each one of us generates tons of garbage every year. The question is "What are we going to do with it all?" Aside from the obvious environmental problems associated with the disposal of tons of solid wastes each year, we are literally destroying acres of wildlife habitat and wasting resources and energy in the process.

Commonly, waste management is one of the last considerations given to a development. Normally the major consideration is "When is my garbage pickup day?" The goal is to integrate waste management planning into the design of the entire project, as well as in the management once the project is completed.

The waste management strategy should start early and be included during the initial planning and the construction of the project. Conscious decisions should be made to reduce the amount of waste generated during construction, and every attempt should be made to export as little as possible. This will not only help alleviate environmental problems associated with waste disposal but save money as well.

Of paramount importance is the overall design of facilities. In many cases, the design of buildings, golf courses, clubhouses, homes, and the like preclude any meaningful waste reuse or recycling because there is no convenient way to do it. If we do not make waste reuse and recycling an easy task in which people can participate, we will never change the present inefficient manner in which we conduct our business. A well-thought-out waste management plan is just as important as any other component of the development. (See Figure 11-12.)

FIGURE 11-12. RIVERBEND GOLF COURSE, MADERA, CA. *Recycling of all materials both in the maintenance facility and on the golf course should be standard practice.*

A waste reduction and management plan should include information concerning planned efforts at minimizing waste of all types from being generated on the site during and after construction. This should include purchase of materials with minimal packaging, precut building materials, buying in bulk, use of brush for wildlife habitat, producing mulches from trees, and reuse of building materials. Additional attention should be focused on a recycling program that includes education and awareness for staff, members, and residents.

9. ENERGY MANAGEMENT

Exploration, extraction, transmission, and use of energy are at the root of many of our environmental problems. Designing facilities that minimize the use of energy will not only help the environment but save money as well. Thoughtful consideration of building design, appliance selection, lighting types, and other issues will result in the construction of truly energy-efficient facilities. (See Figure 11-13.)

When planning a facility or development, one must think beyond a particular vision. The property—its various uses, climate, and vegetational and structural character—must be considered. Thought must be given to all of the seasons of the year, and decisions must be made that make sense from an energy perspective.

When planning decisions are being made, consideration should be given to whether those decisions will waste energy. Are buildings being designed that will be difficult or impossible to keep cool in the summer or warm in the winter? Are highly used areas designed so that they are very dark and hard to light? Is vegetation being planted that will provide shade during the summer? Is vegetation planted on the correct side of buildings to provide maximum shade or sun depending on the heating or lighting requirements? Is every facility adequately insulated? Are energy-efficient appliances and construction products used?

From a golf course perspective, the course design should lend itself to ease of maintenance. The design should not require excessive maintenance that might be

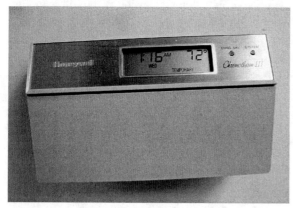

FIGURE 11-13. PGA GOLF CLUB AT THE RESERVE, PORT ST. LUCIE, FL. *There are many simple steps that can be taken to reduce energy use and expenses. Programmable thermostats such as this one are easy to install and can reduce energy bills.*

labor- and energy-intensive as well as economically more expensive. Remember, when the design and construction is completed, the golf course superintendent and staff are left behind to monitor the facility. Unmaintainable bunker designs, excessive use of turf, and inappropriate vegetation selection, for example, will put undue pressure on future land managers and the environment, as well as on waste energy.

An energy efficiency plan should include measures to be taken to minimize waste of energy and energy resources, including steps to conserve energy and maximize efficient use of energy in lighting, buildings, HVAC (heating, ventilation, and air conditioning), equipment and machinery, motors, and vehicles. Additional items to include are as follows:

> Plans for on-site transportation (for example, golf carts). Information concerning the source and type of energy that will be employed for all buildings. Consider alternative forms of energy such as solar or wind.

> Conserving energy through the use of natural lighting, energy-efficient light-bulbs, exterior lighting schedule, thermostat adjustments, window panes, run time adjustment on hot-water heater, and so on.

> Plans to incorporate energy-efficient appliances in kitchen areas, food service centers, changing rooms, restrooms, and so on. This information should cover all large and small appliances, including furnace and air-conditioning units.

> Proposed use and types of vegetation in proximity to buildings, and their role in providing energy-efficient cooling or shading.

> Coils on refrigerators should be cleaned at least once a year.

10. OUTREACH AND EDUCATION

Golf course owners and managers have a vested interest in emphasizing the unique qualities of the course both as a place to work and to visit. Each golf course has the potential to be a model not only for environmental responsibility, but of its unique human and cultural connection with the world around it. The renewed awareness and sense of responsibility of both staff and visitors results in a greater appreciation of their own involvement in the world around them. They then take home with them an ever-increasing commitment to stewardship. Following are some examples of education programs and activities that may be implemented on the property.

Signage

Helping people who use the golf course understand the environmental stewardship actions taken on the course is important. Signage can play an essential role in that effort. Signage may include

➤ Interpretive signage on site (historical, archaeological, life cycles, biological, botanical, etc.).

➤ Identification signs for rare shrubs and trees throughout the golf course.

➤ Strategic photos (of golf course or wildlife), enlarged and hung in the clubhouse, maintenance facility reception area.

Written Materials

Information that is displayed or that can be taken home by golfers, employees, or homeowners is important in order to reinforce the stewardship actions taken on the golf course.

➤ Educational brochures (simply say, for example, "Did you know. . .?").

➤ Seasonal literature.

➤ Daily necessary environmental information (for example, "Red-tailed hawk nesting near #18 tee. Use care and caution.").

➤ Information on poisonous snakes, including pictures in the break room with instructions how to deal with one encountered on-site, particularly by employees.

➤ Pictures and information about endangered species throughout the project during and after construction.

➤ A visitors registry with a place to write comments.

➤ Materials to connect what people see on your site with local natural history exhibits (for example, "For more information on the red-tailed hawk life cycle, visit the _____ Nature Center located at _____.").

➤ Identification guides for birds or mammals to distribute to golfers.

➤ Scorecards that allow for sightings of wildlife to help with wildlife inventory.

➤ The John J. Audubon book, *The Birds of America*, distributed to new members during their enrollment session.

➤ A wildlife article in the monthly newsletter that is received by all members.

➤ One particular bird or species can be featured in the clubhouse each month, with a picture and a detailed summary about the animal habitat and feed habits. Members can look for them as they golf.

Training

➤ Caddy educational training program.

➤ Ranger educational training program.

FIGURE 11-14. *Training sessions are invaluable tools to keep staff aware of both maintenance issues as well as to broaden their environmental awareness and educate them about wildlife on the course.*

> Staff wildlife educational training program.

> A video of the entire construction process could be produced and run continuously in the clubhouse showing how the project came to fruition.

> Nature trails in the habitat areas on the course could be created for members to take a leisure walk and view the wildlife. There could also be plans for sitting benches to be placed along the trails.

Other

> In the pro shop, sell reference materials for local areas of special interest.

> In the pro shop, sell items made from recycled materials.

> Consider using anything that is taken from site (trees, old-home foundations, etc.) as interpretive materials. For example, use a picture of native trees before they are cut, as they are milled, and then as they are used on a split-rail fence, birdhouses, wood piles, or door frames.

> Host fund-raising tournaments with donated rounds of golf to local arts centers, Audubon groups, Audubon International, or the Humane Society.

> Give local press tours of the golf course and explain your environmental efforts.

> Stock lakes with grass carp and game fish.

> Offer birdhouse workshops.

AFTERWORD

The future of Earth and its inhabitants depends on all of us. The decisions that we make in connection to the way we live our lives, the products we purchase, the way we design, build, or manage our buildings, neighborhoods, and communities will all have an impact on our planet, our families, ourselves, and our future. Although this book focuses on golf, I believe it is applicable to all types of properties and all types of developments. It is a book about sustaining life, not just golf. Golf, however, can be a vehicle to deliver and demonstrate that it is possible to use resources and to design, develop, and manage property in ways that not only provide jobs, housing, and recreation but also sustain and even nourish the natural systems that all living things depend on for life.

Once again, let me repeat that there is no "one size fits all" or "cookie cutter" approach to sustainability. We can't plan as if there is; we can't design as if there is; we can't manage as if there is; and we can't govern as if there is. The sustainable answers are right where we are. The sustainable answers are not in this book. What I've attempted to offer here are simply some guidelines and approaches to think about—a reference, if you will. It is up to you to ask the right questions and then incorporate the actions or procedures in ways that are appropriate for the particular piece of land on which you live, work, or recreate. The place itself will give you the correct answers if you will just look, listen, and act as if the lives of your great grandchildren depend on the actions you take today.

Aldo Leopold, who is thought by many to be the father of land conservation practices in the United States, believed that humans play an important role in regard to the productive use and conservation of land. In his essay titled "The Farmer as a Conservationist" (in *The Farmer as a Conservationist*, University of

Wisconsin Press, Madison, Wisconsin, 1939), Leopold said that to practice conservation, landowners need to know a great deal and to apply what they know in practical ways. Leopold refers to this ability as "skill," a talent that cannot be learned solely from books but rather comes from an awareness of the land and a respect for the role of nature. Skill evolves from "a lively and vital curiosity about the workings of the biological engine" and is motivated by "enthusiasm and affection." These are "the human qualities requisite to better land use."

Our commitment to the environment and economic prosperity, and the actions we take today, will be our legacy. Someday we will look back on our past and reflect on what our dreams were for the future and how successful we were in reaching our goals. I believe that each of us is personally and professionally responsible for fostering sustainability and supporting environmental progress. I hope that this book will provide you with some of the tools necessary for you to accomplish your goals in ways that bring you personal satisfaction, as well as benefit the environment for generations to come.

GOLF AND THE ENVIRONMENT RESEARCH

I've worked with many architects, planners, developers, permitting agencies, and others during the past decade. Many of them have told me that they believe the development of public policy for permitting, planning, and managing golf courses should be based in science. The suggestion is that some regulatory requirements, some design principles, and some management approaches are not based on science. The question is this: "If not science, what are those principles based on?" The answers may range from personal opinions to anecdotal "evidence."

To the extent possible, scientifically valid research data should be used to document the facts, and those facts ought to be used as a basis for making decisions regarding regulatory requirements, golf course design criteria, wildlife management practices, and agronomic management. While we still have much to learn in many areas that are connected to the golf course industry, we do know quite a bit already.

By a wide margin, the United States Golf Association has been the leading organization connected to golf in leading research efforts and making them readily available. The USGA has spent millions of dollars toward funding research that has resulted in the development of more resistant turfgrass varieties and research that helps us understand the mechanisms that cause turfgrass to react the ways it does when stressed. They have also funded pesticide and nutrient fate research and wildlife research, and they continue to fund an abundant list of research topics, including funding wildlife research through the National Fish and Wildlife Foundation's Wildlife Links research program.

I have been fortunate enough to serve as a member of the USGA Turfgrass and Environmental Research Committee for a number of years. I can report that I have learned much more than I have taught. As such, I asked Jim Snow, National Director of the USGA Green Section, and Dr. Mike Kenna, USGA Research Director, if they would contribute a chapter for this publication that summarizes some of the work of the USGA in regard to their research efforts. What follows is that summary. We all owe a debt of gratitude to the USGA for funding the research efforts described in this chapter and for the many other contributions that it has made to golf and the environment.

The United States Golf Association Turfgrass and Environmental Research Program Overview*

MICHAEL P. KENNA

USGA Green Section, Research Office, P.O. Box 2227, Stillwater, OK 74076

JAMES T. SNOW

USGA Green Section, National Office, P.O. Box 708, Far Hills, NJ 07931

Despite a dramatic growth in popularity during the past 20 years, golf now faces one of its greatest challenges from people who believe that course maintenance practices have a deleterious impact on the environment. One of the greatest fears is that nutrients and pesticides used to maintain golf courses will pollute drinking water supplies. Many people are concerned about the potential effects of elevated pesticide and nutrient levels on human health. In addition, there is concern for the ecology of surface waters and wildlife health problems associated with the use of pesticides and nutrients on golf courses. Claims have been made that up to 100% of the fertilizers and pesticides applied to golf course turf end up in local water supplies, a claim with no basis in fact. However, a significant emotional reaction from a scientifically illiterate public, unaware of what happens to chemicals in the environment, has increased the urgency and hysteria surrounding the pesticide and nutrient fate issues.

People became concerned about how golf courses affect the environment during a series of widespread droughts that occurred in the late 1970's and early 1980's. Severe drought in California and other western states resulted in extreme

*Reprinted with permission from Kenna, Michael P., and James T. Snow. "The United States Golf Association Turfgrass and Environmental Research Program Overview," in *Fate and Management of Turfgrass Chemicals* (Washington, D.C.: American Chemical Society, 2000), pp. 2–35. Copyright 2000 American Chemical Society.

restrictions on water-use. Golf courses were among the first and most severely restricted operations in many areas, due in part to their visibility and because they were considered non-essential users of water. Similarly, increased golf course construction in the 1980's and 1990's brought golf courses under attack because of the potential impacts on natural areas and the use of pesticides on existing courses. In many cases, anti-development groups made unsubstantiated claims about the negative effects of golf courses in an effort to kill housing developments or commercial real estate development.

As an important leadership organization in golf, the USGA initiated a research program focused on environmental issues in 1989. In particular, university research studies examining the effects of fertilizers and pesticides on surface and groundwater resources were initiated. The studies were conducted on the major pathways of chemical fate in the environment, including leaching, runoff, plant uptake and utilization, microbial degradation, volatilization, and other gaseous losses. The studies were conducted at twelve universities throughout the United States, representing the major climatic zones and turfgrass types. The goal of the program was to build a solid foundation for discussing the effects of golf course activities and turfgrass management on the environment (1).

Since 1991, the Environmental Research Program has evaluated the effects of golf courses on people, wildlife and the environment. The three major objectives of the program were to:

1. Understand the effects of turfgrass pest management and fertilization on water quality;

2. Evaluate valid alternative pest control methods; and

3. Document the turfgrass and golf courses benefits to humans, wildlife and the environment.

TURFGRASS PEST MANAGEMENT AND FERTILIZATION EFFECTS ON WATER QUALITY

Golf course superintendents apply pesticides and fertilizers to the course, and depending on an array of processes, these chemicals break down into biologically inactive by products. There are several interacting processes that influence the fate of pesticides and fertilizers applied to turf. For the purposes of this section, the following seven categories that influence the fate of pesticides and nutrients will be discussed:

1. Volatilization

2. Water solubility

3. Sorption

4. Plant uptake

5. Degradation

6. Runoff

7. Leaching

The role these processes play in the likelihood that the pesticides will reach ground or surface water will be addressed somewhat. The relative importance of each process is controlled by the chemistry of the pesticide or fertilizer and environmental variables such as temperature, water content, and soil type.

Volatilization

Volatilization is the process by which chemicals transform from a solid or liquid into a gas. The vapor pressure of a chemical is the best indicator of its potential to volatilize. Pesticide volatilization increases as the vapor pressure increases. As temperature increases, so do vapor pressures and the chance for volatilization loss. Volatilization losses are generally lower following a late afternoon or an early evening pesticide application rather than in the late morning or early afternoon when temperatures are increasing. Volatilization also will increase with air movement and can be greater from unprotected areas than from areas with windbreaks. Immediate irrigation is usually recommended for highly volatile pesticides to reduce loss.

Nitrogen Volatilization

Only a few studies have evaluated nitrogen volatilization from turfgrass. Nitrogen volatilization depends on the degree of irrigation after the application of fertilizer (2, 3, 4). When no irrigation was used, as much as 36% of the nitrogen volatilized. A water application of 1 cm reduced volatilization to 8%. Branham et al. (5, 6) could not account for 36% of the nitrogen applied one year after a spring application. It was suggested that volatilization and denitrification could be responsible.

In a greenhouse experiment, Starrett et al. (7, 8) investigated the fate of ^{15}N applied as urea from intact soil columns (Table I). Nitrogen recovery averaged 82.4 and 89.7% for single (one 25 mm per week) and split (four 6 mm per week) irrigation treatments. Nitrogen volatilization was higher for the split application; however, this difference was not significant.

Pesticide Volatilization

The volatilization studies determined the amount of several pesticides that volatilized into the air for several days after application (Table II). Reported volatile losses over a one to four-week period, expressed as a percentage of the total

TABLE I

Percentage of Nitrogen Recovered from Intact Soil Cores
for Two Irrigation Treatments

Sample	Weekly Irrigation Regime[1]	
	One 25-mm	Four 6-mm
	——Percent of Total Applied——	
Volatilization	0.9	2.3
Clippings, Verdure	14.3	37.3
Thatch-Mat	11.3	16.7
0–10 cm	13.4	12.6
10–20 cm	7.7	6.4
20–30 cm	7.2	5.6
30–40 cm	7.8	6.7
40–50 cm	7.6	2.2
Leachate[a]	12.3	0.4
Total	82.4	89.7

[1]Each treatment had six replications.
[a]Significantly different (t-test, $P < 0.001$)
Source: Adapted from ref. 8.

applied, ranged from less than 1% to 16% (*9–14*). Results of volatilization studies showed that maximum loss occurred when surface temperature and solar radiation were highest, and that volatile losses were directly related to the vapor pressure characteristics of the pesticide. Thus, examining the physical and chemical properties of the pesticide is a good way to determine if volatilization losses are likely to occur under particular weather and application conditions.

Post-application irrigation has an effect on the volatilization of trichlorfon (*10, 15*). The pesticide was applied once, followed by 13 mm of irrigation, and again separately with no post-application irrigation. The application rate for both occasions was 9 kg a.i. ha^{-1}. Without post-application irrigation, trichlorfon volatile loss totaled 13% compared to 9% when irrigated. Also, withholding post-application irrigation resulted in less conversion of trichlorfon to its more toxic breakdown product, DDVP (Figure 1). It appears that light post-application irrigation may have a small, positive effect on preventing volatile loss of pesticides. However, more research investigating light irrigation on several pesticides is needed to confirm this observed trend.

TABLE II

Summary of Volatile Insecticide Residues Recovered from Putting Green
and Fairway Plots

Pesticide	Volatile Residues % Applied	Comments	Ref.
Trichlorfon	11.6	Applied 9/28/91 on bentgrass fairway, no irrigation following application. Sampled for 15 days.	(10)
	9.4	Applied 7/7/93 on bentgrass fairway, 1.3 cm of irrigation after application. Sampled for 15 days.	(10)
	0.09	Applied 6/4/96 on bentgrass green. Sampled for 29 days.	(13)
Isazofos	11.4	Applied 8/22/93 on bentgrass fairway, 1.3 cm of irrigation after application. Sampled for 15 days.	(10)
	1.04	Applied 10/4/96 on bermudagrass green, 0.6 cm of irrigation followed by 3.94 cm of rainfall over 24 hrs. Sampled 48 hours during cloudy, rainy conditions.	(12)
	9.14	Applied 10/10/96 on bermudagrass green, 0.6 cm of irrigation after application. Sampled 22 hrs, no rainfall.	(12)
Chlorpyrifos	2.7	Applied 10/4/96 on bermudagrass green, 0.6 cm of irrigation followed by 3.94 cm of rainfall over 24 hrs. Sampled 48 hours during cloudy, rainy conditions.	(12)
	11.6	Applied 10/10/96 on bermudagrass green, 0.6 cm of irrigation after application. Sampled 22 hrs, no rainfall.	(12)
	15.7	Applied 6/4/96 on bentgrass green. Sampled 29 days.	(13)
Fenamiphos	0.04	Applied 10/10/96 on bermudagrass green, 0.6 cm of irrigation after application. Sampled 22 hrs, no rainfall.	(12)
	0.25	Applied 10/4/96 on bermudagrass green, 0.6 cm of irrigation followed by 3.94 cm of rainfall over 24 hrs. Sampled 48 hours during cloudy, rainy conditions.	(12)
Carbaryl	0.03	Applied 8/93 to bentgrass green and bermudagrass fairway plots. Value is average over turfgrass and soil types.	(13)
Triadimefon	7.3	Applied 8/23/91 on bentgrass fairway, 1.3 cm of irrigation after application. Sampled 15 days.	(11)
Metalaxyl	0.08	Applied 9/27/96 on bentgrass green. Sampled 8 days.	(13)
Chlorthalonil	0.02	Applied 9/27/96 on bentgrass green. Sampled 8 days.	(13)
Mecoprop	0.08	Applied 9/24/92 on bentgrass fairway, no irrigation following application. Sampled 15 days.	(11)
2,4-D	0.67	Applied 8/93 to bentgrass green and bermudagrass fairway plots. Averaged of turfgrass and soil types.	(14)

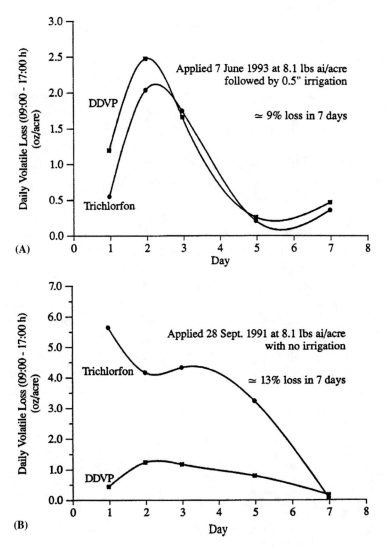

FIGURE 1. *Trichlorfon volatilization from irrigated (A) and non-irrigated (B) bentgrass fairway plots. Source: Reproduced with permission from ref. 9. Copyright 1995 United States Golf Association.*

Water Solubility

The extent to which a chemical will dissolve in a liquid is referred to as solubility. Although water solubility is usually a good indicator of mobility (Figure 2), it is not necessarily the only criterion. In addition to pesticide solubility, the affinity of a pesticide to adhere to soils must be considered (16).

Sorption

The tendency of a pesticide to leach or runoff is strongly dependent upon the interaction of the pesticide with solids in the soil. Sorption includes the process of adsorption and absorption. Adsorption refers to the binding of a pesticide to the soil particle surface. Absorption implies that the pesticide penetrates into a soil particle or is taken up by plant leaves or roots.

This difference is important because pesticides may become increasingly absorbed with time (months to years), and desorption (or release) of the absorbed pesticide may be reduced with time. The unavailable or undetachable pesticide is often referred to as bound residue and is generally unavailable for microbial degradation or pest control.

Factors that contribute to sorption of pesticides on soil materials include (a) chemical and physical characteristics of the pesticide, (b) soil composition, and (c) nature of the soil solution. In general, sandy soils offer little in the way of sorptive surfaces. Soils containing higher amounts of silt, clay and organic matter provide a rich sorptive environment for pesticides. Research conducted during the past eight years (*17, 18, 19*) indicates that turfgrass leaves and thatch adsorb a significant amount of pesticide (see Figure 3).

Adsorption of pesticides is affected by the partition coefficient, which is reported as K_d or more accurately as K_{oc}. A K_{oc} less than 300 to 500 is considered low. The strength of adsorption is inversely related to the pesticide's solubility in

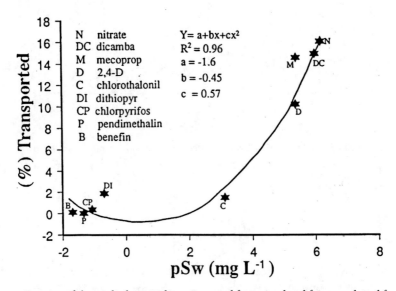

FIGURE 2. *Fraction of the applied pesticides transported from simulated fairway plotted for the log of the water solubility (pSW) of the analyte. Source: Reproduced with permission from ref. 16. Copyright 1998 United States Golf Association.*

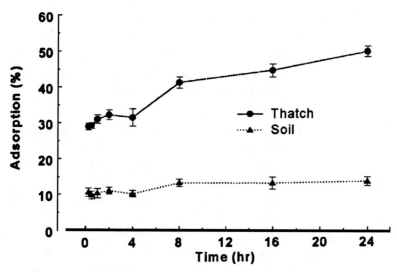

FIGURE 3. *Adsorption kinetics for 2,4-D in thatch and soil. Source: Reproduced with permission from ref. 17. Copyright 1998 United States Golf Association.*

water and directly related to its partition coefficient. For example, chlorinated hydrocarbons are strongly adsorbed, while phenoxy herbicides like 2,4-D are much more weakly adsorbed.

Plant Uptake

Plants can directly absorb pesticides or influence pesticide fate by altering the flow of water in the root zone. Turfgrasses with higher rates of transpiration can reduce the leaching of water-soluble pesticides. In situations where the turf is not actively growing or root systems are not well developed, pesticides are more likely to migrate deeper into the soil profile with percolating water.

Degradation

Degradation occurs because of the presence of soil microorganisms and chemical processes in the turfgrass-soil system. Pesticides are broken down in a series of steps that eventually lead to the production of CO_2 (carbon dioxide), H_2O (water) and some inorganic products (i.e., nitrogen, phosphorus, sulfur, etc.).

Microbial Degradation

Microbial degradation is a biological process whereby microorganisms transform the original compound into one or more new compounds. Each of these new compounds has different chemical and physical properties that make them behave differently in the environment. Microbial degradation may be either direct or indirect. Some pesticides are directly utilized as a food source by microorganisms. In most cases, though, indirect microbial degradation of pesticides occurs though passive consumption along with other food sources in the soil.

Chemical Degradation

Chemical degradation is similar to microbial degradation except that pesticide break down is not achieved by microbial activity. The major chemical reactions such as hydrolysis, oxidation, and reduction occur in both chemical and microbial degradation. Photochemical degradation is an entirely different break down process driven by solar radiation. It is the *combined pesticide degradation* that results from chemical, microbial, and photochemical processes under field conditions that was of the most interest in the USGA sponsored studies.

Degradation rates are also influenced by factors like pesticide concentration, temperature, soil water content, pH, oxygen status, prior pesticide use, soil fertility, and microbial population. These factors change dramatically with soil depth and greatly reduce microbial degradation as pesticides migrate below the soil surface. An interesting result occurred at the University of Florida study when fenamiphos was applied twice at a monthly interval. Although leaching from the first application amounted to about 18%, leaching from the second application was just 4% (20, 21, 22, 23). These results suggest that microbial degradation was enhanced due to microbial buildup after the first application, thereby reducing the amount of material available for leaching after the second application.

In the case of degradation rates, the average DT_{90} (days to 90% degradation) in turf soils generally is significantly less than established values based upon agricultural systems (see Figure 4). Thus, leaching potential for most pesticides is less in turfgrass systems because turfgrass thatch plays an important role in adsorbing and degrading applied pesticides (24, 25).

Persistence of a pesticide, expressed as half-life (DT_{50}), is the time required for 50% of the original pesticide to degrade. Half-life measurements are commonly made in the laboratory under uniform conditions. On the golf course, soil temperature, organic carbon and moisture content change constantly. These factors dramatically influence the rate of degradation. Consequently, half-life values should be considered as guidelines rather than absolute values.

Leaching

The downward movement of nutrients and pesticides through the turfgrass-soil system by water is called leaching. Compared to some agricultural crops, the

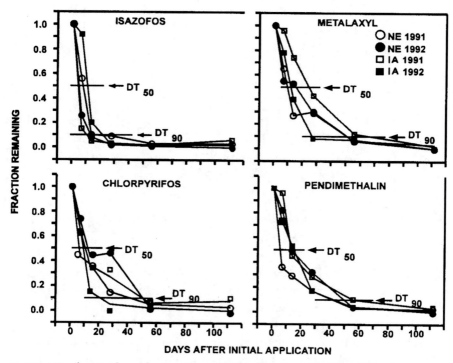

FIGURE 4. *Total pesticide residue in verdure, thatch, and soil as a function of sampling time. Intercepts with 0.5 and 0.1 estimate time to 50 (DT50) and 90 (DT90) percent dissipation, respectively. Source: Reproduced with permission from ref. 25. Copyright 1996 G. L. Horst, P. J. Shea, N. E. Christians, R. D. Miller, C. Stuefer-Powell, and S. K. Starrett.*

USGA-sponsored research demonstrates that leaching is reduced in turfgrass systems. This occurs because of the increase in adsorption on leaves, thatch, and soil organic matter; a high level of microbial and chemical degradation; and reduced percolation due to an extensive root system, greater plant uptake, and high transpiration rates. Separate discussions on nitrogen and pesticide leaching follow.

Nitrogen Leaching

Golf courses use a significant amount of nitrogen (N) fertilizer and there is concern that nitrogen leaching is affecting groundwater supplies. Seven different universities investigated nitrogen leaching, most using bucket lysimeters to measure leaching potential. In general, very little nitrogen leaching occurred when nitrogen was applied properly, i.e., according to the needs of the turf and in consideration of soil types, irrigation regimes and anticipated rainfall. Properly maintained turf grown in a loam soil allowed less than 1% of the nitrogen applied to leach to a depth of 1.2 m (5, 6). Sandy soils are more prone to leaching losses than loam soils. Results averaged over seven leaching projects during the establishment year indi-

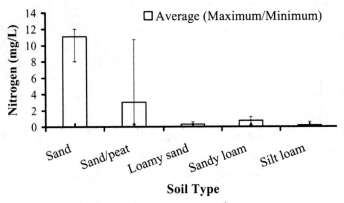

FIGURE 5. *Summary of the nitrogen leaching results (mg L^{-1}) from five soil types reported from USGA-sponsored research studies.*

cate that nitrogen leaching ranged from 11 percent of applied for pure sand rootzones to one percent or less for root zones containing more silt and clay (Figure 5). When more nitrogen is applied than is needed, both the amount and the percentage of nitrogen lost increases. Nitrogen leaching losses can be greatly reduced by irrigating lightly and frequently, rather than heavily and less frequently. Applying nitrogen in smaller amounts on a more frequent basis also reduced leaching losses.

Braun et al. (26) found that nitrogen leaching was significant when applied at heavy rates to newly established turfgrass on pure sand rootzones. For example, they found that 7.6% of an annual application rate of 585 kg N ha^{-1} yr^{-1} (12 lb. N 1000 ft^{-2} yr^{-1}) applied to immature turf grown on a pure sand rootzone leached through the profile (Table III). Leaching was significantly less when peat was

TABLE III

Percent of Total Applied Nitrogen Leached as Nitrate

Rootzone Medium	Nitrogen kg N ha^{-1}yr^{-1}	NO$_3$–N, % of Total N		
		Year 1	Year 2	Year 3
Sand	190	5.37	0.06	2.71
	390	6.31	0.04	3.17
	585	7.55	0.70	4.28
Amended	190	5.37	0.40	0.16
	390	0.91	0.02	0.17
Sand	585	3.37	1.26	2.31

Source: Adapted from ref. 26.

added to the sand (USGA recommended mix), occurring at a level of about 3%. On pure sand, nitrogen concentrations exceeded federal drinking water standards (10 ppm NO_3–nitrogen) several times at the 585 kg rate during the first year, whereas nitrogen concentrations in leachate never exceeded federal standards from the sand/peat mix. Significantly less leaching also occurred when less nitrogen was applied (<380 kg N ha^{-1} yr^{-1}) and when application frequency was increased (22 vs. 11 times annually). During years two and three, on mature turf, much less nitrogen leaching occurred for all treatments. In putting green construction, mixing peat moss with sand significantly reduced nitrogen leaching compared to pure sand rootzones during the year of establishment. Light applications of slow-release nitrogen sources on a frequent interval provided excellent protection from nitrate leaching.

Branham et al. (5, 6, 27) reported that less than 1% of the applied nitrogen leached through a 1.2-m (4-foot) deep profile of undisturbed loam-soil during a 2.5 year period (Figure 6). Most of the nitrogen was recovered in clippings, thatch, and soil. They suggested that the remaining amount volatilized or was lost through denitrification. Starrett et al. (7, 8) observed similar results when nitrogen was applied at moderate rates and lightly irrigated (one 25-mm vs. four 6-mm applications). However, up to 30 times more nitrogen (Table I) was leached after the single 25 mm irrigation application, perhaps in part due to macropore flow caused by earthworm activity. Yates (14) reported that nitrogen leaching from a USGA profile sand-based green was generally less than 1% when nitrogen was applied lightly and frequently.

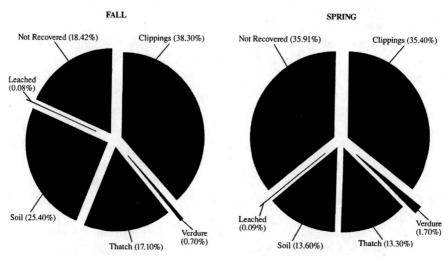

FIGURE 6. *Percent of total nitrogen applied recovered two years after spring and fall applications. Source: Reproduced with permission from ref. 27. Copyright 1994 United States Golf Association.*

Irrigating bermudagrass and tall fescue turf with adequate amounts (no drought stress) of moderately saline water did not increase the concentration or amount of nitrate leached (2). Higher amounts of salinity in the root zone, drought, or the combination of these two stresses caused high concentrations and larger amounts of nitrate to leach from both a tall fescue and bermudagrass turf. This suggests that drought, high salinity, or both impair the capacity of the root system of the turf, and that management modification may be needed to prevent nitrate leaching.

Pesticide Leaching

Pesticide leaching studies were conducted at universities throughout the United States. Treatments were made to a variety of soils and turf species, and plots received varying irrigation regimes or rainfall events. During the first year of the studies, most turf areas were relatively immature. Results showed that very little pesticide leaching occurred with most products, generally less than 1% of the total applied. However, significant leaching occurred with certain products and under certain circumstances (Table IV).

The physical and chemical properties of the pesticides proved to be good indicators of the potential for leaching, runoff and volatilization (27). Products that exhibit high water solubility, low soil adsorption potential, and greater persistence are more likely to leach and runoff. For example, fenamiphos, a commonly used nematicide, is highly water soluble and has low adsorption potential, and its toxic breakdown metabolite tends to persist in the soil. As expected, losses of fenamiphos and its metabolite due to leaching were as high as 18% from a sand-based green in Florida (20, 21, 22, 23), though when all studies are considered, the average loss was about 5%. Soil type and precipitation/irrigation amount also were important factors in leaching losses. Table V shows the effects of soil type and precipitation on leaching of MCPP and triadimefon, two pesticides whose chemical and physical properties indicate a relatively high potential for leaching. Results show significant leaching from coarse sand profiles, especially under high precipitation, and much less leaching from sandy loam and silt loam soils (28).

There are several simulation models currently used to predict the downward movement of pesticides through soil. A good review on pesticide transport models was conducted by Cohen et al. (29). The USGA-sponsored studies indicate that many of these models will need adjustments that take into account the role of a dense turf canopy and thatch layer. For example, the actual leaching loss of 2,4-D was less than the predicted value using the GLEAMS (i.e., Groundwater Loading Effects of Agricultural Management Systems) computer model. Without proper parameter adjustments, the model over-predicted the actual amount leached by 10

TABLE IV

Summary of Total Pesticide Mass and Percent of Total Applied Recovered in Water Effluent from Putting Green and Fairway Lysimeters

Common Name	Trade Name	n	Total Recovered, $\mu g\ m^{-2}$		Percent Recovered	
			Mean	Range	Mean	Range
Fairway Plots						
Chlorothalonil	Daconil	1	0	(0)	0.00	(0.00)
Fenarimol	Rubigan	1	0	(0)	0.00	(0.00)
Metalaxyl	Subdue	1	0	(0)	0.00	(0.00)
Propiconazole	Banner	1	0	(0)	0.00	(0.00)
Triadimefon	Bayleton	8	2,312	(27–11,160)	0.51	(0.01–2.44)
2,4-D	2,4-D	9	155	(0–329)	0.28	(0.00–0.60)
Dicamba	Banvel	2	4,750	(3,700–5,800)	39.58	(30.83–48.33)
MCPP	Mecoprop	6	44,236	(1,006–142,062)	19.34	(0.44–62.12)
Carbaryl	Sevin	8	132	(24–375)	0.01	(0.00–0.02)
Isazofos	Triumph	6	5,590	(5,590)	2.44	(0.00–10.40)
Trichlorfon	Proxol	6	21,527	(5,763–40,341)	2.35	(0.63–4.41)
Putting Green Plots						
Chlorothalonil	Daconil	4	2,961	(749–5,486)	0.08	(0.02–0.14)
2,4-D	2,4-D	7	871	(347–1,808)	2.25	(1.12–3.79)
2,4-D amine	2,4-D	6	46	(0–133)	0.12	(0.00–0.48)
Dicamba	Banvel	7	201	(0–1,173)	3.07	(0.00–19.55)
MCPP	Mecoprop	4	109	(0–329)	0.08	(0.00–0.25)
Carbaryl	Sevin	4	372	(205–642)	0.04	(0.02–0.07)
Chlorpyrifos	Dursban	4	92	(0–193)	0.04	(0.00–0.08)
Dithiopyr	Dimension	4	139	(101–196)	0.24	(0.18–0.35)
Ethoprop	Mocap	1	41,138	(1,138)	0.05	(0.05)
Fenamiphos	Nemacur	4	53,121	(419–199,038)	4.70	(0.04–17.61)
Fonofos	Dyfonate	2	54	(4–103)	0.01	(0.00–0.02)
Isazofos	Triumph	2	123	(41–204)	0.05	(0.02–0.09)
Isofenphos	Oftanol	2	43	(33–53)	0.02	(0.01–0.02)

TABLE V

Effect of Soil Type and Precipitation on the Leaching Loss of Two Pesticides from an Immature Turf, Expressed as Percent of Total Applied

Pesticide	Precipitation	Percent Recovered of Total Applied		
		Sand	Sandy Loam	Silt Loam
MCPP	Moderate	51.0	0.8	0.4
	High	62.1	0.5	1.2
Triadimefon	Moderate	1.0	0.06	0.2
	High	2.4	0.01	0.3

Source: Adapted from ref. *28*

to 100 times, or more, for five of the seven pesticides screened by the computer (*30, 31*).

In summary, the pesticide leaching studies indicate that dense turf cover reduced the potential for leaching losses of pesticides; conversely, more leaching occurred from newly planted turf stands. Generally, sandy soils are more prone to leaching losses than clayey soils. The physical and chemical properties of the pesticides were good indicators of leaching potential. Finally, current pesticide models over-predict the leaching loss of most pesticides applied to turf if valid adjustments are not made to account for the role the turf canopy and thatch.

Runoff

An important finding from the USGA-sponsored research was that pesticide and nutrient runoff pose a greater threat to water quality than leaching. Runoff refers to the portion of precipitation (rainfall) that is discharged from the area through stream channels. The water lost without entering the soil is called surface runoff, and that which enters the soil before reaching the stream is called groundwater runoff or seepage flow from ground water. Pesticides and nutrients applied to golf course turf, under some circumstances, can be transported off site in surface runoff.

Nitrogen Runoff

Three USGA-sponsored studies examined runoff from fairway research plots. In Pennsylvania, runoff experiments were conducted on plots characterized by slopes of 9 to 13%, good quality loam soil, and turf cover consisting of either creeping bentgrass or perennial ryegrass cut at a 12.5 mm (½-inch) fairway height (*32, 33, 34*). Typical of that part of the country, the fairway-type plots received 195 kg N

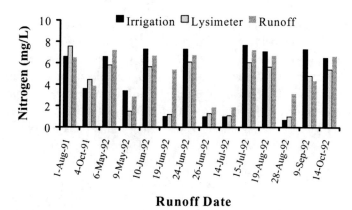

Runoff Date

FIGURE 7. *Concentration of nitrate-nitrogen in irrigation, leachate, and runoff water collected during the 1993 growing season. Source: Adapted from ref. 32.*

ha^{-1} yr^{-1} (4 lb. N per 1000 ft^2 per year). The irrigation water used to simulate rainfall contained a relatively high level of nitrate-nitrogen, ranging from 2 to 10 ppm. They reported that nitrate concentrations in the runoff or leaching samples did not differ significantly from the nitrate concentration in the irrigation water (Figure 7). The study was conducted on excellent quality turf and on soil with a high infiltration rate.

Nitrogen runoff also was measured as part of the studies in Georgia (35, 36). Nitrogen applications were made and 24 hours after a simulated storm event (25 mm applied at a rate of 50 mm hr^{-1}) as much as 40 to 70% of the rainfall left the plots as runoff. A total of 16% (12.5 mg L^{-1}) of the nitrate nitrogen applied at 24 kg ha^{-1} applied to actively growing bermudagrass was found in surface runoff water (Table IV). However, 64% (24.8 mg L^{-1}) of the nitrate nitrogen applied at 24 kg ha^{-1} applied to dormant bermudagrass was found in surface runoff water.

In Oklahoma, the effects of buffer strips and cultivation practices on pesticide and nitrogen runoff were investigated. It was concluded that antecedent soil moisture was the major factor influencing runoff (Table VII). During the first simulated rainfall event in July, soil moisture conditions were low to moderate. After a 50 mm (2 inches) rainfall event, less than 1%of the applied nitrogen was collected in the runoff (37, 38). In August, when the simulated rainfall occurred after 150 mm (6 inches) of actual rainfall the previous week (i.e., high soil moisture), the amount of nitrogen collected after the simulated rainfall averaged more than 8%. When soil moisture was moderate to low in the Oklahoma study, the presence of a 2.4 to 4.9 m (8 to 16 ft.) untreated buffer strip significantly reduced nitrogen runoff, whereas when soil moisture was high, the buffer strips made no difference. In both cases, less runoff occurred when sulfur-coated urea was applied compared to straight urea.

In summary, results from USGA-sponsored runoff studies showed that dense turf cover reduces the potential for runoff losses of nitrogen, and significant runoff losses are more likely to occur on compacted soils. Much greater nitrogen runoff occurred when soil moisture levels were high, as compared to moderate or low. Buffer strips reduced nitrogen runoff when soil moisture was low to moderate at the time of the runoff event. However, buffer strips were ineffective when soil moisture levels were high. Nitrogen runoff was significantly less when a slow release product (sulfur-coated urea) was used compared to a more soluble product (urea).

Pesticide Runoff

In Georgia, studies were conducted on plots with a 5% slope and a sandy clay soil typical of that region (15, 30, 31, 35). Pesticides were applied and 25-mm (1-inch) simulated rainfall events occurred 24 and 48 hours afterward. At a rainfall rate of 50 mm (2 inches) per hour, as much as 40 to 70% of the rainfall left the plots as runoff during simulated storm events. The collected surface water contained moderately high concentrations of treatment pesticides having high water solubility (Table VI). For example, under these conditions, only very small amounts (<1%) of chlorthalonil and chlorpyrifos could be detected in the runoff. However, between 10 and 13% of the 2,4-D, MCPP and dicamba was transported off the plots over an 11-day period. About 80% of this transported total moved off the plots with the first rainfall event 24 hours after pesticide application. Also, the amount of the trichlorfon that ran off the plots was 5.2 times greater when broadcast as a granular product compared to being pressure injected. Finally, the runoff loss of several herbicides was greater when applied to dormant turf as compared to an actively growing turf.

Antecedent soil moisture was a significant factor in determining how much pesticide ran off the plot areas (36, 37, 39). Where soil moisture was low to moderate, buffer zones were effective in reducing pesticide runoff; when soil moisture was high they were not effective except for the insecticide chlorpyrifos (Table VII).

In both Oklahoma and Georgia, best management practice studies investigated how cutting heights and buffers of varying lengths could minimize fertilizer and pesticide runoff. The effect of soil cultivation (core aerification) on runoff potential also was studied. In Oklahoma, a 4.9-m buffer cut at 5 cm (3 inches) significantly decreased the amount of 2,4-D found in runoff water from a 4.9-m treated bermudagrass fairway (Figure 8). However, the results in Georgia that used smaller buffer strips indicated no reduction in the amount of pesticide transported in the surface-water solution (39).

Among the conclusions or trends observed from the pesticide runoff studies were the following: (1) dense turf cover reduces the potential for runoff losses of pesticides; (2) the physical and chemical properties of pesticides are good indicators of potential runoff losses; (3) heavy textured, compacted soils are much more

TABLE VI

The Percentage of Applied and Concentration of Product Transported from Runoff Plots during Rainfall 24 Hours after Application on Heavy Textured Soils with High Antecedent Moisture

Pesticide or Nitrogen Treatment	Application Rate, kg ha^{-1}	Percent Transported	Conc. 24 h after Application, µg L^{-1}
NO$_3$ active growth	24.4	16.4	12,500
NO$_3$ dormant	24.4	64.2	24,812
Dicamba	0.56	14.6	360
Dicamba (dormant)	0.56	37.3	752
Mecoprop	1.68	14.4	810
Mecoprop (dormant)	1.68	23.5	1,369
2,4-D DMA	2.24	9.6	800
2,4-D DMA (dormant)	2.24	26.0	1,959
2,4-D DMA (injected)	2.24	1.3	158
2,4-D DMA (buffer)	2.24	7.6	495
2,4-D LVE	2.24	9.1	812
Trichlorfon[1]	9.15	32.5	13,960
Trichorfon[1] (injected)	9.15	6.2	2,660
Chlorothalonil[2]	9.50	0.8	290
Chlorpyrifos[2]	1.12	0.1	19
Dithiopyr	0.56	2.3	39
Dithiopyr (granule)	0.56	1.0	26
Benefin	1.70	0.01	3
Benefin (granule)	1.70	0.01	6
Pendimethalin	1.70	0.01	9
Pendimethalin (granule)	1.70	0.01	2

[1] Trichlorfon + dichlorvos metabolite.

[2] Total for active ingredient and metabolites.

Source: Adapted from ref. 36.

prone to runoff losses than sandy soils; (4) moist soils are more prone to runoff losses than drier soils; (5) buffer strips at higher cutting heights tend to reduce runoff of pesticides when soil moisture is low to moderate prior to rainfall events; and, (6) the application of soluble herbicides on dormant turf can produce high levels of runoff losses.

TABLE VII

Effect of Low/Moderate versus High Antecedent Soil Moisture Levels on Pesticide and Nutrient Runoff Losses from Bermudagrass Maintained as Fairway Turf, Expressed as a Percentage of Total Applied

Soil Moisture	NO$_3$	PO$_4$	NH$_4$	Dicamba	2,4-D	MCPP	Chlorpyrifos	ref.
Low/mod.	0.09	0.2	0.2	0.35	0.79	0.81	0.04	(38)
	—	—	—	3.1	2.6	1.3		(36)
High	3.1	7.7	5.1	5.4	8.7	9.3	0.025	(38)
	—	—	—	9.7	7.3	9.5		(36)

Source: Adapted from ref. *36, 38.*

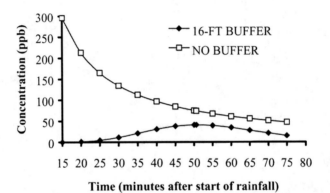

Time (minutes after start of rainfall)

FIGURE 8. *Plot of the predicted concentration of 2,4-D in surface runoff versus time in the 1996 buffer length experiment. Source: Reproduced with permission from ref. 39. Copyright 1998 United States Golf Association.*

ALTERNATIVE PEST MANAGEMENT

Alternative pest management is intended to reduce the amount of pesticide needed to maintain golf course turfgrasses. The USGA provided funding for the development and evaluation of alternative methods of pest control. Research projects focused on the following areas: biological control, cultural and mechanical practices, allelopathy, selection and breeding for pest resistance, and application of integrated pest management strategies.

Biological Control

The microorganisms that inhabit the turfgrass root zone are just starting to be characterized in a way that will lead to positive developments in biological control.

It is important that the mechanisms of biological control be understood thoroughly before products are commercialized. The USGA has sponsored several projects in the area of biological control and we are just starting to understand why some of these organisms fail when used in field situations.

Biological control of turfgrass pests is generally accomplished with a living organism that either lowers the population density of the pest problem or reduces its ability to cause injury to the turf. In this section, a list of potential problems that any organic or biological control agent must overcome to be a commercial success is first covered. After this discussion, biocontrol approaches are investigated to solve some of our common turfgrass disease and insect problems are reviewed.

Potential Problems of Biocontrol

Once laboratory or greenhouse evidence demonstrates that a specific predator or microbial antagonist controls a turfgrass pest problem, additional field research must be performed to determine whether it is a functional biocontrol agent acceptable for commercial use (40). Specifically, sound scientific research must:

1. Determine if the biocontrol agent readily establishes in the turf or surrounding areas.
2. Evaluate the effects of pesticides on the growth and development of the antagonist.
3. Estimate the likelihood of resistance to the effects of the biological agent.
4. Reduce the need for conventional pesticides by providing an adequate level of control.
5. Provide evidence that the biological agent is safe for people, wildlife and the environment.
6. Develop methods for producing commercial quantities with an acceptable shelf life and cost.

The antagonist must be readily established in the turf in order for biocontrol to be effective. This means that the antagonist must become quickly established in the turf and is able to maintain the population level needed to reduce the pest problem. At the present time, repeat applications of large quantities of preparations of the antagonistic organism are usually required in order to achieve and maintain levels of pest suppression that approximate those provided by pesticides. The use of an antagonist must take into consideration how much of the material is required to provide a significant reduction of the pest problem, how long the individual applications will last, and whether the method is economically feasible.

Antagonist growth and development must not be affected by pesticides. Generally, biocontrol procedures alone will not provide satisfactory levels of pest reduction in intensely managed golf course turf. Biocontrol products will probably be used in conjunction with a pesticide program. There are some situations where the pesticides used on the golf course may be toxic to the antagonist or may restrict the growth and development of indigenous species that are necessary for the bio-control species to be effective. Therefore, the impact of pesticides on the growth and development of the antagonist is an important consideration in the selection of biocontrol agents.

Is resistance likely? Many of the pest problems that occur in turfgrass are known to have biotypes that differ in their vulnerability to pesticides, their ability to infest the turf area, or in the environmental conditions needed for optimum growth and development. This means that the biocontrol will need to have a wide range of effectiveness on the various pest biotypes. For this reason, before being sold commercially, an antagonist must be field tested within the prospective marketing regions to determine its level of effectiveness against the target pests in these localities.

The pest reduction level must permit a decrease in pesticide use. A biocontrol system based on the use of a single predator or microbial species is highly specific. Unlike most pesticides, it will not control a wide range of disease or insect problems. The level of pest reduction provided by the antagonist should at least offset pesticide consumption for control of the target pest problem.

The antagonist must be safe for people, wildlife and the environment. Protection of the environment is one of the primary reasons that the concept of biological control has gained much support. Before a biocontrol agent is placed into general use, however, it must be clearly demonstrated that it does not jeopardize the stability of the biological environment or the health of people or wildlife. Ideally, the selected agents should be similar to indigenous microflora so that the danger of introducing potentially damaging organisms is minimal.

Methods for production and formulation must be developed. A commercial product must be easily produced and have a reasonable shelf life in order to be accepted by turfgrass managers. Several effective biocontrol agents cannot be produced in commercial quantities. These biological agents either need a live host to reproduce or the current laboratory production methods available would make the product too expensive to produce.

Disease Biocontrol

There are two general approaches to the biocontrol of turfgrass diseases. First, preparations, containing known microbial species detrimental to the growth and development of a specific pathogen, are used to prevent or control the disease. Second, the use of organic materials, colonized by a complex mixture of microbial species that restrict the pathogen growth and development, are applied to a turfgrass area for disease control. Varying degrees of success have been reported (41) from field and greenhouse-based tests for the control of turfgrass diseases by applying a known microbial agent or complex mixture of bacteria and fungi to the turf area (Table VIII).

TABLE VIII

Examples for Biological Control of Turfgrass Diseases

Disease Pathogen	Antagonists	Location
Brown Patch	*Rhizoctonia* spp.	Ontario, Canada
Rhizoctonia solani	*Laetisaria* spp.	North Carolina
	Complex mixtures	New York, Maryland
Dollar Spot	*Enterobacter cloacae*	New York
Sclerotinia homoeocarpa	*Fusarium heterosporum*	Canada
	Trichoderma harzianum	New York
	Gliocladium virens	South Carolina
	Actinomycetes spp.	New York
	Complex mixtures	New York
Pythium Blight	*Pseudomonas* spp.	Illinois, Ohio
Pythium aphanidermatum	*Trichoderma* spp.	Ohio
	Trichoderma hamatum	Colorado
	Enterobacter cloacae	New York
	Various bacteria	New York
	Complex mixtures	Pennsylvania
Pythium Root Rot	*Enterobacter cloacae*	New York
Pythium graminicola	Complex mixtures	New York
Red Thread	Complex mixtures	New York
Laetisaria fuciformis		
Southern Blight	*Trichoderma harzianum*	North Carolina
Sclerotium rolfsii		
Take-All Patch	*Pseudomonas* spp.	Colorado
Gaeumannomyces graminis	*Gaeumannomyces* spp.	Australia
var. *avenae*	*Phialophora radicicola*	Australia
	Complex mixtures	Australia
Typhula Blight	*Typhula phacorrhiza*	Ontario, Canada
Typhula spp.	*Trichoderma* spp.	Massachusetts
	Complex mixtures	New York
Summer Patch	*Stenotrophomonas maltophilia*	New Jersey
Magnaporthae poae		
Spring Dead Spot	*Pseudomonas* spp.	California
Leptosphaeria korrae		
Sting Nematodes	*Pasteuria* spp.	Florida
Belonolaimus longicaudatus		

Source: Adapted from ref. *41*.

Use of Natural Organic Products. Many natural organic products such as composts, sewage sludge, organic fertilizers and manure-based preparations are colonized by complex mixtures of microorganisms. When some of these materials are applied to turf, the microbial species they carry restrict the growth and development of the resident pathogens. Among the most suppressive composts tested in laboratory and field experiments, brewery and sewage sludge composts have shown the most promise. Organic fertilizers derived from poultry litter also have provided disease suppression in field experiments.

Field tests indicate highly variable results for the reduction of dollar spot incidence in creeping bentgrass golf greens (*40, 41*). Products included sewage sludge materials, brewery and manure composts, and natural organic fertilizers. The natural organic fertilizers contained hydrolyzed poultry feather meal, wheat germ, soybean meal, brewers yeast, bone meal, blood meal, sulfate of potash, and supplemented with species of *Bacillus* and the fungus *Trichoderma viride*. Ammonium nitrate and sulfur coated urea often provided an equal level of dollar-spot control (*41*).

It is important to know something about how the material was produced. Compost that has demonstrated some disease suppressive characteristics are produced under ideal physical and environmental conditions (*41*). The correct starting material composted in this manner allows for the colonization of both mesophilic (moderate temperature) and thermophilic (high temperature) microflora (Figure 9). This complex mixture of microorganisms makes an important contribution to

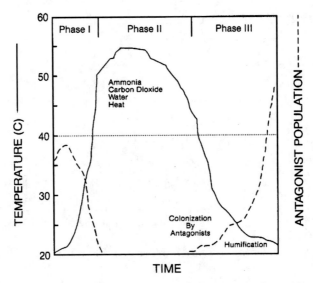

FIGURE 9. *Composts should proceed through three distinct phases involving: Phase I, a rapid rise in temperature; Phase II, a prolonged high-temperature decomposition phase; and Phase III, a curing process where temperatures and decomposition rate decrease. Source: Reproduced with permission from ref. 41. Copyright 1992 United States Golf Association.*

the disease suppressive characteristics of the composted material. Also, composts that have cured for a long period will have a more diverse mesophilic microflora and have the potential to perform better for disease suppression.

Unfortunately, at this time there is no reliable way to predict the disease suppressive properties of composts or organic fertilizers since the nature of these colonizing microbial antagonists is left to chance. It is very important to proceed with caution when using these materials. Even though some research has documented up to 75% control of common turfgrass diseases, there generally is a great deal of variability in their performance. Also, at application rates of greater than 480 kg ha^{-1} (10 lbs. 1000 ft^{-2}) there exists the potential problem of creating an unwanted organic layer above a well-drained putting green or fairway root zone.

Use of Preparations Containing Known Microbial Antagonists. The use of a specific microbial antagonist to reduce the incidence and severity of diseases has been slightly more promising and consistent. Take-all patch of bentgrass has been controlled by infesting the soil with the nonpathogenic fungus *Phialophora graminicola.* Steam-treated preparations of the nonpathogenic fungus *Typhula phacorrhiza* applied as topdressing to creeping bentgrass provided up to 74% control of Typhula blight. The incidence and severity of Rhizoctonia blight of creeping bentgrass golf greens was reduced by inoculating the turf with nonpathogenic *Rhizoctonia* species.

The USGA provided funding for three projects that used specific microbial antagonists to suppress turfgrass pathogens. *Trichoderma harzianum* and *Enterobacter cloacae* have demonstrated promising disease suppression for dollar spot and different *Pythium* species. *T. harzianum* is a fungus that parasitizes *Pythium* blight and other turfgrass pathogens. The current study demonstrates that commonly used fungicides have little effect on the growth and performance of this biocontrol (42). *Enterobacter cloacae* has shown promising results for controlling *Pythium* species by removing turfgrass root exudates (waste products) found in the soil. These compounds stimulate the germination of disease sporangium, and once they are removed, pathogenic species of *Pythium* are less likely to germinate and infest turfgrass roots (43). *Stenotrophomonas maltophilia* (formerly the genus *Xanthomonas*) has provided excellent summer patch control in growth chamber and greenhouse trials. The field research confirms the importance of understanding the population dynamics of the biological control. Populations of the biocontrol agent were maintained above 10^5 cfu g^{-1} of soil; however, as many as 10^7 cfu g^{-1} of soil may be needed to control summer patch on field plots (44).

The USGA also supported a project that is developing a bacterial parasite (*Pasteuria* sp.) of sting nematodes (*Belonolaimus longicaudatus*). The bacterium is very effective in greenhouse trials; however, live nematodes are needed in order for the bacteria to reproduce. Additional field studies were conducted to evaluate natural populations of *Pasteuria* sp. under a variety of turf management levels. Results indicate nematode populations are significantly reduced in turf areas where the bacteria were present (45).

Insect Biocontrol

Biological controls for insect problems in agricultural crops have been used successfully in the United States. Research into the use of biological controls for turfgrass insects recently gained attention because of the push for natural, less toxic, pest control products. Rather than introducing a complex mixture of microorganisms with applications of organic materials, the research effort has focused on increasing our understanding of natural predators and parasites that occur in turfgrass areas. Similar to the preparations of known microbial antagonists to disease, specific organisms such as entomopathogenic nematodes or bacteria are introduced to reduce insect problems.

Natural Predators and Parasites in Turf. The fact that severe insect outbreaks are relatively uncommon in low-maintenance turf suggests that many pests are normally held in check by natural buffers. Environmental stresses such as drought can take a heavy toll on some insects. Natural insect pathogens, including bacteria, fungi, parasitic nematodes, and other disease causing agents, also help to reduce pest populations.

Field surveys have shown that predatory insects are often very diverse and abundant in turf (46). Dozens of different species of ants, ground beetles, spiders and rove beetles feed on the eggs or larval (immature) stages of plant-eating insects. The common tiger beetle was observed to kill as many as 20 fall armyworm caterpillars in a single hour. There is some evidence to suggest that pest outbreaks can sometimes be attributed to inadvertent elimination of natural enemies when using broad-spectrum insecticides. A surface application of chlorpyrifos or isofenphos in June reduced predator populations such as spiders and rove beetles by as much as 60%. Similar work has documented that during a 48-hour period, predators consumed or carried off as many as 75% of sod webworm eggs laid on untreated turf. Chlorpyrifos treated plots had lower numbers of predators and subsequently resulted in significantly reduced consumption of the sod webworm eggs for three weeks (Figure 10).

A better understanding of the interactions between commonly used turfgrass pesticides and beneficial organisms that prey on insect pests is needed. Insecticides and other pesticides are powerful tools that often provide the only method to prevent severe damage from unexpected or heavy pest infestations. Broad-spectrum insecticides kill beneficial insects as well as pests, but fortunately, populations of predators and parasites seem to recuperate relatively quickly following individual applications. Turf managers need to apply pesticides at the proper time and rate, and only as needed to reduce the impact on beneficial organisms.

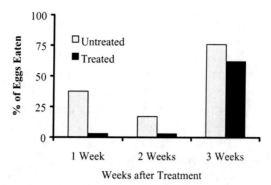

FIGURE 10. *Reduced predation on sod webworm eggs placed in Kentucky bluegrass at one or three weeks after the turf was treated with chlorpyrifos. Predation levels recovered five weeks after application of the pesticide. The difference between treated and untreated plots was statistically significant. Source: Reproduced with permission from ref. 46. Copyright 1992 United States Golf Association.*

Use of Parasitic Agents for Control of Turfgrass Insects. Several interesting biological controls have performed well under ideal conditions (47). Research programs are field testing a variety of organisms to determine which products will establish quickly and have predictable control. In laboratory and greenhouse studies, entomopathogenic nematodes have shown the most promise for controlling grub and caterpillar species. The nematode effectiveness is a function of the species selected and the conditions under which the organism is applied to the turf area. *Steinernema glaseri* and *Heterorhabditis bacteriophora* are effective on white grubs while *S. carpocapsae* is most effective against billbugs, cutworms, webworms and armyworms. Critical conditions include sunlight, irrigation and storage. Applications made in the early morning or evening followed by irrigation were most effective.

Bacteria such as *Bacillus thuringiensis* (Bt) and milky spore disease have been around for many years. The current commercial Bt products are slow to act, have a short residual time in the soil, and are ineffective on larger larvae. In recent years, the U.S. Department of Agriculture has identified a better strain of Bt (*B. japonesis* var. 'buibui') which is effective against the Oriental and Japanese beetle grubs. Milky spore disease against Japanese beetle grubs has been around for decades. Unfortunately, the disease has not been effective for turfgrass areas with high economic value.

Two fungi for controlling turfgrass pests include *Beauveria balliana* and *Metarhizium anisopliae*. Fungi may be more effective because they do not need to be ingested by the target insect. The fungal spore attaches itself to the insect, penetrates the circulatory system, and uses the host as an incubator to reproduce more spores. Research studies on the commercial production, cost and reliability of this type of biological control is just underway.

Cultural and Mechanical Practices

The USGA sponsored a few projects that evaluated the impact of a cultural or mechanical practices on reducing pest infestations. One of the best examples is the research conducted at University of Kentucky (48). Very little was known about the behavior of black cutworms in turf. The study determined where the moths laid their eggs and nightly behavior of cutworms on putting greens. It was found that black cutworm moths laid single eggs on the tips of the putting green leaf blades. More importantly, daily mowing removed 87% of the eggs.

Black cutworms thrived on perennial ryegrass and tall fescue surrounds (48). One source of infestation could be the eggs from putting green clippings strewn in adjacent areas. During nightly monitoring, it was observed black cutworms crawled considerable distances within a single night. Of the caterpillar tracks measured, about half originated from high grass off the putting green and terminated on the putting surface. The average length of the tracks was about 9 meters (30 feet).

These results suggest that black cutworm infestations on putting greens may originate, at least in part, from peripheral areas such as collars and roughs. Since eggs removed from the green can survive in the clippings, it is important to dispose of the clippings well away from the green. In addition, control measures should include a 9-meter buffer zone around the putting green to reduce reservoir populations in the surrounds. Because black cutworms are nocturnal, treatments are best applied at dusk.

Allelopathy

Chemical substances produced by some plants prevent or inhibit the growth of neighboring plants. For example, English walnut (*Juglens* sp.) are known to produce allelopathic substances. In Arkansas, twelve perennial ryegrasses that ranged from moderate to high stand density and zero to 95% endophyte infection were evaluated for their ability to decrease crabgrass populations. Bermudagrass fairway plots were overseeded with new seed lots of the 12 cultivars in the fall of 1994 and 1995. Half of each plot was then overseeded with crabgrass each spring and evaluated for crabgrass suppression. No differences in crabgrass stand could be attributed to any of the 12 cultivars (49).

A basic laboratory evaluation for allelopathy using *Lemna minor* L. (duckweed) measured allelopathic effects of plant tissue extracts on the growth rate of duckweed fronds. Extracts from shoots were applied to duckweed cell plates at three concentrations. The amount of allelopathic inhibition (or stimulation) of duckweed varied with shoot tissue sample season and extract concentration. All cultivars affected duckweed growth, but inconsistently. Perhaps eventually, selection of ryegrass cultivars for crabgrass inhibition may become an important part of IPM programs.

Selection and Breeding for Pest Resistance

Since 1982, the USGA has sponsored turfgrass breeding programs directed toward significantly reducing water use and maintenance costs. Among the maintenance costs, the amount of money spent on mowing, fertilization, and pesticide use is ranked very high. Turfgrass improvement efforts are very important because an integral part of IPM strategies is to use varieties that are well adapted to the local environmental and climatic conditions. Thus, new varieties with better abiotic and biotic stress resistance will have a positive role in IPM practices.

Conventional Breeding

One strategy to accomplish this goal was to improve specific characteristics within each species, such as water use or heat tolerance. This is a long-term approach, however, and can be expected to produce results in small increments over a period of many years. As an example, improved creeping bentgrasses began with vegetative cultivars in the 1920's to 'Penncross' (a seeded polycross) in 1954, to the recently developed seeded varieties.

Another strategy, and one that has the potential to produce a bigger return in a shorter period of time, is to replace stress-susceptible cool season grasses with stress-tolerant grasses that have improved turf characteristics. A good example of this strategy is buffalograss (*Buchloe dactyloides*), which in a short period has been significantly improved for turf quality. Buffalograss now is being used to replace perennial ryegrass (*Lolium perenne*) and Kentucky bluegrass (*Poa pratensis*) roughs in the central United States, resulting in water use savings of 50% or more and a large reduction in maintenance costs. Soon there will be buffalograsses for fairways, producing corresponding savings on those areas. Other non-traditional grasses being improved for turf characteristics are alkaligrass (*Puccinellia* spp.), blue grama (*Bouteloua gracilis*), fairway crested wheatgrass (*Agropyron cristatum*), inland saltgrass (*Distichlis* spp.), and curly mesquitegrass (*Hilaria belangeri*).

Yet another breeding strategy employed has been to expand the range of adaptation or use of existing stress-tolerant turfgrasses, with the hope of replacing less tolerant species. For example, if warm season grasses such as bermudagrass (*Cynodon dactylon*) can be improved for cold tolerance, it could be used to replace bentgrass (*Agrostis* spp.) and perennial ryegrass fairways in the transition zone areas of the United States. This would result in a tremendous reduction in water and pesticide use in these areas.

The last strategy is to develop improved, seeded, warm season grasses, such as bermudagrass, zoysiagrass (*Zoysia* spp.) and buffalograss, which could replace existing vegetatively propagated cultivars and save significant establishment costs. Availability of seeded types also would encourage courses in the transition zone to convert from high maintenance cool-season grasses to stress-tolerant warm-season species.

The USGA has financially supported turfgrass breeding programs in Georgia, New Jersey, Rhode Island, and Pennsylvania for many decades, with significant results. The new programs, initiated in the 1980's, have produced a number of improved cultivars or selections commercially available or released to seed companies for development (Table IX). All exhibit improved turf characteristics, stress tolerance or pest resistance. During the next decade, the number of new introductions will increase significantly, and the golf industry will be in a much better position to conserve and protect our natural resources.

Molecular Genetics

Over the last 75 years, a tremendous amount of effort has been exerted toward improving turfgrass species with conventional plant breeding methods. During the past decade, turfgrass improvement using cell and molecular techniques has been initiated. These new techniques are still in the early stages of development but hold great promise for the future. Biotechnology will enhance breeding efforts to develop turfgrasses that will meet the challenges of the next century in the following ways:

1. Molecular marker analysis

2. Genes with potential for turfgrass improvement

3. *In vitro* culture

4. Genetic engineering

*Molecular Marker Analysis.*Identifying the differences among varieties or cultivars of turfgrass species using molecular genetic analysis has made substantial progress in recent years (50). The new techniques are faster and more accurate than techniques used just a short time ago. Molecular markers linked to important genes controlling a desirable trait should make breeding programs more effective.

Genetic characterization of open-pollinated turfgrass species will present a different set of problems compared to the characterization of asexually propagated cultivars. We need to know something about the breeding behavior and genetics of turfgrass species to establish which genetic characterization techniques should be applied. Is the turfgrass species apomictic? Is it a homogeneous or heterogeneous population? In addition, the statistical analysis techniques to help interpret the tremendous amount of data that can be produced from molecular analysis need

TABLE IX

Turfgrass	University	Varieties and Germplasm Released
Creeping Bentgrass *Agrostis palustris*	Texas A&M University	CRENSHAW (Syn3-88), CATO (Syn4-88) and MARINER (Syn1-88), CENTURY (Syn92-1), IMPERIAL (Syn92-5), BACKSPIN (92-2)
	University of Rhode Island	PROVIDENCE
	Pennsylvania State University	PENNLINKS (PSU-126)
Colonial Bentgrass *Agrostis tenuis*	DSIR-New Zealand and University of Rhode Island	BR-1518 developed
Bermudagrass *Cynodon dactylon*	New Mexico State University	NuMex SAHARA, SONESTA, PRIMAVERA and other seed propagated varieties were developed.
	Oklahoma State University	OKS 91-11 and OKS 91-1
C. transvaalensis	Oklahoma State University	A release of germplasm for university and industry use is under consideration.
C. dactylon X C. transvaalensis	University of Georgia	TIFEAGLE (TW-72), TIFTON 10 and TIFSPORT (TIFTON 94 or MI-40)
Buffalograss *Buchloe dactyloides*	University of Nebraska	Vegetative varieties 609, 315, and 378. Seeded varieties CODY and TATANKA. Three new vegetative selections, NE 86-61, NE 86-120 and NE 91-118, are currently being processed for release.
Alkaligrass Puccinellia spp.	Colorado State University	Ten improved families developed.
Blue grama *Bouteloua gracilis*	Colorado State University	ELITE, NICE, PLUS and NARROW.
Fairway Crested Wheatgrass *Agropyron cristatum*	Colorado State University	Narrow leafed and rhizomatous populations were developed.
Curly Mesquitegrass *Hilaria belangeri*	University of Arizona	A "fine" and "roadside" population was developed.
Annual bluegrass *Poa annua var reptans*	University of Minnesota	DW-184 (MN #184) is commercially available. Selections MN #42, #117, #208, and #234 were released.
Zoysiagrass *Zoysia japonica* and *Z. matrella*	Texas A&M University	DIAMOND (DALZ8502), CAVALIER (DALZ8507), CROWNE (DALZ8512) and PALISADES (DALZ8514)
Seashore Paspalum *Paspalum vaginatum*	University of Georgia	One green type (AP 10) and one fairway type (PI 509018-1) released.

further development and need implementation in order to interpret molecular analysis results (51).

Genes with Potential for Turfgrass Improvement. Molecular and biochemical techniques allow researchers to examine how turfgrass plants respond to abiotic and biotic induced plant stress. Turfgrasses, like all plants, respond to plant stresses by up- or down-regulating genes. Some examples include the production of chitinase in response to disease pressure and cold temperatures (52, 53), the increased presence of desaturases that improve the properties of the cell wall (54), or the production of heat shock proteins in response to high temperatures (55, 56).

With regard to biotic stresses, such as disease problems, research with the chitinase gene demonstrates that genes for disease resistance may be introduced into turfgrass plants (53). However, a great deal more needs to be understood about how these disease-resistant genes will work in an entirely different species. Also, since turfgrasses are perennial, there are concerns that the introduction of a single gene will not produce long-lasting disease resistance.

In Vitro Culture. Tissue or *in vitro* culture already has proven to be a very useful tool in turfgrass breeding programs. The presence of somaclonal variation in many of the commercially important turfgrass species has been documented (55, 57). The presence of this genetic variation has allowed turfgrass scientists and breeders an additional means to improve turfgrass quality through selection of abiotic and biotic stress tolerance.

In vitro culture was used to produce interesting somaclonal variants of seashore paspalum (57). The application of this technique on seashore paspalum is particularly useful because this open-pollinated species produces less than 5% viable seed and is self-incompatible. Conventional breeding methods are limited, and *in vitro* culture produced more than 4,000 regenerants that varied in genetic color, growth rate, density and winter hardiness. More than 100 selections with improved turfgrass traits were selected for further evaluations.

Extensive selection and breeding of regenerated or transformed plants for agronomic characteristics is still required prior to their release as new cultivars. Using parental clones of existing cultivars as the explant material may provide the quickest and most rewarding approach. Work with the six parental clones of "Crenshaw" creeping bentgrass and five new zoysiagrass cultivars is evaluating this approach (58).

Several forage and turfgrass species do not produce economically viable quantities of seed for commercial production. With the development of artificial seed technology through *in vitro* culture, it may be feasible to use this system to propagate parents for commercial production and release of hybrid varieties (59). In addition, if the parents of a commercial variety can be manipulated *in vitro,* the artificial seed method could facilitate the creation of varieties with value-added traits introduced by genetic transformation.

For turfgrass species, *in vitro* culture has been the primary method used to produce somaclonal variants that are screened for an important characteristic under greenhouse or field evaluations. There is hope that *in vitro* culture can be used to actually select for superior somaclonal variants at the cellular level. Embryogenic bentgrass callus was screened *in vitro* for heat tolerance and disease resistance (55). The results of this effort led to the development of HPIS (i.e., host plant interaction system) that allows the disease pathogen and turfgrass species to be cultured together *in vitro*.

Genetic Engineering of Turfgrasses. This research effort has been possible due to the advances made with important food and fiber crops. However, a pleasant surprise is how easily the success with agricultural crops can be applied to turfgrass species. In less than five years, early efforts in genetic transformation have already produced turfgrass parental clones of commercial interest. Herbicide-resistant genes have been successfully introduced into creeping bentgrass (52, 60). Through traditional breeding methods, it now may be possible to incorporate these herbicide resistance genes into putting green bentgrasses. This will allow golf course superintendents to keep annual bluegrass (*Poa annua*) and other weeds out of their greens and fairways with fewer pesticide applications. Potentially, this could reduce water and pesticide use on greens.

It is hopeful that genetic engineering will expedite the development of improved disease and insect resistance in turfgrass varieties for golf courses. Two projects were initiated to introduce chitinase production genes into bentgrass, providing an internal mechanism to help control turfgrass diseases and thereby reduce pesticide use. In 1996, the USGA sponsored a symposium on turfgrass biotechnology, and in 1997 published the proceedings in book form titled, *Turfgrass Biotechnology: Molecular Approaches to Turfgrass Improvement* (61).

Application of Integrated Pest Management (IPM)

This approach relies on a combination of preventative and corrective measures to keep pest densities below levels that would cause unacceptable turf damage. Its goal is to manage pests effectively, economically, and with minimal risks to people and the environment. The process of IPM involves the following steps:

1. Sampling and monitoring turf areas to detect pests and evaluate how well control tactics have worked.
2. Pest identification in order to adequately understand the habits and life cycle of the organism and how it can be managed.
3. Decision making guided by action thresholds based on pest damage that justifies treatment or intervention.
4. Appropriate intervention that determines why a pest outbreak occurred, and if cultural practice adjustments can reduce damage or future outbreaks.

5. Follow-up that includes record-keeping to help predict future pest problems and to plan accordingly. This process also helps to evaluate which management practices work effectively.

6. Education to develop ongoing employee training focusing on pest recognition and agronomic factor that help them to make sound management decisions. Client education on management action to reduce pest problems (i.e., soil tests, aerification, dethatching, fertilization, and tree care) while providing a safe, environmentally responsible golf course.

Although USGA-sponsored research has not specifically addressed investigations on IPM as defined above, most of the research results will help with one or more of the steps outlined above. For example, in North Carolina, with cooperation with Cornell University, extensive research was conducted on the mole cricket behavior (62, 63). The results indicate that mole crickets are capable of avoiding pesticides applied to control them by burrowing deep into the soil until the active ingredient has degraded. A better understanding of mole cricket response to pesticide applications will help determine proper placement and timing of products that enhance contact with the insect.

Research conducted on white grubs (scarab beetle larvae) in Kentucky examined the role of several cultural practices on insect outbreaks (64). Field studies showed that withholding irrigation during peak flight of beetles, raising cutting height, and a light application of aluminum sulfate in the spring helped to reduce severity of subsequent infestations of Japanese beetle and masked chafer grubs. Grub densities were not affected by spring applications of lime or urea, but use of organic fertilizers (composted cow manure or activated sewage sludge) increased problems with green June beetle grubs. Use of a heavy roller was not effective for curative grub control. Soil moisture was the overriding factor determining distributions of root-feeding grubs in turf.

PEOPLE AND WILDLIFE

Pesticides and People

People are concerned about exposure they receive during a round of golf on turf that has been treated with pesticides. Exposure in this situation is caused by pesticide residues on the turf surface that rub off onto people or their equipment during a round of golf. A preliminary risk assessment was conducted for golfers who are exposed to a putting green treated with insecticides. Under the assumptions of this study, the golfer would have received about one-third of the lifetime reference dose considered safe by the USEPA (65). This is not to say that golfers or workers could not receive unsafe exposure to pesticides on golf courses. Under the conditions of this study, though, the golfer would not have been at significant risk.

Other studies that have determined dislodgeable residue levels indicate that less than 1% of the pesticides could be rubbed off immediately after application when the turf was still wet. In addition, the 1% could be reduced significantly by irrigating after the pesticide was applied. After the pesticides dried on the turf, only minimal amounts could be rubbed off. Volatilization studies report that organophosphate insecticides that possess high toxicity and volatility might result in exposure situations that cannot be deemed completely safe as judged by the US EPA Hazard Quotient determination (Table X). Additional biomonitoring studies will be needed to determine the extent of the risk, if any (9, 10, 11, 15).

Golf Course Benefits

Most media attention concerning golf courses tends to focus on the potential negative impacts of turfgrass and golf course management. Although people in our industry know intuitively that there are many benefits associated with turfgrasses and golf courses, the scientific basis for many of these benefits had not been documented. In 1994, through a USGA grant, Drs. James Beard and Robert Green conducted an exhaustive literature search and documented many of these benefits. The results of their work were published in the *Journal of Environmental Quality* (66), and were summarized by and are available from the United States Golf Association.

Wildlife and Golf Courses

Eight years ago, the USGA and Audubon International, Inc. developed the Audubon Cooperative Sanctuary Program (ACSP) to educate everyone involved with the game of golf about the environment. The goal was not to list the things that golf courses did wrong, but teach people what could be done to make the golf course better. The program encourages golf courses to become certified in the following six areas: (1) environmental planning, (2) wildlife and habitat management, (3) water conservation, (4) water quality management, (5) integrated pest management, and (6) member/public involvement.

This certification program has implemented findings from the USGA Turfgrass and Environmental Research Program. It is great to produce research information, but it is more important to put it into practice. Pesticide and nutrient fate, water conservation, and integrated pest management are areas where a significant amount of research has been completed. In order for the golf course superintendent to successfully implement suggested practices from the research studies, the golfer must first be educated about the environment. The ACSP is an important asset in this education effort!

TABLE X

Inhalation Hazard Quotients (IHQs) for Turfgrass Pesticides in the High,
Intermediate and Low Vapor Pressure Group

Group	Pesticide	HQ[1] Day 1	Day 2	Day 3
Group 1: High vapor pressure (i.e., vapor pressures > 1.0 x 10^{-5} mm Hg)	DDVP	0.06	0.04	0.02
	Ethoprop	50.0	26	1.2
	Diazinon	3.3	2.4	1.2
	Isazofos	8.6	6.7	3.4
	Chlorpyrifos	0.09	0.1	0.04
Group 2: Intermediate vapor pressure (i.e., 10^{-5} mm Hg > vapor pressures > 10^{-7} mm Hg)	Trichlorfon	0.02	0.004	0.004
	Bendiocarb	0.02	0.002	0.002
	Isofenphos	n/d[2]	0.02	n/d
	Chlorthalonil	0.001	0.001	0.0003
	Propiconazole	n/d	n/d	n/d
	Carbaryl	0.0005	0.0001	0.00004
Group 3: Low vapor pressure (i.e., vapor pressure < 10^{-7} mm Hg)	Thiophanate-methyl	n/d	n/d	n/d
	Iprodione	n/d	n/d	n/d
	Cyfluthrin	n/d	n/d	n/d

[1]The HQs reported are the maximum daily IHQ's measured, all of which occurred during the 11:00 A.M. to 3:00 P.M. sampling period.

[2] n/d = non-detect

Source: Adapted from ref. 15.

CONCLUSION

The university research investigating pesticide and nutrient fate was the first extensive self-examination of golf's impact on water quality and the environment. What has the environmental research program told us? First, the university research shows that most pesticides used on golf courses have a negligible effect on the environment. The word "negligible" is used because we did find pesticides and fertilizers in runoff or leachate collected from research plots. However, under most conditions, the small amount collected (parts per billion) were found at levels well below the health and safety standards established by the Environmental Protection Agency (EPA). The studies demonstrated that the turfgrass canopy, thatch, and root system were an effective filter or sponge. As one would expect, the results documented that heavy textured soils adsorbed pesticides and fertilizers better than light textured or sandy soils.

The environmental research program has had a positive impact on golf. The program was run in an unbiased fashion, results have been published in peer-reviewed scientific journals, and the message, *be careful and responsible* is getting out to golf course superintendents around the country. Future efforts will focus on scaling up the size of research plots to simulate entire fairways or greens. Some of these studies will be conducted on golf courses. The new projects will document the impact of properly constructed and maintained golf courses on water quality.

The USGA has made progress in understanding the impact that golf courses have on the environment. More is being done to make golf courses both a recreational and environmental asset to the community. An excellent foundation of environmental information, based on scientific investigations rather than emotional rhetoric, has been established. The USGA, and the game of golf, need to keep asking questions and looking for new ways to maintain golf course grasses. More important, efforts should be increased to educate the golfer about environmental issues.

LITERATURE CITED

1. Snow, J. T. *USGA Green Section Record.* **1995**, *33(3), 3–6.*

2. Bowman, D. C.; Devitt, D. A.; Miller, W. W. *USGA Green Section Record.* **1995**, *33(1), 45–49.*

3. Joo, Y. K.; Christians, N. E.; Blackmer, A. M. *J. of Fert. Issues.* **1987**, *4, 98–102.*

4. Joo, Y. K.; Christians, N. E.; Blackmer, A. M. *J. of Soil Sci.* **1991**, *55, 528–530.*

5. Branham, B. E.; Miltner, E. D.; Rieke. P. E. *USGA Green Section Record.* **1995**, *33(1), 33–37.*

6. Miltner, E. D.; Branham, B.E.; Paul, E. A.; Rieke, P. E. *Crop Sci.* **1996**, *36, 1427–1433.*

7. Starrett, S. K.; Christians. N. E. *USGA Green Section Record.* **1995**, *33(1), 23–25.*

8. Starrett, S. K.; Christians, N. E.; Austin, T. A. *J. of Irrg. Drain. Eng.* **1995**, *121, 390–395.*

9. Cooper, R. J.; Clark; J. M.; Murphy. K. C. *USGA Green Section Record.* **1995**, 33(1), 19–22.

10. Murphy, K.C.; Cooper, R. J.; Clark, J. M. *Crop Sci.* **1996**, *36, 1446–1454.*

11. Murphy, K.C.; Cooper, R. J.; Clark, J. M. *Crop Sci.* **1996**, *36, 1455–1461.*

12. Snyder, G. H.; Cisar, J. L. In *USGA Environmental Research Program: Pesticide and Nutrient Fate 1996 Annual Project Reports*; Kenna, M. P., Ed.; USGA Green Section Research: Stillwater, OK. **1996**, pp 109–140.

13. Yates, M. V.; Green, R. L.; Gan, J. In *USGA Environmental Research Program: Pesticide and Nutrient Fate 1996 Annual Project Reports*; Kenna, M. P., Ed.; USGA Green Section Research: Stillwater, OK. **1996**, pp 80–94.

14. Yates, M. V. *USGA Green Section Record.* **1995**, *33(1),10–12.*

15. Clark, J. M. In *USGA 1996 Turfgrass and Environmental Research Summary*; Kenna, M. P.; Snow, J. T., Eds.; United States Golf Association: Far Hills, NJ. **1997**, pp 60–63.

16. Smith, A. E.; Bridges, D. C. In *USGA 1997 Turfgrass and Environmental Research Summary*; Kenna, M. P.; Snow, J. T., Eds. ; United States Golf Association: Far Hills, NJ. **1998**, pp 74–75.

17. Carroll, M. J.; Hill, R. L. In *USGA 1997 Turfgrass and Environmental Research Summary*; Kenna, M. P.; Snow, J. T., Eds.; United States Golf Association: Far Hills, NJ. **1998**, pp 70–71.

18. Turco, R. In *USGA 1997 Turfgrass and Environmental Research Summary*; Kenna, M. P.; Snow, J. T., Eds.; United States Golf Association: Far Hills, NJ. **1998**, pp 79–82.

19. Lickfeldt, D. W.; Branham, B. E. *J. of Environ. Qual.* **1995**, *24*, 980–985.

20. Snyder, G. H.; Cisar, J. L. *Int. Turfgrass Soc. Res. J.* **1993**, *7, 978–983.*

21. Snyder, G. H.; Cisar, J. L. *USGA Green Section Record.* **1995**, *33(1), 15–18.*

22. Cisar, J. L.; Snyder, G. H. *Int. Turfgrass Soc. Res. J.* **1993**, *7, 971–977.*

23. Cisar, J. L.; Snyder, G. H. *Crop Sci.* **1996**, *36, 1433–1438.*

24. Horst, G. L.; Shea, P. J.; Christians, N. E. *USGA Green Section Record.* **1995**, *33(1), 26–28.*

25. Horst, G. L.; Shea, P. J.; Christians, N. E.; Miller, D. R.; Stuefer–Powell, C.; Starrett, S. K. *Crop Sci.* **1996**, *36, 362–370.*

26. Brauen, S. E.; Stahnke, G. *USGA Green Section Record.* **1995**, *33(1), 29–32.*

27. Kenna, M. P. *USGA Green Section Record.* **1994**, *32(4), 12–15.*

28. Petrovic, A. M. *USGA Green Section Record.* **1995**, *33(1), 38–41.*

29. Cohen, S. Z.; Wauchope, R. D.; Klein, A. W.; Eadsforth, C. V.; Graney, R. *Pure & Applied Chem.* **1995**, *67, 2109–2148.*

30. Smith, A. E.; Tilloston, T. R. In *Pesticides in Urban Environments;* Racke, K. D.; Leslie, A. R., Eds.; ACS Symposium Series 522; American Chemical Society: Washington, D.C. **1993**, pp. 168–181.

31. Smith, A. E. *USGA Green Section Record.* **1995**, *33(1), 13–14.*

32. Linde, D. T. *Surface Runoff and Nutrient Transport Assessment on Creeping Bentgrass and Perennial Ryegrass Turf.* M. S. Thesis, Pennsylvania State University, The Graduate School College of Agricultural Sciences, *1993*, p 84.

33. Linde, D. T.; Watschke, T. L.; Borger, J. A. *USGA Green Section Record.* **1995**, *33(1), 42–44.*

34. Linde, D. T.; Watschke, T. L.; Jarrett A. R.; Borger, J. A. *Agron. J.* **1995**, *87, 176–182.*

35. Smith, A. E.; Bridges, D. C. In *USGA 1995 Turfgrass and Environmental Research Summary;* Kenna, M. P., Ed.; United States Golf Association: Far Hills, NJ. **1996**, pp 76–77.

36. Smith, A. E.; Bridges, D. C. In *USGA 1996 Turfgrass and Environmental Research Summary;* Kenna, M. P.; Snow, J. T., Eds.; United States Golf Association: Far Hills, NJ. **1997**, pp 72–73.

37. Baird, J. H. In *USGA 1995 Turfgrass and Environmental Research Summary;* Kenna, M. P., Ed.; United States Golf Association: Far Hills, NJ. **1996**, pp 64–65.

38 . Cole, J. H.; Baird, J. H; Basta, N. T.; Hunke, R. L.; Storm, D. E.; Johnson, G. V.; Payton, M. E.; Smolen, M. D.; Martin, D. L.; Cole, J. C. *J. of Environ. Qual.* 1997, *26, 1589–1598.*

39. Baird, J. H. In *USGA 1997 Turfgrass and Environmental Research Summary;* Kenna, M. P.; Snow, J. T., Eds.; United States Golf Association: Far Hills, NJ. 1998, pp 56–59.

40. Couch, H. B. In *Diseases of Turfgrasses;* Krieger Publishing Company: Malabar, FL. 1995, pp 249–257.

41. Nelson, E. B. *USGA Green Section Record.* 1992, *30(2), 11–14.*

42. Harmon, G. E. In *USGA 1996 Turfgrass and Environmental Research Summary;* Kenna, M. P.; Snow, J. T., Eds.; United States Golf Association: Far Hills, NJ. 1997, pp 92–93.

43. Nelson, E. B. In *Turfgrass Biotechnology: Cell and Molecular Genetic Approaches to Turfgrass Improvement;* Sticklen, M. B.; Kenna, M. P., Eds.; Ann Arbor Press: Chelsea, MI. 1997, pp 55–92.

44. Kobayashi, D. In *1995 Turfgrass and Environmental Research Summary;* Kenna, M. P., Ed.; United States Golf Association: Far Hills, NJ. 1996, pp 50–51.

45. Giblin–Davis, R. M. In *1996 Turfgrass and Environmental Research Summary;* Kenna, M. P.; Snow, J. T., Eds.; United States Golf Association: Far Hills, NJ. 1997, pp 54–56.

46. Potter, D. A. *USGA Green Section Record.* 1992, *30(6), 6–10.*

47. Schrimpf, P. *Lawn & Landscape.* 1997, *18 (3), 66–69, 122.*

48. Williamson, R. C.; Potter, D. A. *USGA Green Section Record.* 1998, *36(1), 6–8.*

49. King, J. W. In *1997 Turfgrass and Environmental Research Summary;* Kenna, M. P.; Snow, J. T., Eds.; United States Golf Association: Far Hills, NJ. 1998, pp 53–54.

50. Kenna, M. P. In *Turfgrass Biotechnology: Cell and Molecular Genetic Approaches to Turfgrass Improvement;* Sticklen, M. B.; Kenna, M. P., Eds.; Ann Arbor Press: Chelsea, MI. 1997, pp vii–xi.

51. Huff, D. R. In *Turfgrass Biotechnology: Cell and Molecular Genetic Approaches to Turfgrass Improvement;* Sticklen, M. B.; Kenna, M. P., Eds.; Ann Arbor Press: Chelsea, MI. 1997, pp 19–30.

52. Anderson, M. P.; Taliaferro, C. M.; Gatschet, M.; de los Reyes, B.; Assefa, S. In *Turfgrass Biotechnology: Cell and Molecular Genetic Approaches to Turfgrass Improvement;* Sticklen, M. B.; Kenna, M. P., Eds.; Ann Arbor Press: Chelsea, MI. 1997, pp 115–134.

53. Zhong, H.; Liu, C. A.; Vargas, J.; Penner, D.; Sticklen, M. B. *In Turfgrass Biotechnology: Cell and Molecular Genetic Approaches to Turfgrass Improvement;* Sticklen, M. B.; Kenna, M. P., Eds.; Ann Arbor Press: Chelsea, MI. 1997, pp 203–210.

54. Baird, W. V.; Samala, S.; Powell, G. L.; Riley, M. B.; Yan, J.; Wells, J. In *Turfgrass Biotechnology: Cell and Molecular Genetic Approaches to Turfgrass Improvement;* Sticklen, M. B.; Kenna, M. P., Eds.; Ann Arbor Press: Chelsea, MI. 1997, pp 135–142.

55. Krans, J. V.; Park, S. L.; Tomaso–Peterson, M.; Luthe, D. S. In *Turfgrass Biotechnology: Cell and Molecular Genetic Approaches to Turfgrass Improvement;* Sticklen, M. B.; Kenna, M. P., Eds.; Ann Arbor Press: Chelsea, MI. 1997, pp 211–222.

56. Sweeney, P. M.; Danneberger, T. K.; DiMascio, J. A.; Kamalay, J. C. In *Turfgrass Biotechnology: Cell and Molecular Genetic Approaches to Turfgrass Improvement;* Sticklen, M. B.; Kenna, M. P., Eds.; Ann Arbor Press: Chelsea, MI. 1997, pp 143–152.

57. Cardona, C. A.; Duncan, R. R. In *Turfgrass Biotechnology: Cell and Molecular Genetic Approaches to Turfgrass Improvement;* Sticklen, M. B.; Kenna, M. P., Eds.; Ann Arbor Press: Chelsea, MI. 1997, pp 229–238.

58. Yamamoto, I.; Engelke, M. C. In *Turfgrass Biotechnology: Cell and Molecular Genetic Approaches to Turfgrass Improvement*; Sticklen, M. B.; Kenna, M. P., Eds.; Ann Arbor Press: Chelsea, MI. 1997, pp 165–172.

59. Brittan–Loucas, H.; Tar'an, B.; Bowley, S. R.; McKersie, B. D.; Kasha, K. J. In *Turfgrass Biotechnology: Cell and Molecular Genetic Approaches to Turfgrass Improvement*; Sticklen, M. B.; Kenna, M. P., Eds.; Ann Arbor Press: Chelsea, MI. 1997, pp 173–182.

60. Lee, L.; Day, P. In *Turfgrass Biotechnology: Cell and Molecular Genetic Approaches to Turfgrass Improvement*; Sticklen, M. B.; Kenna, M. P., Eds.; Ann Arbor Press: Chelsea, MI. 1997, pp 195–202.

61. *Turfgrass Biotechnology: Cell and Molecular Genetic Approaches to Turfgrass Improvement*; Sticklen, M. B.; Kenna, M. P., Eds.; Ann Arbor Press: Chelsea, MI. 1997, 256 p.

62. Brandenburg, R. L.; Villani, M. G. In *USGA 1997 Turfgrass and Environmental Research Summary*; Kenna, M. P.; Snow, J. T., Eds.; United States Golf Association: Far Hills, NJ. 1998, pp 43–44.

63. Brandenburg, R. L. *TurfGrass TRENDS*. 1997, *6(1), 1–8.*

64. Potter, D. In *USGA 1997 Turfgrass and Environmental Research Summary*; Kenna, M. P.; Snow, J. T., Eds.; United States Golf Association: Far Hills, NJ. 1998, pp 39–42.

65. Borgert, C. J.; et al. *USGA Green Section Record*. 1994, *33(2), 11–14.*

66. Beard, J. B.; Green, R. L. *J. of Environ. Qual.* 1994, *23, 452–460.*

THE OLD COLLIER GOLF CLUB: FACILITY CASE STUDY

In an attempt to describe for you the efforts undertaken at one golf course development in regard to the various planning, construction, and management issues described in this book, I offer the following case study about The Old Collier Golf Club, located in Naples, Florida. As you read the case study, keep in mind that the property on which The Old Collier Golf Club golf course was built was originally permitted for an 800-unit development. Imagine what the property would have looked like with 800 homes on it, compared with what it ultimately became.

There are many exceptional golf course projects from which to choose, but I decided on The Old Collier Golf Club for a number of reasons. The Old Collier Golf Club was the first golf course development to achieve the designation of Certified Audubon International Gold Signature Sanctuary. This is the highest level of certification offered by Audubon International. In addition, The Old Collier Golf Club has chosen to use a salt tolerant variety of turfgrass on the greens, tees, and fairways, and is the first golf course in the United States to use this type of turf on the entire golf course. Finally, in conjunction with its innovative use of turfgrass, there is a direct connection between the USGA-funded research that has led to the development of paspalum turfgrass for use on a golf course. Tim Hiers, Golf Course Manager at The Old Collier Golf Club, has stated publicly that, "If it weren't for the research efforts of the USGA, The Old Collier Golf Club would not be here at all."

Therefore, I view The Old Collier Golf Club as an internationally significant demonstration model for appropriate planning, design, and construction that blends nearly all aspects of sustainability, that is based on scientific research, and that has an ongoing monitoring program. As part of the certification requirements,

Audubon International requires the production of a case study for all members of the Gold Signature Program, and the case study for The Old Collier Golf Club follows. It was written by Dr. Joel Howard, who at the time was the natural resource manager of The Old Collier Golf Club. Joel has since moved on and is presently the senior natural resource manager for WCI Communities, Inc., and is overseeing the natural resource management and educational aspects of ten WCI Communities' projects, all of which are enrolled as members of the Audubon International Gold Signature Program.

Facility Case Study: The Old Collier Golf Club, Naples, Florida*

Prepared by

JOEL R. HOWARD, PH.D.
Natural Resource Manager

AN AUDUBON INTERNATIONAL CERTIFIED GOLD SIGNATURE GOLF COURSE

I. Overview

The Old Collier Golf Club (TOCGC), Naples, Collier County, Florida is the first, Audubon International certified, Gold Signature Cooperative Sanctuary golf course. This designation comes under the aegis of the Audubon (International) Signature Program. As with other Audubon International designations, Gold Signature Sanctuary status carries with it a commitment to merging wildlife conservation, habitat enhancement, resource conservation, environmental improvement, and sustainable development. But different from all other levels of affiliation with Audubon International, Gold Signature members establish a partnership with Audubon International *prior* to project location and design. Then, experts from the Audubon International Institute prepare an Environmental Master Plan for all aspects of the property, including very detailed, site-specific strategies for natural

*Copyright 2004, Audubon International. Used with permission.

FIGURE 1. *Hole #11.*

resource conservation and management, architecture, infrastructure, landscaping, and community outreach. The success of any program can be measured by the degree of correlation between initial stated objective and end result or outcome. Regarding the objectives of the Audubon Signature Program, The Old Collier Golf Club exemplifies and validates the concept of co-habitable "common ground" for sustainable economic development and long-term environmental quality.

Environmentally sensitive factors such as regional hydrology, wetlands, and threatened species habitat make this parcel unique and strongly influenced the project design and implementation. The entire Old Collier property consists of roughly 267 acres of mixed upland and wetland habitat bounded to the north by the Cocohatchee River, and to the east, south, and west by major thoroughfares servicing commercial, residential, and institutional development (Figure 2). Prior to construction the parcel was undeveloped except for a storm water management system servicing surrounding residential and commercial properties, and it had been zoned for a planned, 800-unit development. Of the 267 total acres, approximately 53 acres of mangrove and wetland habitat bordering the Cocohatchee River were set aside and remain untouched. The golf course is superimposed on the remaining 214 acres of primarily upland habitat. The project consists of an 18-hole

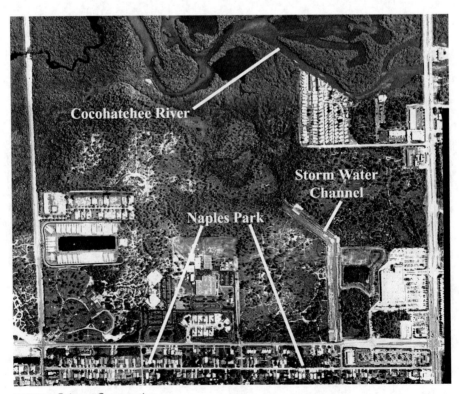

FIGURE 2. *Prior to Construction.*

"golf-only" facility (i.e., no pools, tennis courts, or residents) with 77 acres of irrigated turf; 28 acres of surface water distributed over 11 wholly contained, man-made lakes; and approximately 109 acres of connected native habitat.

II. Water Quality Management

Since the Cocohatchee River (north boundary of the property) is designated as an Outstanding Florida Waterway (OFW), water quality was an overriding factor in The Old Collier Golf Club project from its inception. Succinctly stated, the water quality objective at TOCGC is to maintain or improve the hydrologic standard that was in place prior to property development. In its undeveloped state the property served as a buffer zone between the River and the 400+ acre Naples Park residential development to the south (Figure 2). According to stipulations for development set forth by the South Florida Water Management District, it was necessary to ensure that the golf course project would not alter the existing hydrology of the area. That is to say, the project could neither impede drainage water exiting Naples Park, nor accelerate water movement toward, nor allow overland flow into, the Cocohatchee channel. To protect from direct overland flow into the River, design specifications dictated that, after development, the property must be equipped to retain the total water-equivalent of a 25-year storm falling within the property borders plus the water draining from Naples Park following a storm of that severity.

To control and contain the projected water volume from a 25-year storm, eleven lakes (totaling slightly over 28 acres) were constructed on the property (Figure 3). Underground pipes connect nine of the eleven lakes so that they may act as a unified storm water management system. A portion of the piping system serves as a direct replacement for the original aboveground storm-water drainage channel (labeled in Figure 2). This surrogate storm water channel occurs in the form of a series of three, side-by-side, 72-inch pipes that carry the storm-water influx from Naples Park through two lakes and then to the wetland zone very near the end of the old storm water drain channel. The remainder of the storm water management system consists of single, 24-inch pipes through which storm water accumulations are shared among all lakes and eventually channeled to the river basin in a slow, controlled release. In addition to the storm water management system, water quality is addressed daily by taking full advantage of the "prescription" irrigation system and by using best management practices (BMPs). Water quality BMPs include minimizing overall chemical applications (discussed in the "Integrated Pest Management" section of this report) and implementing operational procedures that isolate turf chemicals from the lakes.

The "prescription" irrigation system is configured such that water application is strictly limited to turfgrass areas. This is achieved by watering turf edges with

FIGURE 3. *Final locations of water management lakes shown with original property.*

FIGURE 4. *Underground pipes for the water management system.*

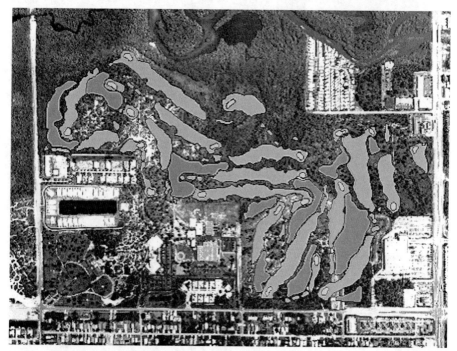

FIGURE 5. *Proposed site plan for TOCGC: January 2000*

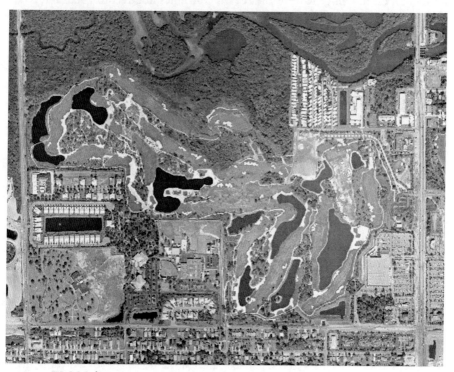

FIGURE 6. *TOCGC during grow-in: January 2001.*

directional sprinkler heads positioned to throw water back toward the center of the grassed areas. While this design serves as a water conservation feature, directional irrigation also impacts the quality of water eventually reaching the Cocohatchee River by filtering irrigation water through dense turfgrass. Also discussed later in this report are the water quality protections incorporated in the Resource Management Center.

III. Water Conservation

Water conservation is probably the single most critical factor impacting sustainable development in Southwest Florida. From 1992 to 2001 southern Florida has incurred an average annual water deficit. Throughout 2001 Lake Okeechobee was at record low levels. The situation was viewed sufficiently problematic that the South Florida Water Management District imposed Modified Phase II water-use restrictions (indicating "severe" water shortage), and was on the verge of moving to Phase III restrictions (indicating "extreme" shortage). Despite this on-going problem, population growth in the region continues at a record pace, and many new housing communities feature golf courses as the major amenity. If development in Southwest Florida is to continue at a sustainable rate, it is imperative to employ every possible tactic to reduce water use.

At TOCGC the very first consideration was to find a variety of grass that would best fit the objective of minimizing water consumption, particularly fresh water consumption. Seashore Paspalum was selected partly because of its deep-rooted character and low water requirement compared to other turf grasses. Seashore Paspalum also has the advantage of being tolerant to water with high Total Dissolved Solids (TDS), including high levels of Sodium Chloride (NaCl), which would be detrimental or even lethal to other turfgrass varieties. TOCGC design took full advantage of these Seashore Paspalum characteristics. Irrigation water is tapped mainly from two sources that are of very little use in supporting the human population in SW Florida. The first pump station installed at TOCGC draws water directly from the Cocohatchee River at the north edge of the property. Since this is a tidal river, during dry-season (winter) months the TDS content of this water often exceeds 25,000 ppm, and in many instances approaches pure seawater with TDS of 34,000 ppm. It is reasonable to assume that about 50% of the seawater TDS load is actual NaCl. The second TOCGC pump station pulls water from a holding pond replenished from an aquifer 587 feet below the surface. The water from this well is naturally high in sulfur and bicarbonates (5200 ppm TDS), which makes it non-potable for humans without substantial treatment; Seashore Paspalum, however, thrives on this water. The well is "artesian" in nature, which means there is sufficient pressure in the aquifer to push the water all the way to the surface without need of an energy-consuming pump. During the first 16 months of managing these water sources a distinct water-use strategy evolved. River water supplements precipitation during the rainy-season (summer months) when river flow is primarily seaward and TDS (salinity) falls between 2,000 and 10,000 ppm. Then, from November through May, the deep well is used as the primary irrigation source.

In any climate where evapotranspiration (ET) exceeds precipitation, chemical "salts" accumulate at the soil surface. During the dry season, TOCGC personnel monitor for signs of physiological wilt (bluish discoloration) in the turf. Soil TDS is sampled and if the level is above 2000 to 3000 ppm it is necessary to initiate a "fresh water" flush of the soil. The process of flushing salts from the turf root zone uses the third source of irrigation water at TOCGC: the on-property lakes. In the event of high soil TDS, the prescription is a full irrigation cycle using lake water. Because this process effectively taps the surficial (shallow) water table, soil salt levels are closely monitored, and fresh water flushes are scheduled only when TDS readings exceed the acceptable threshold.

All irrigation programming takes advantage of the on-site weather station wired directly to the irrigation computer. Evapotranspiration (ET) is monitored daily, and irrigation requirements adjusted accordingly. Irrigation design also plays an important role in water conservation. TOCGC has nearly 2300 sprinkler heads. The heads range from short-throw 720 series to larger 760 series heads. Much of the past year has been devoted to fine-tuning the system to water according to need. The golf course is zoned into several partitions based on a variety of criteria, and corresponding "programs" selectively water these partitions; e.g., all the turf, tees only, greens only, "hot-spots" only, etc. etc. The irrigation programming integrates computer driven ET data with soil probe analysis and visual observation. The measurable result is minimal overall water use, and a virtually insignificant impact on the potable water supply

IV. Wildlife Conservation and Habitat Enhancement

Given that TOCGC is a Gold Signature Sanctuary course, wildlife conservation and habitat enhancement were designed into the property from the earliest planning stages. Pre-construction soil, topographic, vegetation, and animal surveys established baseline data for the property. Using that information as a guide, the golf course was superimposed on the property so as to optimize space distribution between that necessary to create a championship level golf course, and that necessary to retain the greatest possible percentage of continuous, diverse habitat. This process enhanced the carrying capacity for a wide range of mammals, birds, amphibians, reptiles and insects.

FIGURE 7. *A resident gopher tortoise.*

Adjacent to the tidal Cocohatchee River, 50+ acres of the property clearly qualify for designation as "wetlands" under Section 404 of the Clean Water Act. Away from the river, the "upland" portion of the property contains at least 50 acres of prime Gopher Tortoise habitat. As part of the Audubon International Signature Program philosophy, these and other valuable habitat features were identified and isolated during the design and construction phases, and now remain intact for long-term preservation. On numerous occasions during the past two seasons, documented sightings are recorded for adult and juvenile gopher tortoise either in their native scrub oak/pine habitat or making their way across open turf areas. During winter and spring months, adult and fledgling eagles from an adjacent nest are often observed roosting in snags or trees on The Old Collier Golf Club property.

FIGURE 8. *Bald Eagle at TOCGC.*

FIGURE 9. *Habitat juxtaposition as seen from #15 tees.*

FIGURE 10. *Purple martin house.*

As for diversity, the species originally found on the property have been retained. Moreover, maintaining snags, adding birdhouses, creating brush piles, and the substantial addition of open freshwater, grassland, and edge habitats collectively contributes to increased species richness in the form of numerous waterfowl, song birds, ground nesters, and birds of prey that were not observed on the site prior to development. Annual wildlife species and habitat monitoring will document long-term population patterns for both former and new residents.

FIGURE 11. *Classic snag.*

FIGURE 12. *Opportunities abound for cavity nesters.*

V. Integrated Pest Management

A. HISTORICAL PERSPECTIVE

To best explain Integrated Pest Management (IPM) as it is applied at The Old Collier Golf Club, a brief, historical review of pest "control" will be helpful.

Coping with "pests" has always been a problem for agronomists; "pest" being defined as "any agent exerting a deleterious or undesirable effect." For centuries, in the absence of viable treatment options, pests were simply accepted as part of the process. Then, encouraged by apparent successes using powerful chemicals developed in the 1940s, the philosophy for dealing with pests shifted from "acceptance" to "control," and the "control" objective was often times eradication. By the early 1960s, 20 years of widespread, unregulated chemical application had not achieved the desired eradication, but instead resulted in two unexpected consequences: resistance of target organisms to even the most powerful chemicals, and collateral decline of non-target species such as birds and amphibians. Spurred in part by these results, "ecology" and "environment" became household words during the 1970s, and continuing studies revealed that indiscriminant use of chemicals exerted far reaching deleterious effects on all organisms—including humans. These findings signaled the need for a different pest management strategy relying less on chemicals and more on natural "checks and balances." The term which first appeared to identify this strategy was *Integrated Pest Management* (IPM). By the 1990's the term "IPM" had evolved to imply much more of an *ecosystem approach* to managing plant communities. Terms found in the literature from that period (e.g., *Intelligent* Pest Management and Integrated *Plant* Management) reflect the expanded "IPM" perspective.

Regardless of the specific name, IPM represents a major paradigm shift away from the "control" mentality that was prevalent during the 1940s, '50s, and early '60s. Pesticide application programs are often categorized as either "preventative" or "curative." Preventative programs are control oriented, and consist of regular, periodic applications of pesticides to continually keep pests in "check." History proves that the web of ecosystem interactions is so complex that "control" of the entire system or even single components (e.g., an undesirable species) is highly improbable. Shifting from preventative to curative management philosophy requires acceptance of "pests" as endemic, opportunistic organisms competing to survive. This means that, under the curative approach, there will likely always be at least some evidence of pest impacts. Also, under the curative philosophy, treatment to suppress pest-related effects is applied only when pest population levels reach epidemic proportions, and become manifest in the form of damage that surpasses an established threshold level of acceptability. The curative philosophy provides at least three correlated advantages: (1) reduced pesticide use, (2) reduced likelihood of pesticide resistance, and (3) reduced operating costs. Considering these features alone, IPM holds a substantial advantage.

B. IPM AND TOCGC DESIGN

A basic IPM principle is choosing the "right plant for the right place." A key element to successful management of any plant system is to mimic natural processes. The species composition found in "natural" plant communities is the visible end product of environmental "filtering," and the "filter" which separates surviving genotypes from non-survivors is "competition." Of the millions of plant propagules deposited annually, the long-term survivors are those plants whose genetic requirements align most closely with the supply of growth factors (light, heat, water, CO_2, O_2, nutrients) available on that site. When supply matches requirements, the organism is a strong competitor; the strongest competitor becomes the dominant genotype. Conversely, when requirements exceed supply, the genotype cannot successfully survive and reproduce, and therefore holds no prominent place in the system. It could be said that, "the ability of an organism to compete is related to its level of stress." Any organism under stress (conditions not well suited for survival) is a poor competitor. The antithesis being, if environmental conditions are ideally matched (little or no stress), an organism will be a very strong competitor. It follows then, that if one has the luxury of "creating" a managed landscape, it is wise to mimic natural processes and select plant species whose requirements closely match the environmental characteristics. Given that The Old Collier Golf Club site occurs within a region with high potential population and low potential fresh water supply, it made sense to select a grass for the golf course that possessed excellent golf turf characteristics and a tolerance for poor quality water. In accordance with these criteria, Seashore Paspalum was chosen as the grass for use over the entire golf course. As mentioned earlier in the section on Water Conservation, *Paspalum* has a very high tolerance for brackish water. During the SW Florida dry season, one source of water at TOCGC is virtual seawater, usually with total dissolved solid (TDS) content approaching 34,000 ppm. Experience has proved that, while *Paspalum* grows better at lower TDS loads, it is capable of survival using straight seawater. This makes *Paspalum* a strong competitor at TOCGC, thus providing the opportunity to naturally survive attacks from pathogenic organisms.

C. OPERATIONAL IPM AT TOCGC

TOCGC adopts an expanded meaning of "IPM" to reflect that successful plant community management goes well beyond the treatment of "pests." At TOCGC,

"IPM" is understood to mean "Integrated *Plant* Management." "Plant" is taken to include the entirety of the human and material resources comprising the operation (i.e., equipment, people, natural resources, and man-made resources). *Paspalum* as "the right plant in the right place" serves not only to reduce pesticide applications, but also to reduce the consumption of other resources such as fertilizer, water, and time. In addition to genotype selection, turfgrass management that contributes to the overall goal of sustainable development requires an appropriate daily maintenance philosophy, and it also requires wise decisions on the part of all employees everyday.

On a daily basis, IPM at TOCGC is a crew-wide function. Specifically with respect to "pests"; insects, fungi, and weeds are the three broad categories that impact turf quality. As part of their daily assignments crewmembers look for the presence of, among other things, insects, insect damage, bird-peck activity, signs of fungal activity, or discolored turf. On report of any sightings, the Natural Resource Manager or a senior staff member investigates, documents the symptoms or signs, and constructs a list of possible causal agents. Potential problem areas are put on a monitoring list, and suspect sites are revisited daily to determine status. TOCGC is proving to be a working example that the best defense against pests is healthy turf. As of April 2002 (seven months after opening), roughly 98 percent of the intended grass area is covered with dense, uniform turf. The absence of pest problems is noteworthy.

One of the purported advantages of using seawater for irrigation is weed suppression. Since common broadleaf and grass-type weeds are usually not salt tolerant, hypothetically they should not compete effectively with *Paspalum* if exposed to seawater. Based on current evidence at this facility, that hypothesis holds true. The effects of salt-water irrigation were very noticeable during grow-in when grass cover was thin. Weeds occurred in greater numbers on areas where salt water was not applied. Conversely, areas of the golf course where salt water was regularly applied remained virtually weed-free. Now that turf density is high over the entire golf course, despite shifting away from seawater in favor of a second (lower TDS load) water source, weeds are a relatively minor issue in turf areas. Weed suppression activity mostly targets invasive species in the native areas of the property. Brazilian Pepper, Melaleuca, Old World Climbing Fern, and other exotics are removed on a continuing basis.

Also since completion of grow-in, insect pests have shown a similar decline in numbers and impact. The major pests in evidence during grow-in were sod webworm, armyworm, white grub, mole cricket, and billbug. While these species are still present, they seem to exert little significant impact on turf quality, and, again, this negative impact generally occurs only where turf is weaker or less dense. If insect damage does surpass threshold acceptability, it is TOCGC policy to use application rates at the "low" end of the recommended label range. Moreover, to guard against development of pesticide resistance, TOCGC rotates among at least three different modes of action (differing chemicals) in each pest category.

Pathogenic fungi have not been a significant problem in TOCGC *Paspalum*. The most prevalent fungus "season" appears to be January and February. Cooler temperatures, lower light quality, and shorter day-length combine to create poorer growing conditions for *Paspalum*, and the grass is less able to defend against fungal attack. Yellow Patch and Dollar Spot comprise the noticeable fungal activity. While both of these fungi produce lethal effects, TOCGC maintains a different management strategy for each. Yellow Patch outbreaks tend to enlarge quite rapidly, and, while not 100 percent lethal, once infected, turf recovery time can be substantial. As such, Yellow Patch is treated with a fungicide application within 7 days of appearance. Dollar Spot, on the other hand, is generally NOT treated with fungicide. Experience here shows that Dollar Spot is present over the entire golf course, but becomes "visible" only if turf is weakened by an irrigation failure or by low fertility. In the event that Dollar Spot does appear, fertilization and irrigation rates are adjusted accordingly. Higher calcium and potassium rates appear to reduce the incidence of these diseases. Once the grass returns to a healthy condition it seems to resist significant impact from Dollar Spot.

While the long-term environmental advantages of IPM are difficult to measure, existing budget records show that TOCGC IPM philosophy definitely reduces operating costs.

VI. Resource Management Center (Maintenance Facility)

Since the maintenance function of any golf course is closely related with storage and use of fuels, fertilizer, solvents, and pesticides, special consideration must be given to isolating potential contaminants from soil and water. TOCGC's Resource Management Center (RMC) uses special technology and design to accomplish these objectives.

A continuous concrete surface nearly surrounds the RMC (Figure 13). The concrete surface was selected in preference to asphalt for two reasons. First, it lends to the energy efficiency of the RMC complex by reducing absorption of solar radiation (heat storage studies show concrete to be at least 40°F cooler than asphalt). Second, concrete serves as a nearly impermeable surface separating potential contaminants from the soil underlying and surrounding the RMC. Since the integrity of the impermeable surface is dependent in part on its continuous nature, the pad is constructed of 6-inch, steel-reinforced concrete, and is capable of supporting at least 83,000 lbs. gross vehicle weight. With these design specifications, the pad basically has the structural character of a major roadway and readily supports the

FIGURE 13. *Resource Management Center.*

weight of large vehicles such as dump trucks or motorized cranes that service the facility on a regular basis. Interior RMC floors used for equipment maintenance or storage are minimum 4-inch, steel reinforced concrete with a load bearing capacity of at least 3,000 lbs./sq. in., and the concrete surface is coated with chemically resistant urethane (Figures 14a and b).

FIGURE 14a. *Equipment maintenance.*

FIGURE 14b. *Equipment storage.*

(a)

(b)

(c)

FIGURE 15a,b,c. *Equipment Service Facility.*

Also for water quality protection, the Equipment Service Facility (Figures 15a, b, c) has no connection to storm or sanitary sewers. Equipment wash water is collected in two belowground sumps, filtered and chlorinated, and returned to a 1200-gallon storage tank for re-use. The pad is designed to contain a large fuel or wash-water leak. In Figure 15c, the white "arrow" points to the lip of the containment basin.

TOCGC keeps pesticide use to a minimum, however sometimes an application is appropriate. Given that TOCGC is only two miles inland from the Gulf of Mexico, there is almost always a land breeze or a sea breeze in effect. To ensure that the pesticide spray reaches only the intended target, hood and rubber boot assemblies (Figure 16a) surround the booms of the spray apparatus. During application the booms are fully deployed (Figure 16b), and these attachments confine the spray to the area immediately below the nozzles.

Similar to the Equipment Service Facility, the Chemical Storage Building or IPM Control Center (Figure 17a) has no sewer connections; therefore, potential spills are isolated to the space inside the building. A concrete wall divides the building; dry chemicals are stored in one half (Figure 17b), while all liquid chemicals are stored in the Mix/Load area. The Mix/Load bay has a 300-gallon sump plus three 150-gallon elevated storage tanks (Figure 17c). These storage areas plus the capacity of the center-sloping, sealed concrete floor, provide the capability to isolate a liquid spill in excess of 600 gallons; this is 300 gallons greater than any single container in use at TOCGC.

Portable fuel cans, paints, and solvents are stored in fire retardant metal cabinets (Figure 18). Used oil is stored in a separate tank with secondary containment (Figure 19). Periodically, the tank contents are transferred through a specially designed piping system into a transport vehicle to be taken for recycling.

(a)   (b)

FIGURE 16a,b. *Spray apparatus.*

FIGURE 17a. *Chemical storage building.*

FIGURE 17b. *Dry Storage Bay.*

FIGURE 17c. *Mix-Load Bay.*

FIGURE 18. *Fuel can storage cabinet.*

FIGURE 19. *Waste oil storage.*

VII. Energy Efficiency

A. RESOURCE MANAGEMENT CENTER

1. Heating and Cooling

Regardless of season, Southwest Florida's climate is best characterized as sunny, warm, and humid. According to the National Climatological Data Center, annually, nearly 73 percent of days are either clear or partly cloudy. Clear skies and proximity to the Gulf of Mexico contribute to average daily high temperatures of 71°F in January and 90°F in August. In this climate, a work facility that is both comfortable and energy efficient must employ creative design features that inexpensively reduce the absorption of solar radiation and increase the dispersal of accumulated heat. Energy efficiency was one of the primary objectives of facility design at The Old Collier Golf Club.

Among the RMC external design features is a concrete surface covering the vehicular access areas; the lighter color significantly reduces heat accumulation in "paved" areas. This contributes to worker comfort outside the building, and reduces re-radiated heat transfer from paved areas to the RMC building. Palm trees planted around the outside of the RMC block solar radiation from reaching the walls and roof. An aluminum roof provides a highly reflective surface, and extends beyond the exterior walls to form a four-foot eve around the entire building. On the front (south) side of the RMC near the main entrance, the roof extends to become a nine-foot porch. The eves and porch provide a partial barrier diverting solar radiation from building walls and windows. All exterior windows are tinted, double-pane insulated glass. Exterior walls are painted light tan to reduce absorption of solar radiation. Tan (instead of white) was selected as the exterior color to create a better blend with exterior colors of neighboring business buildings.

Of the RMC's 19,000-sq. ft., only the offices, crew room, and equipment repair "clean-room" are air-conditioned (6,000-sq. ft.). In air-conditioned spaces, ceilings have R49 insulation accompanied by R19 insulation in exterior walls. To reduce heat accumulation, the equipment maintenance bay is insulated (but not air-conditioned), and strategically located windows, doors, ceiling fans, and a large gable mounted exhaust fan provide for continuous, rapid air exchange. All air-conditioned areas are outfitted with ceiling fans. Ceiling fans provide a significant cooling effect such that an 80°F room with a ceiling fan effectively feels like 78°F. The air-conditioner unit for the RMC carries a Seasonal Energy Efficiency Ratio (SEER) rating of 18.00, and utilizes a "variable speed air handler." The variable speed air handler is more efficient at removing humidity, and reduces energy consumption by operating only at the minimum speed necessary to meet immediate airflow demand. Electronic air filters reduce energy consumption while providing high quality air to breathe.

2. Illumination

Inside the RMC, T8 fluorescent lights (with electronic ballast) provide the artificial illumination. According to the Virginia State Office of Facilities Management, T8 lamps use up to 20 percent fewer watts than standard T12 lamps, and provide 7-10 percent additional efficiency when outfitted with electronic ballasts. Eight-foot, T8 lamps use up to 33 percent less energy than the most efficiently configured T12 lamps, and T8 lamps have an average life expectancy 25 percent longer than standard T12 lamps. T8 lamps not only have a higher efficacy (lumens/watt) rating, but also provide better color rendering.

Skylights are employed to provide natural illumination to areas of the RMC buildings with no internal ceilings. On clear to partly cloudy days, starting at approximately one hour after sunrise, the amount of natural light transmitted through the skylights is sufficient to provide safe working conditions.

3. Irrigation

The Old Collier Golf Club has two pump stations tapping different sources of brackish water. Each station is Variable Frequency Drive (VFD), which allows the pump system to "ramp-up" slowly thereby decreasing the overall "demand" portion of the electric bill. The VFD system also permits variable motor speeds to supply only the current flow demand. Additionally, irrigation is scheduled during "off-peak" hours as identified in rate information secured from Florida Power & Light (FP&L). "Off peak" hours change by season in SW Florida, so irrigation scheduling is continually reprogrammed to coincide with these fluctuations as updated by Florida Power & Light.

4. Energy Management

A great deal of thought and action has gone toward creating a golf facility that will optimize energy consumption. For example, all water heater circuits are wired with time clocks to limit operation to the first portion of the workday. This is but one of many design elements that give the NRC potential for energy efficiency. However, without a continuing management philosophy that increases employee sensitivity toward habitual energy conservation, the "break-even" point on the initially higher investment (for energy efficient fixtures and features) would occur much later in time. The measurable payoff here at The Old Collier Golf Club is a monthly average energy bill of between $450 and $500 for the entire maintenance facility. This includes electricity for vending machines, microwaves, coffeemaker, ice machine, arc welder, grinders, lights, fans, air compressor, hand dryers, and two 5-ton air-conditioning units.

B. MAIN CLUBHOUSE

As of this writing the main clubhouse is still under construction, so there are no statistics available regarding energy efficiency. Nonetheless, the design takes into consideration the same energy efficient features and factors underlying the RMC. It is anticipated that the result will show the consistently low consumption and cost figures achieved at the RMC. An important difference at the clubhouse will be the cooling system. Total air-conditioned space within the clubhouse is approximately 22,000 sq. ft. The cooling technology employed is "Ice Thermal Storage (ITS)" (Baltimore Aircoil Company). Simply characterized, an ITS unit makes and stores ice at night during off-peak energy hours, and then uses the ice to cool air during the day. Aside from the obvious advantage of operating the energy consumption cycle at night, the ITS unit can be located a considerable distance from the structure being cooled. In this case the ITS is nearly ¼ mile from the clubhouse. Air is circulated between the building and the ITS through underground piping. Given that the line is underground, there is very little line loss over the ¼ mile distance. Also, since the ITS unit is relatively large and readily visible, the remote location eliminates the need to mask or camouflage the unit from view.

VIII. Waste Management

Waste management has been in effect at The Old Collier Golf Club since the inception of design and construction. Low impact, long life span construction materials were selected for buildings. All materials utilized were screened for potential hazards to occupant health, and energy efficiency was paramount in selection of all electrical fixtures. On the golf course, bridge surfaces were constructed of material

FIGURE 20. *Bridge surface constructed from recycled plastic.*

made from recycled plastic (Figure 20). The projected life span of the bridge surface material far exceeds that of wood products used for the same purpose.

Now that The Old Collier Golf Club is operational, the waste management goal is to maximize on-site, green-waste decomposition, and to recycle non-biodegradable materials whenever a market exists.

➤ *Grass clippings.* No grass clippings are shipped off TOCGC property. Walking greensmowers are the only equipment outfitted to catch grass clippings. After being captured in the greensmower baskets, the clippings are emptied behind the green and thoroughly dispersed by broom or blower. Since clippings are comprised of 72 percent–75 percent water it is unlikely that future problems will arise. However, to be certain, the practice is monitored closely.

➤ *Limbs, leaves, etc.* This debris is disseminated in the form of brush piles (Figure 21), throughout the property in upland areas. Brush piles are easily concealed from view, and they create excellent cover for small mammals during the three- to five-year period over which they decompose.

➤ *Aluminum.* Cans are crushed and redeemed for cash every 2 or 3 months.

➤ *Plastic, office paper and magazines.* These materials are carried to county recycling along with aluminum. Recycling trips are made only with full loads, and coincide with other planned travel.

FIGURE 21. *Leaves and tree limbs are spread in brush piles throughout the property.*

➤ *Glass.* Since no glass is used, currently there is no recycling program for this type container. However, when the Clubhouse opens, glass will be added to the current group of recycled materials.

➤ *Cardboard.* A "cardboard only" recycling container is maintained at the RMC, and TOCGC employees understand that *all* cardboard is to be deposited therein. TOCGC pays a fee of $52 per month for the cardboard recycling service.

➤ *Pesticide containers.* All plastic pesticide, fertilizer or other plastic containers are triple rinsed, left to dry, and then stored until a recycling contractor retrieves them. The recycling contractor shreds the containers on-site, at no cost, and ultimately re-uses the plastic fragments to make pallets.

IX. Information and Outreach

During the summer of 2001, in conjunction with The Conservancy of Southwest Florida, approximately 280 children ranging from 2nd to 5th grade toured The Old Collier Golf Club and participated in various ecologically based learning exercises. Also toward the same learning goal, in April and May of 2002, all six, 5th grade classes from Naples Park Elementary School toured TOCGC. The six classes represented approximately 160 children, 15 adults, including six teachers and the school principal.

Because the golf course is grassed with Seashore Paspalum and irrigated with water ranging from 200 ppm to 34,000 ppm dissolved solid content, TOCGC has proved to be of both national and international interest. Visitors have come from China, Switzerland, Great Britain, Canada, Argentina, Dominican Republic, Puerto Rico, Bahrain, Costa Rica, Mexico, and from over 30 of the United States, including Hawaii. Perhaps the largest single agronomy related tour occurred in early April 2002. On that day, thirty-two individuals assembled at TOCGC for a 3-hour tour arranged through the Florida Fruit and Vegetable Association. The group included representatives from the U.S. Environmental Protection Agency, Florida Department of Agriculture, and parties of varied interests from Georgia, Florida, and China.

As time allows, representatives from TOCGC will travel to speaking engagements, seminars, symposia, and professional meetings to share successes and needed improvements. On rare occasions this travel will include individual or company visitations. On-site informational tours for groups or individuals will continue as time and operations permit.

X. Contact Person

For additional information about The Old Collier Golf Club or Audubon International contact:

Mr. Tim Hiers, CGCS
Golf Course Manager
The Old Collier Golf Club
797 Walkerbilt Road
Naples, FL 34110
(239) 593-8522

Audubon International
46 Rarick Road
Selkirk, New York 12158
(518) 767-9051
http://www.audoboninternational.org

REFERENCES

Audubon International. *Sustainable Resource Management Guidelines 1998 and 2000.*

Beatley, T. *Habitat Conservation Planning.* Austin: University of Texas Press, l994.

Bissonette, J. A., and I. Storch, eds. *Landscape Ecology and Resource Management.* Washington, D.C.: Island Press, 2003.

Buttler, T. M., A. G. Hornsby, P. W. M. Augustin-Beckers, L. B. McCarty, D. E. Short, R. A. Dunn, and G. W. Simon. *Managing Pesticides for Golf Course Maintenance and Water Quality,* 1995.

Dodson, R. *Managing Wildlife Habitat on Golf Courses.* Chelsea, MI: Sleeping Bear Press, 2000.

Hatfield, J. L., and B. A. Stewart, eds. *Soil Biology: Effects on Soil Quality.* Boca Raton, FL: CRC Press, l994.

Johnson, K. M., F. Swanson, M. Herring, and S. Green, eds. *Bioregional Assessments.* Washington, D.C.: Island Press, 1999.

Little, C. E. *Greenways for America.* Baltimore: Johns Hopkins University Press, 1995.

Mackay, J. *Audubon International: A Guide to Environmental Stewardship on the Golf Course,* 2nd ed. New York: Audubon International, 2002.

Marquis, K, and B. Smart. *Audubon International: Construction Guidelines for Communities and Golf Courses.* New York: Audubon International, 1999.

Maser, C., R. Beaton, and K. Smith. *Setting the Stage for Sustainability: A Citizens Handbook.* Boca Raton, FL: CRC Press, 1998.

Maser, C. *Vision and Leadership in Sustainable Development.* Boca Raton, FL: CRC Press, 1999.

Meffe, G. K., L. Nielsen, R. Knight, and D. Schenborn. *Ecosystem Management.* Washington, D.C.: Island Press, 2002.

Porter, D. R., R. Platt, and C. Leinberger. *The Practice of Sustainable Development.* Washington, D.C.: Urban Land Institute, 2000.

Rogers, Peter. *America's Water: Federal Roles and Responsibilities.* Cambridge, MA: MIT Press, 1996.

Smart, M., C. Peacock, K. Marquis, and L. Woolbright. *Audubon International. Natural Resource Management Plans for Golf Courses.* New York: Audubon International, 1995.

The Heinz Center. *The State of the Nation's Ecosystems.* Washington, D.C.: The H. John Heinz III Center for Science, Economics and the Environment, 2002.

U. S. Department of Energy. *Fannie Mae's Guide to Buying and Maintaining a Green Home: "Home Performance Power."* Washington, D.C.: USDOE, 2000.

Wilson, A., N. Malin, and P. Yost. Environmental Building News: "Establishing Priorities with Green Building." BuildingGreen, Inc. Brattleboro, VT. 1996, 2001.

Wilson, A., J. Thorne, and J. Morrell. *Consumer Guide to Home Energy Savings.* Washington, D.C.: American Council for an Energy-Efficient Economy, 1999.

INDEX